The Vietnam Experience

The Army at War

by Michael Casey, Clark Dougan, Denis Kennedy, Shelby Stanton,
and the editors of Boston Publishing Company

Boston Publishing Company / Boston, MA

Boston Publishing Company

President and Publisher: Robert J. George
Vice President: Richard S. Perkins, Jr.
Editor-in-Chief: Robert Manning
Managing Editor: Paul Dreyfus
Marketing Director: Jeanne Gibson

Series Editor: Samuel Lipsman
Senior Editor: Gordon Hardy
Design Director: Lisa Bogle
Senior Picture Editor: Julene Fischer
Senior Writer: Denis Kennedy

Picture Editor: Lanng Tamura
Picture Coordinator/Researcher:
Rebecca Black

Text Researcher: Michael Hathaway

Editorial Production: Theresa Slomkowski

Business Staff: Amy Pelletier, Amy Wilson

Special contributors to this volume:
Text Research: Katharine Brady, Jason
Brown, Matthew Hong, Kenneth Jacobson,
Steven W. Lipari, Jonathan Mark, Jennifer
Smith, Michael Youmans

Design: Sherry Fatla, Lynne Weygint

Picture Research: Lauren Chapin, Kathleen
Reidy, Shirley L. Green (Washington, D.C.),
Kate Lewin (Paris),

Editorial Production: Dalia Lipkin, Patricia
Leal Welch

Index prepared by Stephen Csipke

About the editors and authors:

Editor-in-Chief: *Robert Manning*, a long-time journalist, has previously been editor-in-chief of the *Atlantic Monthly* magazine and its press. He served as assistant secretary of state for public affairs under Presidents John F. Kennedy and Lyndon B. Johnson. He has also been a fellow at the Institute of Politics at the John F. Kennedy School of Government at Harvard University.

Authors: *Michael Casey*, author of the chapter on the 25th Infantry Division, was formerly a researcher for *The Vietnam Experience*. He is a graduate of Harvard College. *Clark Dougan* (1st Infantry Division and 199th Infantry Brigade), a former Watson and Danforth fellow, has taught history at Kenyon College. He received his M.A. and M.Phil. at Yale University. *Denis Kennedy* (4th Infantry Division, 11th Armored Cavalry [Regiment], and 23d Infantry Division) received his B.A. at Harvard College. Formerly a researcher for *The Vietnam Experience*, he was also Assistant Editor of Boston Publishing's history of the Medal of Honor, *Above and Beyond*. *Shelby L. Stanton* (173d Airborne Brigade, 9th Infantry Division) is currently a fellow at the Center for Strategic and International Studies. A Vietnam veteran and former captain in the U.S. Army Special Forces, he has researched and written extensively on the war. His books include *Vietnam Order of Battle*, *The Rise and Fall of an American Army*, and *Green Berets at War*. Mr. Stanton also served as chief historical consultant for the book, reviewing the pictures and manuscript, and provided material for the illustrations on pages 96-103.

Historical Consultant: *Vincent H. Demma*, a historian with the U.S. Army Center of Military History, is currently working on the center's history of the Vietnam conflict.

Cover Photo:
Paratroopers of the 173d Airborne Division patrol Phuoc Tuy Province, northeast of Saigon, during a search-and-destroy mission in June 1966.

Library of Congress Catalog Card Number: LC 87-72214

ISBN: 0-939526-23-9

10 9 8 7 6
5 4 3 2 1

Contents

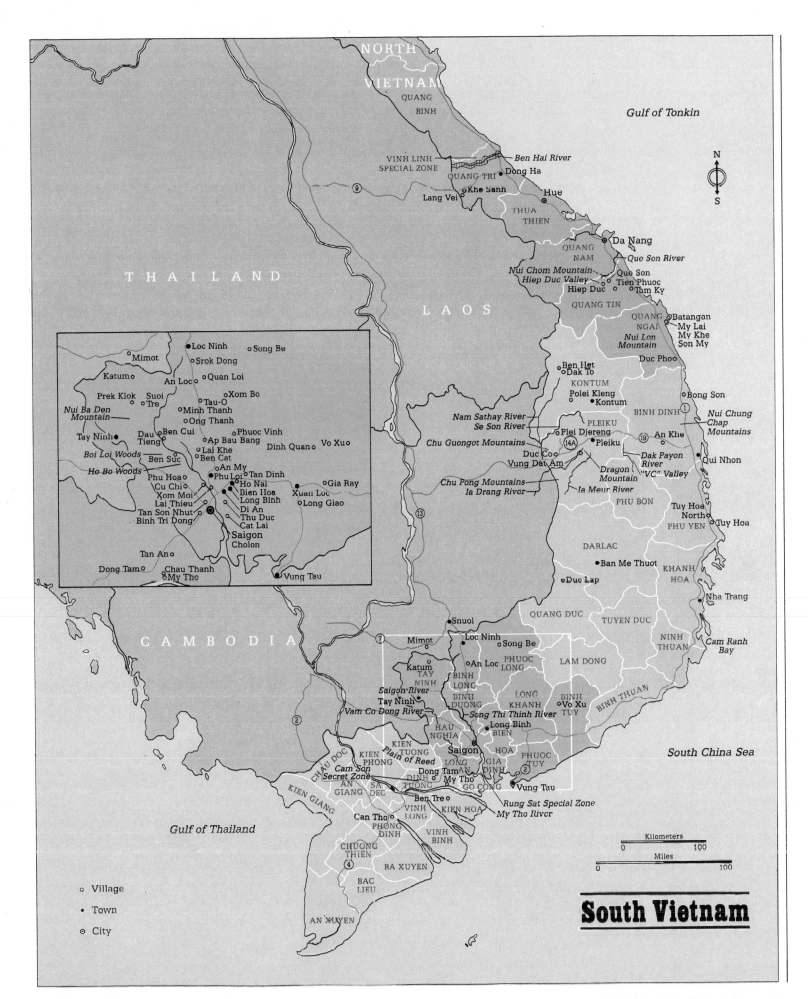

South Vietnam

Legend:
- ○ Village
- ● Town
- ◉ City

Map labels

NORTH VIETNAM

QUANG BINH

Gulf of Tonkin

VINH LINH SPECIAL ZONE

Ben Hai River

QUANG TRI

Dong Ha

Khe Sanh

Lang Vei

Hue

THUA THIEN

Da Nang

QUANG NAM

Quo Son River

Nui Chom Mountain
Hiep Duc Valley

Quo Son
Tien Phuoc

Hiep Duc

Tam Ky

QUANG TIN

QUANG NGAI

Batangan
My Lai
My Khe
Son My

Nui Lon Mountain

Duc Pho

Ben Het
Dak To

KONTUM

Polei Kleng

Kontum

Bong Son

BINH DINH

Nui Chung Chap Mountains

Nam Sathay River
Se Son River

Chu Guongot Mountains

Plei Djereng

Pleiku

An Khe

PLEIKU

Duc Co

Vung Dat Am

Dak Payon River
"VC" Valley

Qui Nhon

Chu Pong Mountains
Ia Drang River

Dragon Mountain

Ia Meur River

PHU BON

Tuy Hoa North

Tuy Hoa

PHU YEN

DARLAC

Ban Me Thuot

KHANH HOA

Duc Lap

Nha Trang

QUANG DUC

TUYEN DUC

NINH THUAN

Cam Ranh Bay

Snuol

Mimot

Loc Ninh

Song Be

PHUOC LONG

An Loc

LAM DONG

BINH LONG

Katum

TAY NINH

BINH DUONG

LONG KHANH

BINII TUY

Vo Xu

BINH THUAN

Saigon River

Tay Ninh

Vam Co Dong River

HAU NGHIA

Song Thi Thinh River

Long Binh

BIEN HOA

KIEN TUONG

Saigon

Plain of Reed

Cam Son Secret Zone

KIEN PHONG

AN GIANG

SA DEC

Dong Tam

DINH TUONG

My Tho

LONG AN

GIA DINH

GO CONG

PHUOC TUY

Vung Tau

South China Sea

Rung Sat Special Zone
My Tho River

Ben Tre

KIEN HOA

KIEN GIANG

CHAU DOC

Can Tho

PHONG DINH

VINH LONG

VINH BINH

Gulf of Thailand

CHUONG THIEN

BA XUYEN

BAC LIEU

AN XUYEN

THAILAND

LAOS

CAMBODIA

Inset map labels

Loc Ninh

Song Be

Mimot

Srok Dong

Katum

An Loc

Quan Loi

Prek Klok

Suoi Tre

Xom Bo

Nui Ba Den Mountain

Tau-O

Minh Thanh

Ong Thanh

Tay Ninh

Dau Tieng

Ben Cui

Phuoc Vinh

Ap Bau Bang

Lai Khe

Dinh Quan

Vo Xu

Boi Loi Woods

Ben Suc

Ben Cat

Ho Bo Woods

An My

Tan Dinh

Phu Hoa

Phu Loi

Cu Chi

Ho Nai

Gia Ray

Xom Moi

Dien Hoa

Long Binh

Xuan Loc

Lai Thieu

Di An

Long Giao

Tan Son Nhut

Thu Duc

Binh Tri Dong

Cat Lai

Saigon

Cholon

Tan An

Dong Tam

Chau Thanh

My Tho

Vung Tau

N

S

The Big Unit War

When the USNS *Gordon* sailed under the Golden
Gate Bridge and steamed into the Pacific Ocean on
June 25, 1965, few of the 4,000 American troops
crowded onto its decks knew their destination, at
least officially. Since late April, when the commanders of the 1st Infantry Division received orders to
prepare a brigade for overseas deployment, the
unit's home base at Fort Riley, Kansas, had been
buzzing with rumors and feverish activity. In early
June flatcars loaded with equipment and supplies
began leaving for the West Coast on a regular basis.
Several weeks later, the soldiers of the division's 2d
Brigade departed by rail and plane, arriving at the
Oakland Army Terminal on June 21 in full combat
gear. By then there could no longer be any doubt. For
the first time since World War II, the division known
as the "Big Red One" was going to war. The destination: Vietnam. After eighteen days at sea, the
soldiers caught their first glimpse of Southeast Asia,
as the *Gordon* approached the sheltered deep-water
harbor at Cam Ranh Bay on July 12. Assigned to

Major General William E. DePuy, commander of the 1st Infantry Division from March 1966 to February 1967, was determined to "shake up" his division.

provide security for the vast new port facility then under construction, the 1st Battalion, 18th Infantry, disembarked, followed by C Battery of the 1st Battalion, 7th Artillery. The rest of the brigade task force then moved south, landing at the port city of Vung Tau two days later. From there the 2d Battalion, 18th Infantry, and the 2d Battalion, 16th Infantry, were airlifted to Bien Hoa Air Base, where they immediately assumed responsibility for the defense of a portion of the perimeter.

In the meantime, the remainder of the 1st Infantry Division at Fort Riley received notice to achieve combat-ready status by September 1. To meet the Pentagon's deadline, two additional regular infantry battalions—the 1st and 2d battalions of the 2d Infantry—were brought in from Fort Devens, Massachusetts, to replace two organic armor battalions slated to stay behind. On September 15 the main body of troops began leaving the United States, and by October 19 the move was complete. After briefly settling into a staging area near Saigon University, the division broke up and established a series of base camps due north of the South Vietnamese capital. While the 1st Brigade dug in at Phuoc Vinh and the 3d Brigade at Lai Khe, the division command set up its headquarters at Di

Preceding page. Soldiers of the 1st Infantry Division take cover during a Vietcong mortar barrage on their fire support base near the Cambodian border in December 1967.

An. The 2d Brigade, which officially rejoined the division on November 1, operated out of its base at Bien Hoa.

Under the command of Major General Jonathan O. Seaman, the division's initial operations were confined largely to patrols and small-scale sweeps of the areas surrounding the camps, an approach that was later criticized. Aside from answering occasional sniper fire, the division made no significant contact with the enemy until November 12, when a battalion task force came under attack during a sweep of National Highway 13 north of Lai Khe. Charged with ensuring the safe passage of the 7th ARVN Regiment from Lai Khe to the village of Bau Bang, the 2d Battalion, 2d Infantry, reinforced by one armored troop of the 1st Squadron, 4th Cavalry, and C Battery of the 2d Battalion, 33d Artillery, had carved out a temporary defensive perimeter just south of Bau Bang on the night of November 11. Shortly before first light the next morning, as the Americans gathered their gear and prepared to move out, a barrage of approximately fifty to sixty mortar rounds slammed inside their camp. A counterclockwise sequence of massed ground assaults followed, as local Vietcong forces attempted to breach the wire first from the south, then the east, and finally the north.

Much to the surprise of some of the U.S. troops, the last and largest of the attacks came directly out of the village of Bau Bang. In the days preceding the battle, battalion medical and civil affairs teams had visited the hamlet twice, never suspecting that they had entered the enemy's lair. When the main assault began around 7:00 A.M., however, it soon became apparent that the covering fire was coming from preestablished positions in and around the village itself. As the VC charged into the perimeter, the Americans responded with a combination of machine-gun, rifle, and direct artillery fire. One group of enemy infantrymen nevertheless managed to push through and destroy a howitzer position before falling back to the village to regroup. Moments later a flight of A-1E Skyraiders swooped in and pummeled a row of recoilless rifle emplacements on the southern edge of town with 500-pound bombs, while gunners inside the camp fired forty artillery rounds into Bau Bang in an effort to silence the enemy's mortars. The bombardment and shelling produced a temporary lull in the action, but it did not prevent the VC from mounting a second attack from the village at 9:00 A.M. Again the American howitzer crews responded with point-blank artillery fire, and again the Air Force assisted with a series of air strikes. Three hours later the Vietcong finally withdrew, leaving nearly 200 dead on the battlefield.

In the wake of the battle of Bau Bang, the division shifted its attention west of "Thunder Road," as Highway 13 came to be called, and joined the 7th ARVN Regiment in a sweep in the vicinity of the Michelin rubber plantation northwest of Lai Khe. Code-named Bloodhound-Bushmaster, the operation resulted in the discovery of a variety of enemy installations, including a munitions fac-

1st Infantry Division

Arrived Vietnam: October 2, 1965   **Departed Vietnam:** April 15, 1970

Unit Headquarters

Bien Hoa *Oct. 1965–Jan. 1966*
Di An *Feb. 1966–Jan. 1967*

Di An/Lai Khe *Feb. 1967–Sept. 1967*
Lai Khe *Oct. 1967–Oct. 1969*

Di An *Nov. 1969–April 1970*

Commanding Officers

Maj. Gen. Jonathan O. Seaman *Oct. 1965*
Maj. Gen. William E. DePuy *March 1966*
Maj. Gen. John H. Hay, Jr. *Feb. 1967*

Maj. Gen. Keith L. Ware *March 1968*
Maj. Gen. Orwin C. Talbott *Sept. 1968*

Maj. Gen. Albert E. Milloy *Aug. 1969*
Brig. Gen. John Q. Herrion *March 1970*

Major Subordinate Units

1st Brigade (1/2, 1/26, 1/28)
2d Brigade (2/16, 1/18, 2/18)
3d Brigade (2/2 [mech], 1/16 [mech], 2/28)
1st Battalion, 5th Artillery
8th Battalion, 6th Artillery
1st Battalion, 7th Artillery
6th Battalion, 15th Artillery
2d Battalion, 33d Artillery
Battery D, 25th Artillery
1st Aviation Battalion (Airmobile)
162d Aviation Company (Airmobile)

173d Aviation Company (Airmobile)
C Troop, 16th Cavalry (Air)
3d Squadron, 11th Armored Cavalry
5th Battalion, 60th Infantry (Mechanized)
1st Squadron, 4th Cavalry
Company F, 52d Infantry
Company I, 75th Infantry
1st Engineer Battalion
1st Medical Battalion
1st Supply & Transport Battalion
121st Signal Battalion

1st Administration Company
701st Maintenance Battalion
1st Military Police Company
337th Army Security Agency Company
242d Chemical Detachment
266th Chemical Platoon
17th Military History Detachment
1st Military Intelligence Company
43d Public Information Detachment
44th Public Information Detachment

3,146 KIA
(Casualty figures are "Vietnam Era.")

18,019 WIA

11 Medals of Honor

---

tory, repair shops, and an extensive base camp tunnel complex. It also produced the first major confrontation between Vietcong Main Force units and the Big Red One. Known as the battle of Ap Nha Mat, the engagement pitted the 2d Battalion, 2d Infantry, against a 1,200-man, four-battalion force later identified as the 272d VC Regiment. It began shortly after noon on December 5, when the 2/2 stumbled upon a heavily fortified base camp and training area eight kilometers west of Highway 13. Pinned down by thunderous volleys of automatic-weapons fire that cut some of the surrounding trees in half, the Americans immediately called in air strikes and artillery to break the attack. In response, the Vietcong resorted to the "hugging" tactics that would become a trademark of their encounters with U.S. forces, closing in so tightly that forward air controllers could not easily distinguish their own soldiers' positions from enemy ones. Only the bravery of a few individual soldiers, who repeatedly exposed themselves to hostile fire in order to mark their locations with smoke grenades, spared the battalion from annihilation. Guided by the markings, subsequent air strikes proved deadly accurate, blasting the VC out of their well-concealed bunkers and preparing the way for a counterattack by the men of the 2/2, the "Ramrod" battalion. As the American troops charged forward, the bulk of the enemy force broke contact and fled, leaving behind only a few scattered snipers to cover their retreat. The 2/2 remained in the area for two more days, conducting detailed searches that uncovered numerous equipment and supply caches as well as approximately 300 enemy bodies.

During the next few months the 1st Infantry Division continued to expand its arc of operations, exploring the territory north and northwest of Saigon that would be its hunting ground for the next four years. In early January 1966, the 3d Brigade moved into Hau Nghia Province and the Cu Chi District in Operation Crimp. In February the division made its first forays into the Boi Loi Woods during Operation Mastiff and the Long Than District in Operation Mallet, both long-time Vietcong strongholds. And in early March Operation Hattiesburg took the 2d Brigade into Tay Ninh Province. Although in each instance contact with enemy forces was limited and sporadic, the division command believed that the large quantities of weapons and supplies the men seized dealt the VC a severe blow.

DePuy takes command

On March 15, 1966, Brigadier (soon to be Major) General William E. DePuy took over the 1st Infantry Division, as Gen. Seaman moved on to assume command of II Field Force, Vietnam. A former regimental operations officer and battalion commander with the 357th Regiment, 90th Infantry Division, during World War II, DePuy held a number of prestigious Army staff positions in the postwar period, leading to his appointment in 1962 as director of special warfare in the office of the deputy chief of staff. Ordered to Vietnam in May 1964, he served for two years as the chief of operations for Military Assistance Command, Vietnam (MACV), working closely with General William C. Westmoreland in planning the expanding American war effort.

According to a variety of sources, including DePuy himself, the decision to place him in charge of the Big Red One reflected a growing conviction at MACV headquarters that the division "simply wasn't carrying its weight." "It didn't have a very mobile mentality," DePuy later recalled, whereas "the command in Saigon was very mobility-minded because we'd been fighting a countrywide war. MACV commander Gen. Westmoreland didn't want to bring a division all the way from the United States and have it sit around in little camps and just patrol around them. He wanted them to go up into Tay Ninh Province, and up to Song Be, and down to Vung Tau, and over to Xuan Loc, or wherever it was necessary to go to get into the war."

Nor was a lack of mobility the only problem DePuy perceived. He also observed that many soldiers had not been properly trained and, as a result, "they were stumbling into battles." On several occasions, on-hand reserves had been unprepared for immediate commitment, insufficiently controlled, or simply unavailable during engagements with the enemy. As one former battalion operations officer put it, "General DePuy thought that too many men were being killed needlessly."

Determined to shake up the division and "get it moving," DePuy immediately replaced most of the brigade and battalion commanders who had served under Seaman with men of his own choosing. The personnel changes temporarily undermined morale among the senior officer corps and led to widespread criticism of the general's methods. "He went to the extreme and relieved battalion commanders for practically no cause, never giving them a chance," asserted General Bruce Palmer, Jr., the deputy commander of U.S. Army, Vietnam. But others saw it differently. "I think he received more blame than he deserved," recalled General Melvin Zais, who became the new assistant division commander of the Big Red One on May 1, 1966. "In getting rid of people, he got a reputation for being a ruthless man who fired people left and right. It wasn't quite that way. He was trying to build his own team, like a new manager on a baseball team." Among the "galaxy of stars," as Zais put it, that DePuy brought in were Colonel Sidney B. Berry, Jr., who assumed command of the 1st Brigade; Brigadier General A. E. "Ernie" Milloy, who took over the 2d Brigade and became the division's commander three and a half years later; and Colonel Alexander M. Haig, who commanded the 1st Battalion, 26th Infantry.

Even before the new team was in place, DePuy began moving the division around, even when he "didn't have a very good excuse to do so," in order to instill a "mobile

---

First Infantry Division troops face enemy fire after being dropped into a landing zone near Trung Lap forty kilometers north of Saigon, January 8, 1966.

mentality." He also made sure that his combat troops were well schooled in the techniques of jungle warfare. Widely regarded as one of the Army's most brilliant tacticians, he introduced the division to tactics designed to enable troops to search a large area without massing in any one spot. Yet to DePuy, all of this was only preparatory to the main task of finding, fixing, and destroying the enemy. "He was a very bright, very brave, very aggressive commander," Zais noted, "and he really went after the Vietcong and the North Vietnamese."

Nevertheless, the first few operations initiated by DePuy resulted in only limited encounters with enemy forces. On the night of April 12, during Operation Abilene, Company C of the 2d Battalion, 16th Infantry, became embroiled in an intense four-hour firefight with the D800 VC Battalion in the dense jungle sixty-four kilometers northeast of Saigon. But otherwise the search-and-destroy mission produced no significant contact. Minor squad- and platoon-size actions also characterized Operation Birmingham, a multibattalion sweep of northern Tay Ninh Province in late April.

Frustrated by the division's continuing inability to engage the enemy, MACV directed DePuy to draw up plans for a four-battalion air assault on the suspected Communist headquarters in the South, the Central Office for South Vietnam (COSVN). Code-named Hollingsworth, the surprise attack was scheduled to begin on May 7. But the outbreak of a series of torrential thunderstorms, signaling the approach of the summer monsoons, grounded the operation before it could get under way. Forced to seek his quarry elsewhere, DePuy sent his troops north to Loc Ninh in response to fresh intelligence indicating an impending four-regiment attack on the local Special Forces/CIDG (Civilian Irregular Defense Group) camp. After a month of fruitless sweeps through the area surrounding Loc Ninh, however, Operation El Paso I was called to a halt.

El Paso II

In early June, DePuy decided to plunge the division even more deeply into Communist-dominated territory in Operation El Paso II. Though the stated objective of the campaign was to prevent the 9th VC Division from mounting a major offensive during the upcoming monsoon season, the more immediate goal was to lure enemy Main Force units into battle. Much to the satisfaction of both DePuy and the Saigon command, this time the Vietcong obliged.

The first substantial contact occurred on the afternoon of June 8, six days after the operation officially began, when the 272d VC Regiment ambushed a convoy of tanks and armored personnel carriers along Route 13 just outside the village of Tau-O. A Troop of the 1st Squadron, 4th Cavalry, was passing through a narrow section of the road where dense jungle growth pressed in on both sides when the lead tank hit a mine, halting the column. Moments later two battalions of enemy infantrymen attacked from the

west behind a barrage of mortar and recoilless rifle fire, while a third battalion struck the cavalry's rear. Intense combat raged for five hours until the arrival of a relief column from the 2d Battalion, 18th Infantry, finally forced the enemy to withdraw. A sweep of the battlefield the following day revealed nearly 100 Vietcong killed in action (KIA), including the commander of the 272d Regiment's 1st Battalion. American losses were thirteen killed and thirty-eight wounded.

Three days later, the 2d Battalion, 28th Infantry, unexpectedly ran into a battalion of the 273d VC Regiment at a rubber plantation northwest of Loc Ninh. The action began shortly before nine o'clock on the morning of June 11, when Company A of the 2/28 came under rifle fire from a small hill as it prepared to sweep the village of Loc Thien on the plantation grounds. An hour later, after repeated attempts to overrun the hill were repulsed by small-arms and machine-gun fire, Company C was dispatched from Loc Ninh to join the fight. But before the reinforcements could link up with their sister company, they too came under heavy fire from another hill.

Realizing that they were up against a sizable and well-entrenched enemy force, the company commanders called for heavy mortar and artillery support, then readied their troops to assault the VC emplacements. Again Company A failed to make much headway, while Company C's advance up the second hill almost ended in disaster. Hit by steadily intensifying machine-gun fire and showered with grenades, the men of Charlie Company fell back in disorder and were nearly encircled before the commitment of the company's reserve platoon broke the enemy's counterattack. The Americans then regrouped and charged up the hill, storming the VC trench lines by late afternoon.

In the meantime, the commander of the 2/28, Lieutenant Colonel Kyle W. Bowie, sent the last of his reserves, Company B, to the aid of Company A. After intensive artillery bombardment and a series of air strikes, the fresh troops of Bravo assaulted the first hill and overran the enemy's bunkers in furious hand-to-hand combat. The Vietcong scattered and fled, many making their way through a gap in the allied lines created by the panicked flight of an attached South Vietnamese CIDG platoon. Left behind on the two hills were the bodies of ninety-eight enemy soldiers. By contrast, the 2d Battalion, 28th Infantry, suffered thirty-three killed and an equal number wounded. In a grinding war of attrition in which the enemy seemed willing to sacrifice ten men for every American killed, victory at the Loc Ninh rubber plantation was costly.

During the next two weeks the 1st Infantry Division encountered only sporadic resistance as it continued its search-and-destroy missions in War Zone C. Then on June 30 the enemy struck again, ambushing an armored task force along Highway 13 between An Loc and Loc Ninh. B Troop of the 1st Squadron, 4th Cavalry, reinforced by a rifle platoon from Company C of the 2/18 Infantry, was return-

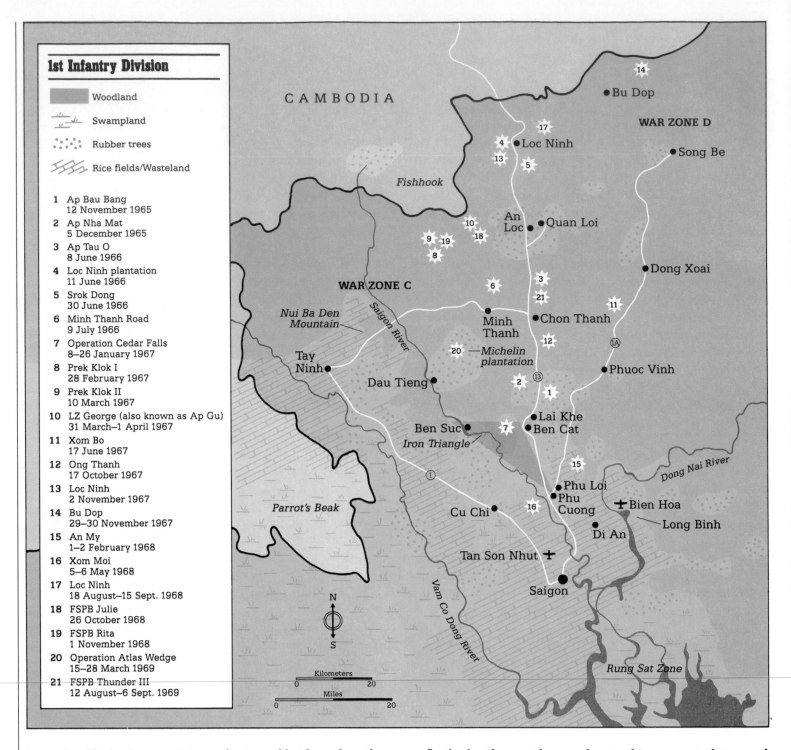

1st Infantry Division

	Woodland
	Swampland
	Rubber trees
	Rice fields/Wasteland

1. Ap Bau Bang
   12 November 1965
2. Ap Nha Mat
   5 December 1965
3. Ap Tau O
   8 June 1966
4. Loc Ninh plantation
   11 June 1966
5. Srok Dong
   30 June 1966
6. Minh Thanh Road
   9 July 1966
7. Operation Cedar Falls
   8–26 January 1967
8. Prek Klok I
   28 February 1967
9. Prek Klok II
   10 March 1967
10. LZ George (also known as Ap Gu)
    31 March–1 April 1967
11. Xom Bo
    17 June 1967
12. Ong Thanh
    17 October 1967
13. Loc Ninh
    2 November 1967
14. Bu Dop
    29–30 November 1967
15. An My
    1–2 February 1968
16. Xom Moi
    5–6 May 1968
17. Loc Ninh
    18 August–15 Sept. 1968
18. FSPB Julie
    26 October 1968
19. FSPB Rita
    1 November 1968
20. Operation Atlas Wedge
    15–28 March 1969
21. FSPB Thunder III
    12 August–6 Sept. 1969

ing to Loc Ninh after repairing a destroyed bridge when the 271st VC Regiment sprang its trap near the village of Srok Dong. The Vietcong had taken up position along a mile-long stretch of "Thunder Road" bracketed on both sides by thick jungle undergrowth and rice fields. As soon as the column came within range, the enemy soldiers unleashed a torrent of recoilless rifle and machine-gun fire that quickly disabled all four of the troops' tanks, tearing the turret-top cupola off one and decapitating its commander. The Americans retaliated with heavy machine-gun fire, followed by a series of artillery barrages and helicopter gunship runs, but they could neither break the attack nor suppress the intensity of the enemy's fire.

As the battle raged on and casualties mounted, several of the troops' armored personnel carriers headed back toward a crossroads just south of the ambush site to evacuate the wounded and replenish ammunition supplies. There they met up with sister C Troop, which had been racing toward the action from a point farther down the road. Amid steady bombardment from enemy mortars, a traffic jam ensued as the tanks and APCs tried to maneuver around one another. Despite successive hits on C Troop's lead tank, the relief column finally snaked its way through the clogged junction and rumbled forward, laying down a heavy base of fire in every direction. The reinforcing APCs then moved onto the narrow shoulders of the road and formed a shield around the remnants of B Troop, while the tank crewmen manually swiveled their damaged turrets toward the enemy and fired off sixty rounds. A short time later Companies A and B of the 2d Battalion, 18th Infantry, arrived on the scene, but by then the bulk of the enemy force had already slipped away.

Although the official combat after-action report for Operation El Paso II described the battle of Srok Dong as "one of the classic engagements of the Vietnam conflict," resulting in the "sound defeat" of the 271st VC Regiment, Major General DePuy offered a more sobering appraisal. "This was a complete surprise," he later reported to General Westmoreland. "U.S. forces nearly lost this battle." The 1st Infantry Division commander was nevertheless determined to regain the tactical initiative and soon began laying plans to draw the enemy into a trap of his own. The result, in DePuy's words, was "the last and most violent" engagement of El Paso II—the battle of Minh Thanh Road.

Capitalizing on intelligence indicating that the elite 272d VC Regiment had moved into north central Binh Duong Province, DePuy and 1st Brigade commander Colonel Sidney B. Berry, Jr., conceived a three-phase operation using the 1st Squadron, 4th Cavalry, as bait. After information was leaked through the local Vietnamese that a small armored convoy would be traveling along the road between Minh Thanh and An Loc, Phase I began on July 8 with a B-52 strike and airmobile feint to the northeast of the suspected enemy location. The next morning Task Force Dragoon, including B and C troops of the 1/4 Cav as well as Company B of the 1st Battalion, 2d Infantry, set off along Minh Thanh Road, inaugurating Phase II. Meanwhile, a multibattalion reaction force moved into prearranged position, ready to commence Phase III if and when the Vietcong struck.

The plan worked almost to perfection. After moving along without incident for two hours, the armored column came under attack precisely where the division command had expected. Firing from roadside drainage ditches and deep foxholes in the surrounding jungle, the VC raked the convoy with a relentless stream of rocket, mortar, and recoilless rifle fire that destroyed one tank and four APCs and severely damaged several others. Enemy infantrymen then sprang up and attempted to overrun the task force, only to fall prey to a ferocious display of American firepower superiority. Using the road as a fire coordination line, the division's eight-inch 105MM and 155MM howitzers blanketed the north side of the road with more than 2,000 artillery rounds, while the Air Force assisted with more than ninety bombing sorties on the south side.

In the meantime Col. Berry's 1st Brigade reaction force closed in on the enemy's flanks—the 1st Battalion, 18th Infantry, and the 2d Battalion, 2d Infantry, by foot from the west; the 1st Battalion, 28th Infantry, by air from the east. To complete the encirclement of the VC regiment and to prevent escape, the 1st Battalion, 16th Infantry, later as-

saulted by helicopter into blocking positions to the enemy's rear. On every front the American infantrymen met with stiff resistance from well-entrenched Vietcong covering forces. After hacking their way through the tangled jungle, the "Swamp Rats" of the 1/18 had to slice their way through a network of fortifications on the enemy's west flank, while the 1/28 was similarly stalled by a heavily defended bunker complex on the east flank. The soldiers of the 1/16 found the going equally tough, colliding with a VC rear guard unit as they closed in from the north. In the fierce firefight that ensued, battalion commander Lieutenant Colonel Rufus G. Lazzell was struck in the chest by a fifty-caliber machine-gun round and had to be flown out. His place was taken by Col. Berry, who immediately called for artillery support and ordered the 2d Battalion, 2d Infantry, to reinforce the position. By the time the 2/2 arrived, however, many of the enemy had already withdrawn from the battlefield, taking advantage of the thick jungle cover to elude the Americans' tightening ring. Even so, the engagement had proved exceedingly costly to the 272d VC Regiment. In addition to the 239 KIA recorded by body count, eight members of the unit were captured and numerous weapons as well.

Four days later, on July 13, Operation El Paso II came to a close. During the course of the campaign the 1st Infantry Division fought four pivotal battles against all three regiments of the 9th VC Division. The heavy losses inflicted on these units severely disrupted enemy plans for a major monsoon offensive and earned for the 1st Squadron, 4th Cavalry, the first Presidential Unit Citation awarded to the division during the war. Perhaps most important of all, the forty-two-day operation clearly demonstrated the division's willingness and ability to pursue the enemy aggressively within his own domain. After El Paso II, questions about the performance of the division faded as the 1st Infantry went on to establish a reputation as one of MACV's hardest-fighting units.

Search and destroy

During the late summer and early fall of 1966 the pace of action diminished as the 9th VC Division withdrew to hidden base camps deep in War Zone C, replenished their ranks with fresh replacements from North Vietnam, and for the most part avoided contact with the Big Red One. The two units did not clash again until early November, when the entire 1st Infantry Division joined Operation Attleboro in western Tay Ninh Province. Called into action after the 196th Infantry Brigade (Light) and 25th Infantry Division became embroiled in a furious battle with four enemy regiments—the 70th, 271st, and 272d VC regiments and the 101st NVA Regiment—the 1st Infantry Division assumed control of the operation under orders from MACV on November 6. A short time later the 3d Brigade of the 4th Infantry Division and the 173d Airborne Brigade also joined the fight, making Attleboro the largest U.S. operation to that date. Faced with such an overwhelming show of force, the Vietcong soon retreated west, leaving behind more than 800 dead as well as several large caches of weapons, ammunition, and supplies.

Encouraged by the success of Attleboro, and convinced that they now had the enemy on the run, General Westmoreland and his staff immediately began planning similar multibrigade search-and-destroy operations for the coming year. Among the ambitious aims of the 1967 MACV counteroffensive were the reopening of Highway 1, the neutralization of War Zones C and D, and the systematic extension of government control over the civilian population. The ultimate goal, however, was nothing less than the wholesale destruction of all VC and NVA Main Force units northwest of Saigon.

The only remaining questions were when and where to strike first. Against the advice of Major General DePuy, who wanted to plunge directly into War Zone C, II Field Force commander Gen. Seaman, who had recently earned his third star, decided to begin with a thrust into the long-time VC stronghold known as the Iron Triangle, a wedge of jungle and rice fields roughly bounded by the Saigon River, the Song Thi Thinh, and Thanh Dien Forest. Code-named Cedar Falls, Seaman's plan called for a corps-size "hammer-and-anvil" operation involving twenty maneuver battalions. After the 25th Infantry Division and the 196th Infantry Brigade (Light) established set positions along the winding Saigon River, the 1st Infantry Division, the 173d Airborne Brigade, and the 11th Armored Cavalry would sweep through the Triangle from east to west, pinning the enemy against the awaiting blockers. The celebrated "Iron Brigade," the 3d Brigade of the Big Red One, and the paratroopers of the 173d were to spearhead the drive with an opening attack on the fortified village of Ben Suc, believed to be the nerve center of enemy activities in VC Military Region IV.

Following four days of massed B-52 Arc Light strikes, the operation kicked off on the morning of January 8, 1967. The skies were clear but it was still dark as sixty helicopters, packed with soldiers of Lt. Col. Alexander M. Haig's 1st Battalion, 26th Infantry, set off from the airstrip at Dau Tieng for Ben Suc. Flying in two giant V formations at eighty miles per hour, the troop carriers swept over the heavily forested terrain at treetop level and dropped into the village without warning. The stunned inhabitants of Ben Suc crowded together and watched in eerie silence as the American troops poured out of the transports, expecting battle. But aside from occasional sniper fire and a few

On July 10, 1966, one day after the battle of Minh Thanh Road, a 1st Infantry Division M48A3 tank retrieves the gutted shell of an APC (right), hit by recoilless rifle fire in an ambush by the 272d VC Regiment. American artillery and air strikes devastated VC forces after the ambush.

scattered mines, they met no resistance. After a thorough search of the hamlet revealed an elaborate underground supply complex, with tunnels and storage rooms extending three levels below some houses, the 6,000 villagers were evacuated to a refugee camp at Phu Loi. Bulldozers, "tankdozers," and demolition teams of the 1st Engineer Battalion then moved in and razed the entire village, ensuring that Ben Suc would never again serve as an enemy base.

The "hammer" phase of Cedar Falls similarly failed to generate much contact, as Vietcong Main Force units chose to evade the onrushing American forces rather than confront them. Instead the success of the operation had to be measured in terms of enemy installations discovered and destroyed. By the time Cedar Falls terminated on January 26, U.S. and ARVN troops operating in the Triangle had uncovered 1,100 bunkers and 500 tunnels, including one huge four-level labyrinth that turned out to be the long-sought-after headquarters of VC Military Region IV. They had also seized a wide array of enemy weapons and equipment, as well as enough rice to feed 13,000 troops for a year. Yet while the campaign may have dealt the enemy

a severe logistical blow, it did not deter the VC from filtering back into the Iron Triangle as soon as the Americans departed. As they proceeded to rebuild their base camps and supply network, it soon became apparent that in the future, as in the past, the area one MACV official likened to "a dagger pointed at Saigon" would remain a center of Communist military operations in South Vietnam.

Preparations for the long-awaited drive into War Zone C were already under way when on February 10 Major General DePuy relinquished command of the 1st Infantry Division to Major General John J. Hay. A veteran of the famed 10th Mountain Division, which saw action in Italy during World War II, Hay served for two years as the commanding general of the Berlin Brigade and, briefly, as commander of the 11th Infantry Brigade. Ordered to Vietnam in January 1967, he barely had time to unpack his bags before he was placed in charge of the Big Red One and received plans for the biggest operation to date.

Villagers of Ben Suc await their evacuation. Nearly 6,000 people were uprooted to a refugee camp at Phu Loi as part of Operation Cedar Falls, January 1967.

Dubbed Junction City, the multidivisional campaign called for the 1st Infantry Division, the 173d Airborne Brigade, and two brigades of the 25th Infantry Division to create a giant inverted horseshoe bracketing War Zone C to the east, north, and west. A third brigade of the 25th Infantry Division, backed by the 11th Armored Cavalry, would then push through the open end of the horseshoe from the south. With no avenue of escape, the Vietcong would either have to stand and fight or be crushed by the tightening vise of the advance.

By mid-February the blocking forces were on the move, the 25th Infantry Division taking up position along the Cambodian border on the western side of War Zone C while the 1st Infantry Division set up along provincial Route 4 to the east. On February 22 the 1st Brigade of the 1st Infantry Division and the 173d Airborne Brigade sealed off the northern edge of the horseshoe with a massive air assault that featured the only major U.S. combat jump of the Vietnam War. The next day the 2d Brigade of the 25th Division and the 11th Armored Cavalry swept into action, eager to take on the resilient 9th VC Division, now reinforced to a strength of four regiments by the addition of the 101st NVA Regiment.

After five days of fleeting contact, the first significant engagement of the operation occurred on February 28, when Company B of the 1st Battalion, 16th Infantry, ran into the 2d Battalion, 101st NVA Regiment, near Prek Klok at the western tip of the horseshoe. Pinned down by intense rocket and machine-gun fire as they moved through the jungle toward Prek Klok Stream, the men of Bravo pulled back, formed a circular defensive perimeter, and held off the enemy until a combination of artillery fire and fifty-four air strikes finally broke the attack. Two weeks later, on the night of March 10, a battalion of the 272d VC Regiment launched another attack near Prek Klok, this time at the construction site of a future Special Forces camp manned by the 168th Engineer Battalion; the 2d Battalion, 2d Infantry (Mechanized); and the 2d Battalion, 33d Artillery. Organized in a giant "wagon train" circle to protect the engineers building the camp, the APCs of the 2/2 blunted the ground assault with a ferocious hail of machine-gun fire. The 2/33 Artillery further decimated the advancing NVA with more than 5,000 rounds of direct artillery fire, while the Air Force assisted with 100 air strikes. At five o'clock the following morning the fighting sputtered out, as the shattered enemy force abandoned any hope of penetrating the American perimeter and withdrew into the jungle.

On March 18 Junction City entered its second phase, as MACV assigned each committed unit a specific area of operation. Soon thereafter the 1st Infantry Division began receiving reports that a large enemy force had been sighted within its sector, close to the Cambodian border. In response, on the afternoon of March 30 the 1st Battalion, 26th Infantry, air-assaulted into a clearing due west of An Loc designated Landing Zone George. As the "Blue Spaders" fanned out to secure the position, they quickly discovered that the LZ was surrounded by an extensive network of abandoned fortifications. They also found signs, written in English and posted on trees, warning them to keep out. Their arrival had obviously been expected, even though the enemy was nowhere to be seen.

The next morning the 1st Battalion, 2d Infantry, helilifted into LZ George, allowing the 1/26 to probe more deeply into the surrounding woods. Shortly after noon, the battalion reconnaissance platoon came under heavy fire north of the LZ and called for assistance. Without consulting the battalion commander, Col. Haig, and without waiting for the customary artillery and aerial support, reserve Company B rushed out to extract the embattled platoon. By the time Haig realized what was happening, Bravo had also been pinned down by intense enemy fire. Sensing imminent disaster, Haig landed his command helicopter near Bravo's position and called for reinforcements. The subsequent arrival of Company A finally broke the attack, permitting the U.S. troops to retreat to the battalion perimeter before nightfall.

Further strengthened by the addition of the 1st Battalion, 16th Infantry, the American force at LZ George now waited for the enemy to make the next move. Most of the night passed quietly. Then, shortly before 5:00 A.M., an intense barrage of heavy mortar fire slammed into the battalion fire support base, signaling the onset of a mass ground assault. The mortars were so close that the troops could hear the rounds leaving the tubes, one soldier reported, and they were firing so fast they "sounded like loud, heavy machine guns." Fifteen minutes later, as the mortar fire subsided, soldiers of the 271st VC Regiment charged out of the woods and attacked the northeastern sector of the 1/26 perimeter, deeply penetrating positions manned by Company C. Although hit three times by enemy fire, Charlie Company commander Captain Brian H. Cundiff rallied his men to shoulder the attack until the recon platoon and Company B moved up and helped reestablish the American lines. In the meantime, division gunners saturated the battle area with 15,000 rounds of artillery fire, while Air Force jets streaked in and unleashed their bombs within six meters of the battalion perimeter. As the intensity of the assault diminished, Captain Cundiff led his men in a sustained counterattack that drove the remaining enemy troops into full retreat.

The most severe blow yet dealt to the 271st VC Regiment, the lopsided battle at LZ George cost the enemy nearly 600 soldiers, compared with 17 American KIAs. Though artillery and aerial firepower played a decisive role in the victory, the courageous acts of individual soldiers did not go unrecognized. In addition to Captain Cundiff, who earned a Distinguished Service Cross, 48 members of the 1st Infantry Division were awarded Silver Stars and 121, Bronze Stars for their actions at LZ George.

Back to the border

On April 15 the 1st Infantry Division ended its activities in Operation Junction City and began preparing for a follow-up sweep of the Iron Triangle. Reinforced by elements of the 25th Infantry Division and the 11th Armored Cavalry, the division launched its new campaign, called Manhattan, with a series of coordinated air and ground assaults on April 23. Again the Americans found ample evidence of the enemy's presence, including hundreds of freshly dug bunkers and several large caches of weapons and supplies. Contact with the Vietcong forces was minimal, however, and after two weeks Operation Junction City was called to a halt.

In June the division entered the previously unexplored jungles of War Zone D in Operation Billings, a multibrigade search-and-destroy mission that resulted in back-to-back battles between the 1st Battalion, 16th Infantry, and the 271st VC Regiment. The first took place on June 14, two days after the operation began, when Company B of the 1/16 came under fire as it approached a wood line near the village of Xom Bo. Unable to move, the company called in artillery and air strikes and finally managed to extract itself after several hours of intense combat.

Intelligence gleaned from a captured VC soldier set the stage for the second battle of Xom Bo three days later. The prisoner told interrogators that four companies of the 271st VC Regiment had set up an ambush site at a bean-shaped landing zone two kilometers north of the previous day's firefight. As a result, the division command canceled a planned air assault into the area and instead prepared to storm the LZ by foot. On the morning of June 17, a force consisting of Companies A and B of the 1st Battalion, 16th Infantry; Company B of the 2d Battalion, 28th Infantry; and the 1/16 Reconnaissance Platoon set out to foil the trap. They found the enemy shortly after noon, when the lead troops came under heavy automatic-weapons and small-arms fire just south of the landing zone. The Americans immediately pulled back and formed a defensive perimeter, using giant ant hills and clusters of bamboo for cover. Moments later the VC launched a three-pronged ground assault, only to be halted in their tracks by a relentless hail of artillery, air strikes, and helicopter gunship fire. Within ten minutes the worst of the fighting was over, as the VC fell back and the battle devolved into an occasional exchange of mortar rounds.

In the wake of Billings the pace of action subsided, as the 1st Infantry Division entered a prolonged "turnover" period that brought changes of leadership at virtually every level of the command structure. After devoting most of the summer to training his new men, Gen. Hay finally decided to put them to the test in a major campaign scheduled to kick off in late September 1967. Code-named Shenandoah II, the operation aimed at clearing Highway 13 from Lai Khe to Loc Ninh, the most dangerous stretch of "Thunder Road" and a favored hunting ground of the 271st VC Regiment. As conceived by Hay, the operation would be preceded by an elaborate "psyops," or "psychological operations," campaign throughout the populated areas bordering Highway 13. Two full brigades, the 1st and the 3d, would then conduct a reconnaissance-in-force west of the road as far as the Michelin rubber plantation, seeking out and eliminating any enemy troop concentrations.

Perhaps because of the relative inexperience of many of the troops involved, the first major engagement boded ill for the operation. Known as the battle of Ong Thanh, it began on the morning of October 17, when Companies A and D of the 2d Battalion, 28th Infantry, tripped into an ambush along a well-worn jungle trail nineteen kilometers northeast of Lai Khe. Two platoons were completely cut off and unable to move. Deprived of effective artillery support by the enemy's "hugging" tactics, the Americans were forced to withdraw in small groups of two and three under constant fire from a reinforced battalion of the 271st VC Regiment. By midafternoon, when the firing finally ceased, fifty-three U.S. soldiers lay dead and another fifty-eight had been wounded. Among those killed were battalion commander Lieutenant Colonel Terry D. Allen, Jr., whose father had commanded the 1st Infantry Division during World War II, and 1st Brigade chief of operations Major Donald W. Holleder, a former all-American football player at West Point.

At the end of October the focus of Operation Shenandoah II shifted north to Loc Ninh, following an attack by the 273d VC Regiment on the local district headquarters compound and Special Forces camp. Hoping to intercept the enemy force before it fled across the Cambodian border, on the morning of October 29 Major General Hay dispatched the 1st Battalion, 18th Infantry, to the Loc Ninh rubber plantation, four kilometers west of the attack site. The 1/18 became embroiled in a running battle with the 165th NVA Regiment. The fighting carried over into the next day, when a combination of artillery and air strikes forced the enemy to scatter and flee.

On the night of October 31, the Special Forces camp and airstrip at Loc Ninh were hit again, this time by the 1st and 2d battalions of the crack 272d VC Regiment. Charging across the airstrip in three successive waves, the enemy were met by a wall of high-explosive direct artillery fire that broke the attack almost as soon as it began. Another seemingly suicidal attempt to breach the camp perimeter two nights later met with the same result. The area around Loc Ninh then grew quiet until November 7, when the 1st Battalion, 26th Infantry, came under attack from a battalion of the 272d VC Regiment during a sweep eight kilome-

The look of war. Moments after a thirty minute firefight that killed six and wounded twelve, soldiers of Company B, 1st Battalion, 16th Infantry, 1st Infantry Division, await evacuation during Operation Billings in June, 1967.

The Big Red One

America's oldest Army division, the 1st Infantry Division was formed in the spring of 1917 as the United States prepared to enter World War I. Originally known as the First Expeditionary Division, the unit was composed of 14,000 men organized into four infantry regiments. Of these the 2d Infantry Regiment boasted the longest lineage, having seen service in every major American war since its inception in Pennsylvania in 1808. The 16th Infantry and 18th Infantry regiments traced their roots to the early years of the Civil War, while the 28th Infantry Regiment had fought in the Philippines following its formation at Vancouver Barracks, Washington, in 1901.

Under the command of Major General William I. Sibert, the division landed in Brittany and immediately set out for Paris. On July 4, 1917, the soldiers of the 2d Battalion, 16th Infantry, entered the streets of the French capital, where they were greeted by shouts of "*Vives les Teddies!*" and showered with flowers and cologne. After parading down the city's boulevards to the tomb of Lafayette, the column halted to pay homage to the French for their support a century and a half earlier during the American Revolution. It was there that one member of General John J. Pershing's staff uttered the memorable phrase, "*Lafayette, nous sommes arrivés.*" ("Lafayette, we are here.")

After officially changing its name to the 1st Infantry Division on July 6, the division joined the grinding war of attrition on the western front. Nearly a year later, on May 28, 1918, the division won the first major American victory of the war when the 28th Regiment—thereafter known as the Black Lions of Cantigny—stormed and captured a German garrison occupying the small village of Cantigny. Three weeks later, on July 18, 1918, French commander Marshall Ferdnand Foch called upon the Americans to take Sois-

World War I soldiers of the 1st Division wait for orders to advance from their positions in the Argonne Forest.

sons. The division succeeded, penetrating seven miles into German lines at a cost of 7,000 casualties—a sacrifice that prompted Foch to thank the Americans "for the blood so generously spilled on the soil of my country." By the time the war ended in November 1918, 22,320 members of the division had been killed or wounded in action.

During the course of its participation in World War I, the 1st Infantry Division had accrued its first seven campaign streamers, its men had been awarded five Medals of Honor, and the unit had acquired a nickname that would endure throughout the years: the "Big Red One." According to one story, the nickname derived from the large numeral 1 that was painted on each of the division's supply trucks to distinguish them from identical models belonging to the British. A second and more colorful explanation, however, claims that the Big Red One made its first appearance as a makeshift shoulder patch designed by a general officer during the division's early training days in the summer of 1917. Convinced that the new unit needed an appropriate insignia, the general reportedly cut a rough number 1 from his red flannel underwear and sewed it onto his sleeve. After the division arrived in Europe, a lieutenant attached the flannel 1 to an olive drab piece of cloth taken from the uniform of a captured soldier, creating the patch that would eventually be approved for wear by all soldiers of the 1st Infantry Division.

After World War I, the division remained in Europe as an occupation force until September 1919, when it returned to the United States and separated into various posts along the Atlantic seaboard. More than twenty years passed before the Big Red One was again called to action in August 1942. Again designated the First Infantry Division, the unit was deployed to the Mediterranean in early November

to join in the first Allied invasion of North Africa. On the eve of battle division commander Major General Terry Allen, whose son was later killed in Vietnam, exhorted his troops by vowing that "nothing in hell must delay the 1st Division." As it turned out, nothing did. The "Fighting First" marched through Oran, Algeria, and secured Tunisia by May 1943, defeating the vaunted Nazi Afrika Korps along the way.

After fending off a German Panzer division in Sicily in July 1943, the Big Red One returned to England to prepare for the long-awaited Allied invasion of France. On D-day—June 6, 1944—the First Infantry Division stormed ashore at Omaha Beach and then moved on to the bloody battle of St. Lô. In the months that followed the division drove across northern France and laid siege to Aachen, taking the German fortress-city by direct assault on October 21, 1944. After breaching the Siegfried Line, the division

D-day, 1944. Men of the 1st Division take cover from withering German fire during the invasion of Normandy.

crossed the Rhine River at Remagen Bridge on March 16, 1945, and closed the Ruhr Pocket. By May 8, when the Germans surrendered, elements of the Big Red One had pushed all the way across the border to Cheb, Czechoslovakia.

The overall performance of the 1st Infantry Division in World War II was just as impressive as it had been in World War I. Suffering 21,023 casualties, the division added seven more campaign streamers to its colors and its men earned sixteen Medals of Honor. After the war it remained in Germany for ten years on occupation duty before returning to Fort Riley, Kansas, in the summer of 1955. It would be ten more years until the 1st Infantry Divison again wore its big red patch in combat, this time on the battlefields of Vietnam.

ters northeast of Loc Ninh. Though sustained artillery fire and air strikes eventually compelled the enemy to break contact, eighteen Americans were killed in the action, including Blue Spader battalion commander Lieutenant Colonel Arthur D. Stigall.

On November 19 the 1st Infantry Division terminated Operation Shenandoah II, having achieved its principal objectives. Not only had it succeeded in extending friendly supply lines nearly to the Cambodian border, but in the process it had inflicted staggering losses on three Main Force enemy units, including the vaunted 272d VC Regiment. Nevertheless, the willingness of the enemy to sacrifice so many troops in a futile attempt to seize Loc Ninh puzzled the American command. At the time, the most likely explanation seemed to be that the Communists were desperate for a battlefield victory that would discredit the Thieu regime in the wake of the recent presidential election. Only later did the allies come to recognize the real goal of the enemy's Loc Ninh campaign—to lure the 1st Infantry Division away from Saigon in anticipation of the 1968 Tet offensive.

1968

Like many American units, the 1st Infantry Division operated primarily as a reaction force during the Tet offensive, rushing to the aid of besieged ARVN units at Ben Cat, Chau Thanh, Di An, Lai Thieu, and Thu Duc. In addition, the 1st Battalion, 18th Infantry, and A Troop of the 1st Squadron, 4th Cavalry, were hurled into the battle of Saigon, initially joining the fight at Tan Son Nhut airfield and then staying on for a week of mop-up operations throughout the Capital Military District. The 1st Battalion, 28th Infantry, also became heavily involved in the fighting, taking on elements of the 273d VC Regiment in a savage two-day battle in and around the village of An My, thirty-two kilometers north of Saigon. Scattered though the fighting was, by mid-February the division had accounted for more than 1,500 enemy killed, among the largest totals it had yet recorded in a single operation.

On March 8 Major General Keith L. Ware, a former Medal of Honor winner and the first Army draftee to rise to the rank of general, took command of the Big Red One, as Maj. Gen. Hay moved on to become deputy commanding general of II Field Force, Vietnam. Three days later the division joined with other American and South Vietnamese forces to launch Operation Quyet Thang (Resolved to Win), a counteroffensive interdiction campaign in Binh Duong Province. Though the month-long operation produced no major contact, the division discovered and destroyed one extensive VC base camp and seized a variety of weapons, equipment, and supplies.

In early April all units in III Corps Tactical Zone combined to inaugurate the largest operation of the war, code-named Toan Thang (Certain Victory). Designed to preempt future attacks on the Saigon area, the campaign involved forty-two American and thirty-nine South Vietnamese infantry and tank battalions deployed in a ring surrounding the capital. Even though the operation did not prevent the enemy from launching its "Mini-Tet" offensive in early May, it did ensure that friendly forces were well positioned to respond.

Assigned to guard the northern approaches to Saigon, the 1st Infantry Division reacted swiftly to the new wave of attacks, driving enemy forces from several villages in the vicinity of their Di An base camp. In the largest of these engagements, elements of the 1st Squadron, 4th Cavalry, and the 1st Battalion, 18th Infantry, tangled with a large NVA force just outside the village of Xom Moi. The action began on the afternoon of May 5, when B Troop of the 1/4, or "Quarter Cav," spotted several enemy soldiers inside a sparse wood line bordered by dry rice fields. A brief exchange of rapidly intensifying fire followed, as more Communist troops exposed their positions inside the tree line. "It seemed as if there were thousands of NVA in those woods," recalled First Lieutenant Michael J. Bache, one of the platoon leaders in the Quarter Cav. "Some were moving among the trees and the rest were dug in with overhead cover."

Moving into a box formation, with its tanks across the front and armored cavalry assault vehicles (ACAVs) in the rear, D Troop surged forward. "My platoon was on the right," Bache recounted. "We went from the paddies into the brush and trees where, between the eroded ground and the thick bamboo, we had trouble staying on line." The NVA quickly took advantage of the armored troop's disorganization, isolating and destroying one tank. The Americans then pulled back and called in a series of air strikes to soften the enemy's resistance. But the NVA held their ground. "Every time we moved into the woods," said First Lieutenant Joseph F. Scates, another platoon leader, "We got hit hard."

In the meantime, A Troop of the 1/4 Cav, under orders to stand by as a reaction force, raced toward the battle site. As soon as it arrived, the two troops reassembled and again advanced on the tree line. At that point many NVA troops jumped out of their holes and began to flee. Though the Americans initially tried to pursue them, darkness was falling and visibility was poor. "We were having trouble seeing the NVA," Lt. Bache remembered, "but they were having no problems finding us." A flame thrower unit was then called in to help the armor extract itself, and thus the battle eased for the night, as the cavalrymen withdrew to their nearby base camp.

The next morning the armored troops returned, reinforced by a platoon from Company B, 1st Battalion, 18th Infantry. Much to their astonishment, the NVA were still there. "I found it strange to believe," said Major Paul A. Lucas, assistant operations chief of 1st Squadron, 4th Cavalry. "I couldn't understand why the NVA hadn't left.

They knew they were no match for our firepower." Before reentering the wood line, the Americans dispatched a psyops team to fly over the area and warn the enemy that they were about to be "attacked relentlessly" if they failed to surrender within five minutes. When no one came out, the tanks rumbled forward, firing. Behind them came the infantrymen of the 1/18, dropping grenades into bunkers and spider holes to eliminate any enemy soldiers the armor had missed. By late afternoon only a few small pockets of resistance remained, as much of the enemy force had at last fled the armored attack, and by nightfall the battle was over.

The next few months passed quietly, as Communist forces avoided contact and concentrated on recouping the staggering losses incurred during the Tet and Mini-Tet offensives. Though the 1st Infantry Division continued to conduct extensive reconnaissance-in-force missions under the aegis of ongoing Operation Toan Thang, much of the division's energy was devoted to a series of land clearance and road construction projects along the Binh Long-Binh Duong provincial boundary and in the vicinity of Lai Khe. Heavy fighting did not resume until late August, when the

An M60 machine gunner of the 1st Battalion, 28th Infantry, lays down supporting fire in fighting at Thu Duc, east of Saigon, during the Tet offensive, February 1968.

NVA and VC initiated another series of attacks on the Special Forces camp and airstrip at Loc Ninh.

Called upon to reinforce elements of the 11th Armored Cavalry, men of the 1st Battalion, 2d Infantry, arrived in the area on the morning of August 22 and promptly found themselves fighting a battalion-size NVA force eight kilometers east of Loc Ninh Village. Following a series of brief, intense firefights, the battalion pulled back to evacuate its wounded and then began moving toward its prearranged overnight position. Along the way the scout leader of Company D found a communications wire leading up a hill and called it to the attention of company commander Captain Oliver B. Ingram, Jr. Moments later the hillside erupted in violence, as the NVA opened fire with small arms and mortars from three sides. "Then they just started coming from behind every tree," recalled First Lieutenant Lee F. Jones, the 2d Platoon leader. "A squad here, a squad there, they advanced downhill."

After ordering his men to form a defensive perimeter, Captain Ingram crawled back and rejoined them, then called in air strikes and artillery. The supporting fires seemed to have little effect, however, as the enemy continued to advance on Delta Company's position with steadily intensifying firepower. "They just kept walking toward us," said Lt. Jones. "It looked as if we were going to be overrun. We were told to pop smoke, which we did, and air strikes were dropped within fifty yards of our position— so close you could feel the heat." The close air support finally checked the NVA charge, allowing Delta Company to extract itself at dusk.

The next morning Company D again moved up the hill, preceded by the battalion recon platoon and backed by Companies A and C. Hit by heavy mortar and sniper fire as they entered a wood line some 900 meters from the top, the soldiers of the 1/2 slowly pressed forward until they reached a ridge line where the NVA came into view. "There seemed to be an enemy behind every tree," remembered Specialist 4 Evan Harr, the radioman for Company D. "You could just about pick out the officers by their clean, starched uniforms." The NVA laid down a heavy base of fire, then mounted a ground assault against the positions held by the recon platoon and Company D. Again air strikes and artillery were requested, and this time they did the job with devastating effect. Within an hour all firing had ceased, as the battered remnants of the enemy force retreated down the hillside.

In mid-September the action around Loc Ninh picked up again, as three battalions of the Big Red One—the 1st Battalion, 2d Infantry; the 1st Battalion, 28th Infantry; and the 1st Battalion, 16th Infantry—fought a series of skirmishes against an NVA force estimated to be a regiment inside the Loc Ninh rubber plantation. During this engagement, on the afternoon of September 13, the command helicopter carrying General Ware and seven members of his staff was shot down, killing everyone aboard. The assistant division commander, Major General Orwin C. Talbott, was immediately named Ware's successor.

In October 1968 the division relinquished the northern portion of its tactical area of responsibility (TAOR) to the 1st Cavalry Division (Airmobile), as MACV moved to bolster its forces northwest of Saigon. Elements of the 1st Infantry Division nevertheless continued to operate in the area, joining forces with the 1st Cav soldiers to establish a network of interlocking fire support patrol bases (FSPBs) astride the main enemy infiltration routes leading through War Zones C and D. With plans already under way for another major attack on Saigon in early 1969, the North Vietnamese immediately began probing these new defenses, launching successive multibattalion attacks against FSPBs Julie and Rita at the end of October. Although both assaults were quickly repulsed, enemy activity along the Cambodian border continued to preoccupy the 1st Infantry Division as the year ended.

Winding down

During the first two months of 1969 contact with enemy forces was light, as the division increasingly focused its attention on pacification and road-clearance operations within its newly delimited TAOR. Included among the latter was a herculean effort to reopen the road from Phuoc Vinh to Song Be, which had been cut off by the Vietcong for more than three years. Beginning in mid-January, combat engineers of the 1st Engineer Battalion cut giant swaths out of the thick vegetation bordering the route, allowing construction crews to transform what had formerly been a single-lane pass into a major thoroughfare. In the meantime, infantrymen of the 1st Brigade conducted extensive sweeps of the surrounding area, ensuring the security of the mission.

In March, following the outbreak of the enemy's 1969 Spring offensive, B and C Troops of the 1st Squadron, 4th Cavalry, teamed up with the 11th Armored Cavalry and elements of the 1st Cavalry Division (Airmobile) to sweep the Michelin rubber plantation in War Zone C. Codenamed Atlas Wedge, the counteroffensive caught the 7th NVA Division by surprise. In the past, the plantation had served as a haven for enemy forces operating northwest of Saigon because the U.S. and South Vietnam did not want to destroy its economically valuable rubber trees. For Atlas Wedge, however, the long-standing restrictions on fighting in the plantation were temporarily lifted. As a result, the North Vietnamese marched directly into the advancing American armor, triggering a series of violent clashes that resulted in the death of more than 400 enemy troops.

During the late spring and summer of 1969, in accordance with MACV's new emphasis on "Vietnamization," the division devoted an ever-growing share of its time, energy, and resources to the task of preparing the Army of the Republic of Vietnam (ARVN) for the eventual departure of U.S. combat troops. Under the auspices of a program called "Dong Tien" (Progress Together), joint operations with the 5th ARVN Division became increasingly common, as the Big Red One strove to familiarize its South Vietnamese counterparts with American military doctrine and tactics. In addition to providing training in the techniques of helicopter mobility and tactical air support, the division began to send out mixed ambush patrols, to man its fire support bases with ARVN as well as U.S. troops, and to establish combined tactical operation centers throughout its area of responsibility.

Yet if the war was winding down for the soldiers of the 1st Infantry Division, it was far from over. Beginning in mid-August, the 2d Battalion (Mechanized), 2d Infantry, became involved in a series of fierce battles along Highway 13, as NVA forces attempted to stem the flow of U.S. and South Vietnamese supplies into War Zones C and D. The first occurred on August 12, two days after now-Major

General A. E. Milloy took command of the division, when a large resupply convoy fell into an ambush just north of Fire Support Base Thunder III. Posted nearby, Companies A and C of the 2/2 immediately responded, racing to the scene of action and driving the enemy into the jungle before they could overrun the column of trucks.

Two days later the NVA struck again in the vicinity of FSB Thunder III, blowing up two 1,500-gallon fuel tankers en route from Quan Loi to Long Binh. Again Companies A and C were called upon to break the attack, with additional fire support provided by helicopter gunships and tactical air strikes. After a third ambush on August 20 met with similar results, the NVA decided to alter its tactics. In the early morning hours of September 5, enemy sappers launched a three-pronged assault on FSB Thunder III in an attempt to penetrate the headquarters of the 2/2. Though several of the enemy managed to breach the wire and blow up an armored personnel carrier, by dawn the attack had been repulsed.

In the months that followed, the division continued to work closely with the 5th ARVN Division, setting up small-unit ambushes, searching villages, combing the country-side for enemy cache sites. Contact with enemy forces was minimal, however, as the NVA and Vietcong reduced the scale of military operations in anticipation of a total U.S. pullout. A similar anticipation could also be seen in the attitude and performance of many soldiers of the 1st Infantry Division. War-weary, demoralized, and deprived of any sense of mission, some now openly referred to their unit as the "Big Dead One."

On December 15, 1969, three days after President Nixon publicly announced the commencement of the third phase of troop withdrawals, Maj. Gen. Milloy was told to bring his division home. Precisely four months later, on April 15, 1970, Operation Keystone Blue Jay came to an end as the last remaining elements of the 1st Infantry Division departed for Fort Riley. When it left, the division carried with it a host of unit and individual awards for gallantry in action, including 11 Medals of Honor, 67 Distinguished Service Crosses, and 905 Silver Star medals. Over the course of its involvement in the Vietnam War the division suffered more casualties than it had in World War II and nearly as many as in World War I. The 20,770 soldiers killed or wounded on the battlefields of Vietnam became part of the proud legacy of the Big Red One.

ARVN soldiers begin an assault from Hueys of the 1st Infantry Division's 162nd Aviation Company, 1970. By then, a priority of the Division was "Vietnamizing" the war.

The Fire Brigade

To many other American fighting men they were known as "the Herd" because of their high esprit and close bond to each other. To Nationalist Chinese soldiers who watched admiringly as they trained over Taiwan they were *Tien Bing*, or "Sky Soldiers." Within their own ranks, they came to be called "Two Shades of Soul," a sign of the harmony that existed between black and white paratroopers at a time of racial strife in America. These three nicknames reflect the qualities of the men of the 173d Airborne Brigade, the first U.S. Army combat unit sent to Vietnam.

The elite 173d Airborne Brigade was a relatively new organization, formed in mid-1963 from the assets of the 2d Airborne Battle Group (Reinforced), 503d Infantry, a well-regarded unit of paratroopers based in Okinawa since 1960. Because the brigade contained the 1st and 2d battalions of the 503d Infantry, it retained a close association with its predecessor. The 503d Parachute Infantry had conducted the first American airborne operation in the

Pacific during World War II, parachuting into New Guinea's Markham Valley to engage entrenched Japanese forces in 1943. The regiment's greatest moment of glory came when it jumped onto the Japanese-held Philippine island of Corregidor, known as "The Rock," early on the morning of February 16, 1945, completely surprising its defenders, who had expected an amphibious attack. After fighting for eleven days, the Allies retook Corregidor from the enemy, and the 503d earned an enduring appellation: "the Rock Regiment." Twenty years later, the 173d Brigade troopers, cursing the dangerously hard drop zones on Okinawa, called their modern island base the Rock.

The brigade's training was constant, tough, and realistic. Every man in the brigade, from general to private, was a parachutist. So outstanding was the unit's airborne school that U.S. Marine Anglico (naval gunfire coordination) teams and Navy Underwater Demolition teams (which became the SEALs of Vietnam) received their parachute training there. Brigadier General Ellis W. Williamson kept his 4,000-man brigade training intensively throughout Okinawa and adjacent regions. The men also underwent extensive airborne, guerrilla, and jungle warfare training in the Philippines, Taiwan, Korea, and Thailand.

The unit had been designed as a hard-hitting, self-sufficient fire brigade able to strike anywhere in the western Pacific on short notice. Wherever the paratroopers landed, they were ready to fight instantly because their own heavy equipment, ranging from tactical rafts to artillery, was dropped with them. From the moment their aircraft took off from Okinawa the paratroopers could, within two hours, be jumping into the rough mountains of Taiwan. In three hours, they could be hitting the silk over the snowy hills of Korea or the tropical Philippine rice fields. In six hours, brigade parachutists could be descending over the jungles of Vietnam.

In country

It was to this last destination that the paratroopers were ordered to counter the Communists' Winter-Spring offensive of 1965. They landed in transport planes between May 2 and May 7. Their assignment was to defend the critical airfield complex at Bien Hoa, near Saigon, and the coastal landing site of Vung Tau. It was a "temporary" assignment, but the rapid escalation of American forces quickly turned it into a long-term one.

Soon, the men came face to face with the bitter reality of war. At 3:00 P.M. on May 22, several of the paratroopers patrolling outside the Bien Hoa air base tripped a VC booby trap, wounding one soldier in the neck. A second

was injured later that day when he fired an M79 round on a hut he suspected of housing VC. The round bounced off the hut, however, and exploded near the grenadier. The two became the first of more than 10,000 casualties the brigade suffered during its six years in Vietnam.

Although trained as paratroopers, the soldiers of the 173d reached their Vietnam battlefields primarily by helicopter. Their first large helicopter assault took place during the third week of May, when they were ordered to clear a suspected VC operating base nineteen kilometers outside Bien Hoa. Except for some sporadic sniper fire, the assault was uneventful.

In June, the 173d was boosted to three battalions with the attachment of the 1st Battalion, Royal Australian Regiment. During the next few months, the paratroopers and their Aussie comrades conducted joint sweep missions throughout War Zone D, the major Vietcong stronghold northeast of Saigon. The first sallies into the region met with little resistance. Then, on November 8, 1965, during Operation Hump, the Vietcong suddenly counterattacked. Early that morning the 1st Battalion, 503d Infantry, had taken up position in dense jungle when three battalions of Vietcong regulars stormed their lines with human wave assaults.

The fighting was at such close range that supporting artillerymen were at first unable to fire for fear of hitting their own troops, and reinforcements were unable to help because too few helicopters were available. The American paratroopers were on their own. Specialist 4th Class Jerry W. Langston remembered the fierceness of the fight. He and a group of troopers were protecting some wounded men on a hill near a small jungle creek when "the woods seemed to get up and charge at us. The VC had bushes and branches tied to their backs and they started blowing bugles and charged us from three sides. They came down off the hill behind us, from the flank, and across the creek to our front. The fighting was close in, real close. We were really cut off and there didn't look to be much chance left."

Langston crawled to the radio operator, who had already been hit in the right arm and left leg but continued to report the unit's situation. Then he was hit again and the radio was destroyed. Attempts to evacuate the radioman failed and he died. Langston crawled on and got to a handset held by a platoon sergeant who had been using it when he was killed. Langston kept calling for help.

"Each time the VC came at us they blew their bugles," Langston remembered. "That shook us up at first, then it just made us mad. I remember one of our men down the hill from me. While we were trying to move the wounded out, he stayed right where he was, holding off the VC and trying to buy us time. He got hit and tried to crawl up to us,

---

173d Airborne Brigade

Arrived Vietnam: May 7, 1965

Departed Vietnam: August 25, 1971

Unit Headquarters

Bien Hoa *May 1965–Oct. 1967*

An Khe *Nov. 1967–April 1969*

Bong Son *May 1969–Aug. 1971*

Commanding Officers

Brig. Gen. Ellis W. Williamson *May 1965*
Brig. Gen. Paul F. Smith *Feb. 1966*
Brig. Gen. John R. Deane, Jr. *Dec. 1966*

Brig. Gen. Leo H. Schweiter *Aug. 1967*
Brig. Gen. Richard J. Allen *April 1968*
Brig. Gen. John W. Barnes *Dec. 1968*

Brig. Gen. Hubert S. Cunningham *Aug. 1969*
Brig. Gen. Elmer R. Ochs *Aug. 1970*
Brig. Gen. Jack MacFarlane *Jan. 1971*

Major Subordinate Units

1st Battalion, 503d Infantry (Abn)
2d Battalion, 503d Infantry (Abn)
3d Battalion, 503d Infantry (Abn)
4th Battalion, 503d Infantry (Abn)

Company D, 16th Armor
E Troop, 17th Cavalry (Armored)
3d Battalion, 319th Artillery (Airborne)
335th Aviation Company (Airmobile)

173d Support Battalion (Abn)
173d Engineer Company
534th Signal Company
173d Signal Company

1,748 KIA
(Casualty figures are "Vietnam Era.")

8,747 WIA

12 Medals of Honor

but he was hit again and killed. Then something hit me in the forehead and I went out. When I came to, the rest of the platoon had broken through and were charging back down the hill through the VC, driving them off."

All around the American perimeter, the enemy charges had been repulsed. The main fighting ended late in the afternoon. Sporadic machine-gun and sniper fire against the paratrooper positions continued throughout the night even though the Vietcong slowly withdrew. As the VC retreated, American artillery and air power could at last be used without endangering the troopers. The VC left 403 bodies on the battlefield. The next day, the paratroopers cut a landing zone in the dense foliage to evacuate their wounded. Operation Hump was the brigade's first real encounter of the war, demonstrating its ability to meet Main Force Vietcong units under unfavorable conditions and in difficult tropical terrain.

The 173d Airborne Brigade found new utility when General Westmoreland made it MACV's primary reaction force for any sector threatened in Vietnam, although the brigade remained based at Bien Hoa. In this role, the paratroopers helped to break the Vietcong siege of Duc Co in the central highlands in December 1965. The roads into Kontum had also been cut off by the Communists, and the 173d brought the first convoy in more than five weeks into that provincial capital. The brigade became the first U.S. combat formation to strike the Vietcong in the Mekong Delta (on Operation Marauder near the Cambodian border in January 1966). The next month, Gen. Williamson passed the colors to Brigadier General Paul F. Smith, a veteran of two combat jumps during World War II.

Throughout 1966, the 173d Airborne Brigade operated all over III Corps trying to find and destroy Vietcong forces and base camps. The VC were frustrating opponents, offering heavy resistance to initial air assaults when the helicopters and men were most vulnerable, then melting back into the jungle to elude further searches by the paratroopers. To help find this elusive enemy, General Smith formed the brigade's first long-range reconnaissance patrol (LRRP) platoon from selected volunteers on April 25. The brigade's detection abilities were enhanced when it was joined by a scout dog unit, the 39th Infantry Platoon, in the fall. While not infallible, the dogs provided patrols with an added edge in point and flank security.

The addition of the 4th Battalion, 503d Infantry, which arrived from the United States on June 25, 1966, further strengthened brigade combat power. The so-called Geronimo battalion was sent north into the Da Nang area on October 8 during Operation Winchester to bolster the Marine defenses there, an assignment they carried out for two months. The brigade had already been the first Amer-

Paratroopers disembark from a Huey near Ben Cat in December 1965. Though the men of the 173d were parachute-qualified, most landings were made by helicopter.

icon ground unit to enter War Zone D, the Iron Triangle, and the Mekong Delta, and Winchester made it the first brigade to send men into all four corps tactical zones.

The war for these men was not all bullets and bombs. Wherever the brigade went, they helped rebuild schools, construct bridges, repair roads, and administer dental and medical care to needy villagers. The paratrooper civic action program slogan became "Help Protect Yourself by Helping the 173d." Away from war the brigade also worked to retain its parachutist proficiency with training jumps, sometimes involving entire battalions.

In the field, the brigade continued to scour the heart of War Zone D, floating down streams in rubber rafts and landing high atop the thick jungle on helicopter-delivered aluminum treetop pads, which allowed the men to look for the enemy from above. The brigade's constant patrolling and skirmishing activity continued throughout 1966, involving them in Operation Attleboro and a variety of smaller actions.

Cedar Falls

In December Brigadier General John R. Deane, Jr., took over the brigade. Soon after, MACV launched Operation Cedar Falls against VC in the Iron Triangle. Gen. Westmoreland ordered the 173d to assist in the multidivisional search-and-destroy operation, which began in January 1967. Instead of massing for battle as MACV had hoped they would, the guerrillas avoided large-scale combat. The brigade employed its reconnaissance element, Troop E of the 17th Cavalry, to conduct airmobile search-and-destroy missions across the rice fields in the southwestern portion of the triangle along the Saigon River. Their riskiest missions came at night, when twelve-man patrols backed by artillery support took positions in the inundated paddies and tree-lined canals. Their purpose was to ambush enemy soldiers leaving the area and call in artillery to finish them off. The brigade's participation in Operation Cedar Falls was typified by the experience of one of these small patrols.

Late on the afternoon of January 16, a patrol led by Sergeant Michael J. Howard set up an ambush near a footbridge known to be used heavily by the Vietcong. Employing claymore mines, machine guns, and automatic rifles, the men covered the bridge, the canal it crossed, and an adjoining trail. The ambush prepared, the men lay motionless in the thick brush, some on each side of the canal, and observed strict silence while waiting for nightfall. All was still until a Vietcong soldier walked into the

ambush zone at about seven-thirty. The squad opened fire and killed him instantly. About an hour later another guerrilla came down the same route, but it was so dark that no one saw him until he was in the center of the ambush. Several rounds rang out but missed. The guerrilla brandished a grenade, but before he could throw it, another burst of fire hit him and he dropped out of sight, moaning briefly until his grenade exploded under him.

Between the first and second ambushes, the troopers had observed several lights flashing on and off as the VC signaled to each other. The men guessed that the second soldier had been a scout sent to investigate before a larger force crossed the bridge. Soon afterward, the troopers' supposition was confirmed when they were fired on by about fifteen enemy soldiers. The enemy fire wounded Specialist 4th Class William E. Collins, who lay on the southern side of the canal, and momentarily pinned down the rest of the patrol. The paratroopers regrouped and heaved grenades, allowing two specialists named Phillips and Moye to reach the wounded man. With ammunition already low, the Americans held their fire to conserve bullets. Sergeant Howard then crossed the canal and gave Phillips and Moye a pocket flashlight to help them aid Collins, who was in shock from the wound to his cheek. Howard radioed back to another sergeant, Bolen, that they needed two more soldiers to cover them while they administered first aid.

Fortunately the grenades had quieted the Vietcong, who moved away from the troopers. Phillips lifted Collins onto the canal's bank, where he performed mouth-to-mouth resuscitation. When a dustoff helicopter arrived ten minutes later, guided to the men by a trip flare, Howard, Phillips, and another man struggled through the chest-high muddy water to carry Collins to safety.

The men returned to their positions, and much later two Vietcong soldiers wandered directly in front of Specialist Fourth Class McDonald's M60 machine gun. McDonald opened fire but his weapon jammed. Sergeant Howard fired his M16, but mud had jammed his rifle. Seeing this, Sergeant Bolen fired his M16, killing one but only wounding the other. Bolen chased him to the brush at the canal's edge and killed him. The remainder of the night was uneventful and helicopters lifted the patrol out the next morning. Sp4 Collins, a nineteen-year-old native of Houston, Texas, died in the hospital a week later. The bullet, which the patrol thought had only pierced his cheek, had lodged in his brain.

Operation Cedar Falls ended ten days later with mixed results. Although the Vietcong had avoided MACV's intended knockout punch, the Americans uncovered huge stores of rice and weapons, destroyed hundreds of bunkers and tunnels, and found a valuable stack of significant VC intelligence documents.

The brigade's proficiency during the operation in small-unit tactics reinforced its value for the hard campaigning

"Geronimo"

Though the use of the troop-carrying helicopter in Vietnam threatened to make the combat parachute jump only a memory, some paratroopers still got a chance to put their airborne training to use in the war. On February 22, 1967, almost 800 men of the 173d Airborne Brigade staged a drop over Katum into War Zone C during Operation Junction City. It was the brigade's first—and last—combat jump and the largest of the war.

Above. *At first light, soldiers of the 173d board an Air Force C-130 at Bien Hoa for their mission. Right. Tethers securely fastened to the static line overhead, the men anxiously await the call to jump. Opposite. Parachutes float over a clearing near the Cambodian border as the 173d soldiers begin their airborne assault.*

that followed. The next multidivisional operation, Junction City, aimed to encircle the 9th VC in War Zone C. It was heralded by a spectacular mass parachute drop conducted shortly after dawn on February 22 by men of the brigade. It was the only large combat jump of the war; 780 paratroopers, mostly from the 2d Battalion, 503d Infantry, the Paragon battalion, jumped over Katum near the Cambodian border to cut off enemy escape routes from War Zone C. Soon after the 2d Battalion landed safely in the drop zone, the rest of the brigade flew to the battlefield by helicopter and completed the airborne brigade's portion of the encirclement.

The 173d Airborne Brigade fought in Junction City until April 13, 1967. Throughout the operation, the troopers maintained daily contact with the enemy using airmobile assaults, search-and-destroy missions, and night ambushes and inflicting casualties and logistical losses on the Vietcong. Enemy resistance tapered off during March and April, and the next month the brigade returned to the base at Bien Hoa, where it rested, trained, and provided local security.

The toughest test

The 173d Airborne Brigade had gained a reputation as a highly skilled combat formation, available for deployment into the most dangerous locations. That reputation was soon to be tested. On the afternoon of May 23, MACV ordered General Deane to prepare his airborne brigade for immediate deployment to the Pleiku area in the central highlands, where the 4th Infantry Division had encountered entrenched North Vietnamese regiments near the rugged western border. Two hundred and eight Air Force sorties were used to transport 2,239 soldiers and 2,700 tons of equipment rapidly into II Corps Tactical Zone. Soon after arrival, the paratroopers began clashing with the North Vietnamese in the high mountain ranges and deep river valleys. The brigade also took responsibility for protecting the coastal rice harvest in the Tuy Hoa region of II Corps.

Firing their weapons, men of the 2d Battalion, 503d Infantry, move through jungle clouded by artillery fire during Operation Junction City on March 31, 1967.

When Brigadier General Leo H. Schweiter assumed command of the 173d Airborne on August 23, his brigade was fighting enemy forces scattered from the central highlands to the shores of the South China Sea. To provide a central command post nearer the action, in October he moved the main brigade headquarters to An Khe, the old 1st Cavalry Division base camp on the vital inland highway leading to Pleiku. That month the brigade was strengthened by the arrival of its fourth American maneuver battalion, the 3d Battalion, 503d Infantry, the Rock from Fort Bragg. When Main Force NVA units were discovered deeply entrenched in the treacherous mountain ridges near Dak To in mid-November, Gen. Schweiter's 5,228 paratroopers were ready to tackle them.

The action around Dak To was part of Operation MacArthur, in which the 4th Infantry Division assumed operational control over the 173d Airborne Brigade. After a series of pitched firefights, the operation culminated in the bloody contest for Hill 875 near Cambodia, a five-day battle, the toughest brigade encounter in Vietnam.

On the morning of November 19, the 2d Battalion of the 503d Infantry moved into assault positions on Hill 875, the top of which was held by the 17th NVA Regiment. While Companies C and D stormed the bamboo-covered northern slope, Company A cut out a landing zone at the base of the hill. NVA troops entrenched lower on the hill opened with heavy machine-gun fire on the two attacking companies in a steep area covered with fallen logs. At first the paratroopers pushed forward, throwing grenades at bunkers and firing on the NVA concealed in holes. The NVA, however, quickly escalated their barrage on the advancing Americans, firing 57MM recoilless rifles and B40 rockets from higher trenches. The paratroopers had reached a spot only 100 meters from the hill's crest, when a combination of explosions and automatic-weapons fire cut through them and drove them back with heavy losses. The two companies were forced to dig in and consolidate their positions.

Farther down the hill, Company A, commanded by Captain Michael Kiley, was having a difficult time cutting an LZ out of the high jungle. At 2:00 P.M. a brigade supply helicopter dropped in chain and cross saws and other cutting equipment to speed the work. Just after the equipment hit the ground, the NVA launched a massed attack against the company's rear and right flank. Only the firing of machine guns at the company's guard posts gave the rest of the men any warning. Captain Kiley ordered his company to consolidate, but it was his last transmission. NVA mortar and automatic-weapons fire prevented the men from joining up, and Captain Kiley was killed by a burst of AK47 fire. Pressing the attack, the camouflaged NVA soldiers charged through their own mortar fire. Most of the paratroopers were killed or wounded in the sudden vortex of close fighting.

The survivors of Company A scrambled up the hill toward the relative safety of the perimeter of Companies C

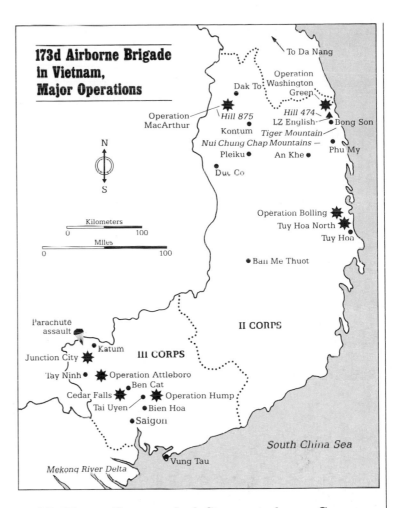

and D. Platoon Sergeant Jack Siggers took over Company A and posted a rear guard on the trail to cover the withdrawal of his remaining paratroopers. But the NVA kept coming, and the rear guard was quickly forced to scramble up the slope as well. Initially the men of Companies C and D fired on the retreating members of Company A, but after hearing cries of "Friendly! Friendly!" they helped pull them inside their perimeter to reinforce the position. Their combined effort finally stopped the main NVA assault, but sniper fire from the high trees and mortar rounds continued to harass the troopers. Most of the mortar shells burst in the trees with little effect, but others came through the jungle canopy and fell among the troops.

Air strikes and supporting artillery prevented the NVA from overrunning the shrunken battalion perimeter during the night. The close air support led to one of the worst accidents of the war, however, when a fighter-bomber pilot mistakenly dropped a 500-pound bomb inside the troopers' perimeter. The flare he was relying on to guide him had drifted over the men of the 503d, causing the errant strike. It killed forty-two men and wounded forty-five.

Early next morning the brigade's 4th Battalion, 503d Infantry, set out to reinforce the shattered 2d Battalion. It took them until nightfall to reach them. Sniper fire prevented all but one medevac helicopter from landing. On the morning of November 21, the two battalions renewed the assault. Leading the group, Captain Jim Muldoon's Company A, 4th Battalion, moved through a ravine and then started uphill. Just as the men were climbing out of the ravine, a mortar barrage crashed down on them. Captain Muldoon decided the only way out was up. One-third of the company had already fallen dead or wounded, but the paratroopers grimly proceeded to crawl forward through the tangled remnants of shattered bamboo and timber. Muldoon's decision to advance proved sound, for the mortar fire began to fall behind them.

The paratroopers crept to within fifty meters of the NVA trenches atop the hill before a machine gun opened fire on them and hand grenades began hurtling toward them. The men slowly gained more ground and one platoon worked its way into the trench system. Sergeant Joseph Decamto of the center platoon crawled toward the trenches while Specialist Fourth Class John H. Deatherage covered him with a machine gun. The two men knocked out one bunker and killed its five occupants, but since Sergeant Decamto did not have a radio, Captain Muldoon was unaware the team was in the NVA trench works.

Most of the company was still pinned down by NVA machine-gun fire. One of the men, a staff sergeant named Terraza, crept up and fired two M72 light antitank weapons (LAWs) at one enemy fortification, but the rounds barely damaged the bunker slits. Another band of paratroopers rushed the final meters to the bunker and pitched grenades at it but had to run downhill when the NVA defenders hurled the incoming grenades back at them. The company first sergeant, Fraizer, then worked his way up to the bunker under the covering fire of Terraza and Private First Class Dennis Adams. Fraizer got so close to the bunker that the red-hot shell casings ejecting from the NVA weapons burned him. He fired into the bunker but was unable to silence the enemy.

The men were so close yet so far from taking the hill. That evening, constant enemy automatic-weapons, rocket, and mortar fire forced the paratroopers to withdraw farther down the hill. After a full day of softening up the hill with more artillery and air strikes, the brigade attacked again on November 23, Thanksgiving Day. This time, the men gained the crest of the hill but without the satisfaction of having defeated the enemy; the Communists had abandoned their positions, sneaking away sometime in the previous thirty-six hours.

The conquest of Hill 875 during November 1967 was one of the most critical and brutal battles fought by the 173d Airborne Brigade. President Johnson awarded the coveted Presidential Unit Citation to the brigade for its heroic performance. Although the paratroopers emerged with their morale high, the cost was great. In one month the brigade lost 192 killed and 642 wounded; the hill battle alone claimed 158 lives and another 402 casualties. Combined with noncombat losses, this represented one-fifth of the brigade's strength. Since a unit suffering casualties of 10 percent is usually considered unable to function effectively, the airborne brigade had proved its mettle under the most adverse circumstances. Enemy losses were even more staggering: an estimated 1,500 were killed.

Defending Tuy Hoa

After the battle of Hill 875, the brigade deployed emergency task forces to secure Ban Me Thuot and Kontum, also under attack that fall. But with the paratroopers on these extended operations in western Vietnam, the local VC were able to join NVA reinforcements near the coastline and slip unnoticed into the populated area. At the outbreak of the Communist Tet offensive at the end of January 1968, they attacked the city of Tuy Hoa. After the Communists hit American artillery positions on the outskirts of town on the night of January 30, a reaction force composed of elements from the 503d Infantry's 4th Battalion counterattacked by helicopter just before dawn. Enemy fire struck the first CH-47 approaching an LZ at the Tuy Hoa airfield, destroying one of its engines and setting it afire. Its men landed safely, though, and with the rest of the paratroopers they dropped their rucksacks, picked up extra ammunition, and pushed outside the wire toward the VC-held artillery compound.

The first troops rushed the enemy positions, throwing grenades until the VC abandoned their bunkers. The troopers recaptured the compound and its radar site but not without losing Lieutenant Colonel Robert E. Whitbeck, the artillery battalion commander, killed by a North Vietnamese AK47 round. The troops who reached his body came under fire from the Phu Yen Rehabilitation Center's northern tower, which looked into the artillery compound. The early morning skies had not yet brightened and so the men were able to see North Vietnamese muzzle flashes in the tower. Covered by fellow paratroopers, Lieutenant Lawrence D. Greene stopped the fire with a LAW. General Schweiter then set up his command post on the bunker where Lt. Col. Whitbeck had been killed, but more enemy mortar fire forced the command group to take cover inside the bunker.

The paratroopers then moved to the neighboring town of Tuy Hoa North, defended only by a sorely pressed group of South Vietnamese soldiers holed up on the opposite side of town. One paratrooper called "Killer" Mahon ran forward and surprised a number of VC occupying foxholes facing away from the paratroopers. Mahon jumped into one spider hole, grabbed an AK47 rifle, and killed the occupants with their own weapon. He then leaped into the next hole, but a VC was waiting for him and they exchanged fire. Mahon was wounded, but the enemy soldier lay dead.

Troops of the 173d Airborne Brigade move cautiously from a trench to rescue a wounded soldier during the bloody battle for Hill 875, near Dak To, in November 1967.

Mahon's action sparked a firefight along the village's hedges and huts. Enemy fire killed Lieutenant Greene, soon after wounding his radio operator. When one platoon seized a graveyard at the top of a hill on the village outskirts, they were able to support the men inside the town. But enemy return fire escalated with rounds ricocheting from the tombstones. The paratroopers were forced to pull back to regroup for their next move.

Company D commander, Captain Jimmy Jackson, ordered CS gas grenades thrown into Tuy Hoa North to provide a screen for his attacking company. The town was soon shrouded in a pall of smoke and tear gas. Covered by the fire of ARVN troops who had been brought forward, the paratroopers donned gas masks and charged down a hill toward the town. Although smoke partially masked their view, Vietcong soldiers opened fire and hit several men as they reached the first hootches. Making matters worse, the gas masks were hot, causing the men to sweat, which restricted their vision. Often the VC guerrillas emerged behind the advancing troops from spider holes and doorways, and the masked paratroopers could see them only dimly. The men's reaction time was slowed, and in a series of individual encounters in the yards and alleys between the houses, several of them were felled by enemy fire.

When Jackson's company reached the middle of the village, the attack stalled. Those paratroopers not pinned down by the heavy fire had been either wounded or killed. A sergeant major named Arthurs was about to sprint across a sixty-meter-wide open field to shuttle more grenades to the forward lines when he looked up in astonishment to see Gen. Schweiter. All he could think to say was, "General, you shouldn't be down here, there's a lot of firing going on!"

Ignoring the bursts of AK47 sniper fire over his head, Gen. Schweiter approached the front lines to be briefed on the situation. When wounded paratroopers staggered from the hut behind him, he immediately began escorting them to medical evacuation helicopters. Schweiter determined that further advance against such heavy resistance would probably destroy the unit completely, so he ordered the men to withdraw. Company D had been reduced from more than 150 men to an effective strength of 2 officers and 38 enlisted men. The next day air strikes were called in to pummel Tuy Hoa North, while tanks and reinforcements arrived and retook the village. Thanks in large part to the troopers' efforts, the village was safely back in South Vietnamese hands.

The brigade's reaction during the Tet maelstrom was characterized by rapid response, aggressiveness, and bravery. Brigade officers were at the head of their troops, with colonels killed and wounded alongside their privates. While the action at Tuy Hoa faded in comparison to the larger battles at Hue and Saigon, it exemplified the 173d Airborne Brigade's constant elan and courage.

Expansion and pacification

In February 1968 the brigade activated its 74th Infantry Detachment (Long-Range Patrol) and a combat tracker dog outfit, the 75th Infantry Detachment. During the next month the brigade assumed responsibility for the coastal II Corps provinces of Binh Dinh, Phu Yen, and Phu Bon. This region became the brigade's permanent tactical area of operation for the remainder of the war. The brigade situated its forward command post at LZ English just north of Bong Son along Highway 1 to control the vital rice fields of the Bong Son Plains.

On March 20, Brigadier General Richard Allen took charge of the brigade. A paratrooper veteran of World War II, Allen entered the Army as a private and rose to first sergeant before becoming an officer. On April 5, his command was increased to 6,436 men with the attachment of the separate 1st Battalion, 50th Infantry (Mechanized), and its M113 armored personnel carrier, giving the paratroopers extra armored mobility. This mechanized battalion stayed with the unit until October 1969, during which time the airborne brigade matched the size and power of a light division.

In June 1968, as the brigade celebrated its fifth anniversary, the U.S. Army recognized the 173d's combat engineering accomplishments by selecting its engineer company as the Army's best. The 173d Engineers' achievement underscored the essential role of the brigades' support units. The 173d Support Battalion, 173d Engineer and 534th Signal companies, 39th Infantry Platoon (Scout Dog), and the 51st Chemical, 172d Military Intelligence, 24th Military History, 404th Army Security Agency, and 46th Public Information detachments all provided excellent service throughout the war. In addition, the brigade utilized its own artillery (the 3d Battalion, 319th Artillery) and reconnaissance (Company D, 16th Armor, and Troop E, 17th Cavalry) units in addition to the 74th Infantry Detachment and Company N of the 75th Infantry. The brigade even had its own aviation platoon, nicknamed Casper, which flew virtually every type of helicopter mission, from medical evacuation to combat assault.

As the airborne brigade consolidated its operating area, the North Vietnamese and Vietcong reduced their activity to a combination of sporadic mortar or rocket attacks, ground probes, and sapper demolitions. During the summer and fall of 1968, the 173d concentrated on securing Phu Yen Province in Operation Bolling (later redesignated Dan Hoa), which had begun the previous fall. The brigade also continued Operation Cochise, which they had initiated at the end of March. During the ten-month operation, the troopers helped pacify the critical rice bowl section of

Vietnamese children mingle with 173d paratroopers and local militia during a pacification operation, Washington Green, in Gia An, Binh Dinh Province, December 1969.

lowland Binh Dinh Province. Brigade units were also engaged in the yearlong Operation Walker around An Khe. During December, Brigadier General John W. Barnes took command of the brigade.

To help carry out the major pacification programs being implemented in northern Binh Dinh Province, the brigade started Operation Washington Green on April 15, 1969, a long-term effort by brigade forces participating with ARVN soldiers to bring stable South Vietnamese government authority to the area. The brigade's function was simple: to provide military security in the vicinity of selected hamlets and to assist South Vietnamese officials as they tried to win the loyalty of the province's populace. Phase I, which lasted until June, initially aimed at pacifying sixteen hamlets, but when the men met with unexpected progress in the early stages the brigade was able to aid a total of twenty-four.

The restraint and respect accorded the villagers by the 173d Airborne Brigade helped make the first stage of Washington Green a success. The improved local stability in turn enabled the brigade to make an objective evaluation of the local South Vietnamese forces charged with defending the area. The Americans determined that these forces lacked essential military skills and were too weak to provide adequate defense. The next stage of Washington Green, which began on July 1, was intended to improve the local defense forces. The brigade's mission remained the same, providing security for designated hamlets, but the number of hamlets was increased to thirty-four. Brigadier General Hubert S. Cunningham, who assumed command of the brigade in August, emphasized the strengthening of the Vietnamese Regional, Popular, and District forces. He organized hundreds of paratroopers into advisory teams, which instructed twenty-seven Regional Force companies and fifty-two Popular Force platoons. The advisers trained their counterparts in a variety of military skills, including marksmanship, ambush techniques, night patrolling, weapons care, and sentinel duty.

The brigade began to see results when suspected Vietcong sympathizers came out of the mountains and gave up the guerrilla cause to rejoin their families in the secured villages. The Americans had expected another Communist Tet offensive in January 1970. Its failure to materialize was considered to be at least in part the result of the paratroopers' pacification efforts. The brigade decided to employ half its strength in direct pacification chores and use the other half to give overall security for the program and to provide a responsive capability in case of enemy buildups. Two battalions of the 503d Infantry were released from purely advisory and pacification support duties and reverted to a combat role. Thus, the 503d Infantry's 1st and 4th battalions rendered pacification support for the Phu My and Tam Quan districts, respectively, while the 2d and 3d battalions conducted field operations in the nearby mountains.

Fighting on

The troopers patrolling the highlands saw their share of action in January 1970, when they attacked the 8th NVA Battalion on Hill 474. The battle for Hill 474 developed into a prolonged, bitter, two-month ordeal. At the end of the fighting, the enemy battalion had been reduced to a third of its original strength and was forced to divide into small groups attached to local VC forces. By rendering the North Vietnamese battalion combat-ineffective, the 173d freed itself from most concerns about the enemy in the adjacent mountains.

On May 10, Washington Green entered a fourth phase, in which the brigade accelerated Vietnamese territorial force training. The troopers spent the summer familiarizing regular ARVN personnel and selected territorial officers in the U.S. with reconnaissance and security techniques. Brigadier General Ray Ochs took over the brigade in August and shifted its priority to destruction of the Vietcong infrastructure. This effort was severely hampered by the withdrawal of the 4th Infantry Division from Pleiku in November, for the 173d was ordered to fill the vacuum and defend the entire Highway 19 axis in the central highlands. The 2d Battalion of the 503d Infantry was moved to An Khe for the purpose. After twenty months of providing support to South Vietnam's pacification program, Operation Washington Green was terminated on the last day of the year.

When Gen. Ochs was transferred to the United States in January 1971, he was replaced by Brigadier General Jack MacFarlane, a dynamic former engineer officer who received his commission from Engineer Officer Candidate School. The 503d Infantry's 1st Battalion gradually scaled down tactical operations and left Vietnam on April 27. In the meantime, the other battalions of the 503d Infantry conducted intensive reconnaissance-in-force missions through the treacherous enemy strongholds of northern Binh Dinh Province. The men walked miles of foot trails under the scorching tropical sun seeking out elusive NVA/VC troops but made only light contact.

On April 2, 1971, the 2d Battalion encountered a large force of North Vietnamese regulars in a fortified base camp atop a ridge west of Phu My in the Nui Cung Chap Mountains. The troopers of the 4th Battalion were called upon to reinforce. Company D took the lead when it landed in an LZ late that evening. The first helicopter to land was met by enemy fire but managed to spill out a group of hard-fighting troops who peppered the dense jungle with enough fire to provide cover for the rest of the men as they arrived. At first light the next day, Company B of the 2d Battalion attempted to reach the top of the ridge. Some of the hardest fighting of the campaign ensued on the steep hillside as the North Vietnamese clung to their positions, raining grenades and automatic-weapons fire down the slope.

The battle raged eight days, each side determined to outlast the other. The 173d's advance was led by troops like Specialist 4th Class Dennis A. Terschak, who crawled through heavy elephant grass to within two meters of an enemy machine-gun nest, waited for the right moment, and assaulted the emplacement, destroying the nest. Air strikes and a multitude of artillery barrages finally routed the NVA soldiers from their fortified positions.

Even though men of the brigade knew they would be sent home that summer and had little fighting time left, the fierce action proved that the 173d was still willing to fight well. During July the remaining three battalions began to disengage in preparation for redeployment to the United States in August. On August 25, without much fanfare, the unit was withdrawn from the Republic of Vietnam.

"The Herd"—the 173d Airborne Brigade, the Army's first combat formation sent into Vietnam—left a remarkable fighting legacy. Its early airmobile searches of War Zone D and the Iron Triangle, the parachute assault into War Zone C, and the critical battle of Dak To were all destined to become landmarks in Army service during the Vietnam conflict. The brigade proved to be tough and efficient, living up to the valiant reputation of the regular Army paratrooper in wartime. However, its most telling success was its transformation late in the war from a hard-hitting combat formation into a flexible unit dedicated to pacification in a particularly brutal war. The brigade's Vietnam service, largely free of drug, racial, or war crime problems, was a lasting tribute to the quality of its men.

Soldiers of the 173d Brigade return sniper fire during a mission near the Ai Lao River, fifty kilometers northwest of Bong Song, on March 29, 1970.

Five Days on Hill 875

In November 1967, the 173d Airborne Brigade, the 4th Division's 1st Brigade, and two ARVN battalions waged a grueling month-long battle with the 1st NVA Division along the triple-canopied mountain ridges near Dak To. The climax of this struggle was a bloody five-day assault by paratroopers of the 173d Airborne Brigade on Hill 875, near the Cambodian border. Waiting for them atop this hill was the crack 174th NVA Regiment, well protected in fortified bunkers connected by trenches and tunnels.

The battle for Hill 875 began on the morning of November 19 with near disaster for the paratroopers. NVA troops, hidden in their vegetation-covered bunkers, cut apart Companies C and D of the 2d Battalion, 503d Infantry, and through a flanking maneuver, decimated Company A, which had been held in reserve farther down the hill. Though the paratroopers fought valiantly, the riddled companies were forced to fall back, the men desperately digging defenses with their knives and helmets.

For two days the paratroopers remained virtually trapped within their perimeter, periodically fighting off waves of NVA attackers. Though air support and artillery fire prevented the NVA from overrunning the paratroopers' position, U.S. helicopters could not land to provide supplies or evacuate the wounded. Six relief helicopters were shot down during the first day, and the paratroopers received no food or water for over fifty hours. It was a nightmarish scene as mortars, grenades, and sniper fire from the nearby North Vietnamese rained down upon the paratroopers. One shaken defender later remembered, "You didn't know where to go, you didn't know where to hide. You slept with the corpses. I slept under Joe. He was dead, but he kept me warm."

The weary paratroopers received reinforcement—the 4th Battalion, 503d Infantry (Airborne)—on the evening of the twentieth, and the next afternoon, they again took the offensive. Their grenades, flame throwers, and recoilless rifles, however, proved ineffective against the fortified bunkers. Instead, individual paratroopers crawled through the dense undergrowth toward the enemy. When close enough, they tossed twenty-pound satchel charges into the bunkers or dumped in napalm, igniting the fluid with grenades. Again, though, NVA firepower forced the paratroopers to pull back with some units suffering staggering casualties: Bravo Company saw half of its men killed or wounded.

Air strikes pummeled the top of Hill 875 all day on November 22, as the paratroopers prepared for a final assault. At eleven o'clock the next morning, Thanksgiving Day, the troops stormed from their positions with cries of "Airborne!" and "Geronimo!" There was no fight. The North Vietnamese had withdrawn during the night. After suffering 158 men killed and 402 wounded, the 173d Airborne Brigade had captured the hill. That afternoon, the exhausted troops sat on the top of the fortress and celebrated a heartfelt Thanksgiving.

A radio-telephone operator from the 173d Airborne Brigade rushes past his buddies to a more secure firing position during the fight for Hill 875 on November 22, 1967, the fourth day of the battle.

One of the 173d's command groups operates from atop a recently captured NVA bunker on the hill, November 22. The North Vietnamese built most of the bunkers three to six months before the battle, giving the underbrush time to grow and camouflage the structures.

Paratroopers of the 173d Airborne Brigade file past the stacked bodies of fellow paratroopers killed during the assault on Hill 875. For the first two days of the battle, NVA fire prevented helicopters from landing and removing the dead and the wounded.

Above. *After five days of fierce fighting, an exhausted paratrooper from the 173d Airborne Brigade rests against a charred tree trunk on Hill 875.*

Opposite. *Having finally reached the summit of Hill 875, troopers of the 173d Airborne Brigade rest amid discarded rifles and rucksacks and contemplate the battle.*

Highland Regulars

On the morning of July 28, 1965, Major General Arthur S. Collins, Jr., gathered his command staff at his headquarters at Fort Lewis, Washington, to listen to President Lyndon Johnson's press conference from the White House. Johnson was expected to announce the nation's new course of action in Vietnam, and like most in the military, Collins was interested in learning the commander in chief's plans for deployment of troops. "I was sure as I'm sitting here now that he was going to call in the Guard and Reserve to demonstrate the U.S. determination to do what was necessary," Collins later recalled. The president did announce the deployment of more troops to Vietnam but to the general's surprise added, "It is not essential to order reserve units into service now."

Most other military men shared General Collins's shock at the president's plans. U.S.-based divisions were typically under strength in peacetime, particularly in areas of combat support such as engineering, signal, and logistical units. Standing mobiliza-

Major General William R. Peers (right), commander of the 4th Infantry Division during heavy fighting in 1967, converses with Lt. Col. James R. Hendrix near Dak To in November 1967.

tion plans called for an infusion of reservists with these essential skills to bring the divisions up to full strength. But President Johnson's decision not to call up the reserves or National Guard meant that regular Army units would be bolstered not by trained reservists but by a widening pool of recruits and draftees. Such news presented a special challenge to General Collins, for one of the first units likely to go to Vietnam was his new command, the 4th Infantry Division.

Gearing up

The "Ivy Division"—so called because of the Roman numerals of its title and the four connected ivy leaves on its official patch—was created during World War I and served in France, where German soldiers were said to have spoken with fear of the "soldiers with the terrible green crosses." In World War II the "Fighting Fourth" landed at Utah Beach on D-day and took part in the liberation of Paris and the final assault on Germany. After a stint in Germany during the Korean War, the division arrived at its new base in Fort Lewis, Washington, where it became part of the Strategic Army Corps charged with rapid deployment to trouble spots anywhere on the globe.

In 1965, however, the 4th's strength had been compromised by the demands of a war to which it had not yet been committed. So many in the ranks of the division had been

dispatched to Vietnam and Europe to replenish other units that in the summer of 1965 the total strength at Fort Lewis stood at only about 7,000, with a glaring lack of middle-level officers, such as captains and lieutenants as well as NCOs. Though such deficiencies were common in other American divisions, it was especially disturbing for one that would soon be in Vietnam.

As it prepared for war, the 4th was scheduled to receive thousands of new men, mostly draftees, for assignment. Collins insisted that they be trained with the division—a departure from standard procedure in which men joined units only after completing basic. So 8,000 inductees were sent to Fort Lewis and assigned to brigades even before starting training. Preparation was mostly at the company and battalion level. Given the emphasis on small units in Vietnam, Collins later decided, the move was profitable. "We had cohesive units where the new men knew their fellow soldiers, NCOs, and officers right from the start, and vice versa."

As the ranks of the division swelled, training became more geared to the battlefield ahead. Collins led a refresher course in tactics for his battalion and brigade commanders. An NCO leadership school trained fire team and squad leaders. A mock jungle village on the base grounds gave the men a feel for their next environment. Though most of his men had gone through a crash course of training, Collins felt confident of their capability.

Finally, after rebuilding itself for Vietnam service, the 4th Infantry Division was ready to embark from Tacoma. On July 21, 1966, 5,000 men of the 2d Brigade—and Clarence, a boa constrictor adopted as a mascot—boarded the USNS *General John Pope* as the division band played "Auld Lang Syne" and friends and relatives bade them good-bye. The parting was more reminiscent of the departures by unit of World War II soldiers than what became the journey of the individual GI to Vietnam. During the voyage the men were given a smattering of further training, including an introduction to Vietnamese language and customs, but there was still much to learn.

On August 14 the *Pope* arrived at Qui Nhon, where the men and supplies were transferred to C–130 transport planes and flown to Pleiku City, in the central highlands close to the Cambodian border. By nightfall the 2d Brigade—comprising the 2d Battalion, 8th Infantry; 1st Battalion, 12th Infantry; and 1st Battalion, 22d Infantry—had arrived at the base camp prepared by its advance team at the foot of Dragon Mountain, sixteen kilometers south of Pleiku. The tent city was planted in the mud, for it was the height of the summer monsoon season. (Early in 1967 the camp was renamed Camp Enari, in honor of First Lieutenant Mark Enari, the posthumous recipient of the division's first Silver Star in Vietnam.)

While the 2d Brigade expanded its camp in the rain, the other two brigades and attached units of the division arrived in Vietnam. The 1st Brigade debarked at Nha

4th Infantry Division

Arrived Vietnam: September 25, 1966   **Departed Vietnam:** December 7, 1970

Unit Headquarters

Pleiku *Sept. 1966–Feb. 1968*	Pleiku *April 1968–Feb. 1970*	An Khe *April 1970–Dec. 1970*
Dak To *March 1968*	An Khe/Pleiku *March 1970*	

Commanding Officers

Maj. Gen. Arthur S. Collins, Jr. *Sept. 1966*	Maj. Gen. Charles P. Stone *Jan. 1968*	Maj. Gen. Glenn D. Walker *Nov. 1969*
Maj. Gen. William R. Peers *Jan. 1967*	Maj. Gen. Donn R. Pepke *Nov. 1968*	Maj. Gen. William A. Burke *July 1970*

Major Subordinate Units

1st Brigade (1/8, 3/8, 3/12)	Company K, 75th Infantry	4th Battalion, 42d Artillery
2d Brigade (2/8 [Mech], 1/12, 1/22)	4th Aviation Battalion	2d Battalion, 77th Artillery
3d Brigade* (2/12, 2/22, 3/22)	2d Battalion, 34th Armor*	4th Engineer Battalion
3d Brigade** (1/14, 1/35, 2/35)	1st Battalion, 69th Armor**	4th Medical Battalion
1st Squadron, 10th Cavalry	2d Battalion, 9th Artillery	4th Supply & Transport Battalion
Company E, 20th Infantry	5th Battalion, 16th Artillery	124th Signal Battalion
Company E, 58th Infantry	6th Battalion, 29th Artillery	704th Maintenance Battalion

2,531 KIA	15,229 WIA	11 Medals of Honor
(Casualty figures are "Vietnam Era.")		

*Transferred to 25th Infantry Division, August 1967.   **Arrived from 25th Infantry Division, August 1967.

Trang and trucked overland to Tuy Hoa, eighty kilometers north, where it established its headquarters. MACV ordered the brigade to operate in the lowlands and rice fields along the coast, where it remained until February 1967.

While MACV had determined the ultimate destination of the 1st and 2d brigades before they had even left the United States, the assignment of the 3d Brigade was still unknown when it set sail on September 22. It may have seemed natural to place it in II Corps with its two sister units and thus maintain the unit's integrity. However, a third brigade was already operating independently in II Corps: the 3d of the 25th Infantry Division, stationed at Pleiku since its arrival at the beginning of the year. The rest of the 25th ended up farther south, in III Corps, defending the area west of the capital.

Because the 3d Brigade of the 25th Infantry Division was so entrenched in Pleiku, and because that division was clamoring for another brigade, MACV decided on an unusual compromise. The 25th got a third brigade—that of the 4th Infantry Division, not its own. In return the 4th received operational control of the 3d Brigade of the 25th Infantry Division. Thus a new brigade of fresh troops augmented the seasoned troops of the 25th, while at least one veteran brigade operated with the 4th in the highlands. "Because soldiers identify closely with their division, I was concerned lest the transfer adversely affect morale," MACV commander General William Westmoreland later wrote, "but the effect proved to be minimal." Some in both "bastard brigades" probably disagreed with the general, but in Vietnam divisional identity seldom seemed to be as immediate or heartfelt as brigade or battalion camaraderie. Almost immediately upon its attachment to the 25th Infantry Division, the 3d Brigade of the 4th Infantry Division was thrust into action, entering War Zone C in Tay Ninh Province west of Saigon, for Operation Attleboro. Serving as an enemy rear base area near the Cambodian border and situated astride the main approach to Saigon, War Zone C was always a heavily contested area. The 3d Brigade saw steady action there for the next year.

While its 3d Brigade remained in III Corps with the 25th Infantry Division, II Corps became home to the rest of the 4th Infantry Division. At 31,200 square kilometers, II Corps was the largest of South Vietnam's four military regions. The 1st Cavalry Division (Airmobile) at An Khe and the Capital and 9th Infantry divisions of South Korea, stationed along the South China Sea, were also located in the Corps, but the 4th was the only division in the western highlands along the Cambodian and Laotian borders.

The placement of a division of 15,000 men in the hills along the border represented the growing importance of the area in American and South Vietnamese strategy. For years North Vietnam had been shipping supplies and men to the south on the Ho Chi Minh Trail, which wound through Laos and Cambodia and crossed over into South Vietnam at several points, many in the highlands. The dark river valleys and thick rain forests of II Corps had become major supply and staging areas for the enemy, whose bid for military and political control of the terrain threatened to split South Vietnam in two. The 4th Infantry Division's task was to screen the border as the first line of defense against infiltration and to preempt any offensive on the more populated lowlands.

From Pleiku the 2d Brigade moved west to Vung Dat Am, where it built a camp called the Oasis. There with the 3d Brigade of the 25th Infantry Division it took part in its first

The Famous 4th

The 4th Division was one of the oldest divisions in the U.S. Army, but it remained in the United States during the first few years of World War II. Finally arriving in England in 1944, Ivy commanders learned they were about to take part in the long-awaited invasion of France. On the morning of June 6, the division stormed ashore at Normandy as part of the D-day assault and pushed inland to help liberate Paris. Moving westward toward Germany with the American First Army, the 4th captured Munich by late April 1945, gathering some 50,000 prisoners along the way. The troops were called home after V-E Day for deployment to the Pacific, but victory there changed those plans. More than 22,000 men of the division were killed or wounded in the war, and for their service in Europe all three of the division's infantry regiments, the 8th, 12th, and 22d, received Distinguished Unit Citations.

Arriving home from World War II, soldiers of the 4th Infantry Division gather in jubilation as their transport nears New York Harbor on July 10, 1945.

operation, Paul Revere III, a series of sweeps near the border in Pleiku Province. Almost a month later, on October 18, the operation concluded without any battles between the 2d Brigade and the enemy.

The experience, however, led the 4th Infantry Division to mount large-scale operations on its own, offensive forays designed to preempt any NVA movement from the highlands to the more populous areas of South Vietnam. In Operation Paul Revere IV, the 2d Brigade of the 4th worked again with the 3d of the 25th, but this time the 4th Infantry Division assumed overall command. Sweeping across the razorback ridges and snake-infested rain forests of the border area in southern Kontum Province on search-and-destroy missions, the green troops soon got their first tastes of combat. On October 27, Company A of the 1st Battalion, 12th Infantry, was dug in for the night when it was attacked by a reinforced NVA company. Artillery and air strikes finally repelled the enemy. The next evening an NVA battalion hit the positions of Companies B and C of the 2d Battalion, 8th Infantry. The Americans turned back the waves of enemy attackers, but three American helicopters were shot down in the battle.

That the North Vietnamese could nearly defeat these 4th Infantry Division companies showed that American Army units were still struggling to get the upper hand in combat. Reports for 1966 indicated that 88 percent of all firefights involving Army units were initiated by the enemy, usually from fortified positions. Almost half of these encounters were ambushes. Though the U.S. forces were growing in number, they had yet to gain proficiency in the field.

Into the forests

In January 1967 a new division commander arrived at Pleiku to succeed Arthur Collins. Major General William R. Peers, fifty-two years old, had served with the OSS in Burma in World War II and later as a special assistant for counterinsurgency to the Joint Chiefs of Staff. Ironically, however, his new command required little knowledge of guerrilla tactics. In the highlands the primary enemy was not the ragtag Vietcong guerrilla but the well-equipped NVA regular, reminiscent of Peers's World War II foe. "The tactics used by the NVA forces were closely akin to those used by the Japanese forces in WWII," the general later reported. "This, in turn, resulted in the use of rather formalized tactics by U.S. and ARVN forces. Accordingly, the war in the highlands could be considered as a somewhat conventional jungle war."

According to Peers, the key to success in the highlands was a "maximum of flexibility" in a broad range of areas such as logistics, manpower, and tactics. Predictability in operations and planning allowed the enemy to get the upper hand. Consequently, 4th Infantry Division patrols pushed out in all directions into the remote areas near the border to engage the NVA, not waiting for the enemy to come to them. Of a 160-man company, at least 125 were always expected to be in the field, with the rest ready to replace them on short notice. At least two of the three companies then in an infantry battalion were to be on patrol at any given time. "We worked on the basis that all of the battalions were out all the time," Peers recalled.

Peers also implemented various procedures to prevent his units from being surprised or from sustaining heavy losses. One guideline, for example, stated that companies in the field should not wander more than a kilometer or one hour's travel away from each other, whichever was less. The NVA's aim, Peers believed, was to "get some outfit separated and then try to isolate it and go to work on it. So we always had it so another unit could get into it right away. This really paid us high dividends." Despite such safeguards, however, NVA ambushers were still able to cut off some American units in the field.

Peers's flexible tactics were quickly put to the test, for 1967 was perhaps the most significant year for 4th Infantry Division border operations. The first operation of the new year was Paul Revere V, later renamed Sam Houston, which sent the American battalions into the forests in search of the 1st and 10th NVA divisions, believed to be near the Cambodian border somewhere in Pleiku and Kontum provinces. The men of the "Funky Fourth," as soldiers began calling their division, moved from Pleiku to the jagged ridges west of the Se San River, within thirty-two kilometers of Cambodia. There they brushed against pockets of NVA troops, and throughout January small skirmishes flared in the triple-canopy jungle. Tangled undergrowth and trees 6 or 7 feet in diameter and up to 250 feet tall made movement treacherous and plunged the jungle floor into virtual darkness. Local VC guerrillas, pesky adjuncts to the formidable NVA, mined roads and harassed American units in the area.

Reports from the seven reconnaissance teams that were constantly in the field revealed an increasing NVA presence in Kontum and further infiltration from Cambodia during the Tet truce, February 7 to 11. U.S. patrols uncovered several enemy bunkers and underground complexes containing both ammunition storage facilities and hospitals. The 1st Battalion, 12th Infantry, and 1st Battalion, 22d Infantry, were warned of possible heavy combat with the NVA as they crossed the Nam Sathay River to operate in the slender pocket formed by the river and the border. To take up their former positions between the Nam Sathay and Se San, the 1st Brigade moved from Tuy Hoa and was in place around Plei Djereng by February 21.

As the Americans pressed toward the border and established firebases, enemy scouts shadowed them and monitored their movements. At 6:30 P.M. on February 12, Company C, 1st Battalion, 12th Infantry, fanned out in search of the enemy. Two squads had gotten no more than 100 meters to the south before they came under heavy automatic-weapons fire. The Americans pulled back toward their firebase and called in artillery and air strikes, but the NVA employed hugging tactics to close in, forcing the troops to direct mortars and bombs perilously close to their own position.

In the early afternoon the remainder of the battalion airlifted in. Heavy NVA fire greeted the men as the heli-

copters set down. The two companies clambered out and started toward the besieged Company C, but the NVA quickly pinned down two platoons of Company B. As casualties mounted, Company A formed a corridor from the perimeter to allow for the evacuation of the wounded of Company B. Finally, at 8:00 P.M., after hammering the enemy with mortars and air strikes, the Americans were able to reach Company C, and the NVA slipped away in the darkness. A sweep of the area the next day uncovered 113 NVA bodies and four wounded; American losses were twelve killed and thirty-two wounded.

Thus began a week that featured six major engagements with the NVA, each involving at least a full battalion. Units of both the 1st and 2d brigades continued to clash with NVA regulars, but for the most part the North Vietnamese dictated the time, place, and conditions of battle. Whereas during Operations Paul Revere III and IV most enemy attacks were against American fixed positions, the majority of firefights during Sam Houston involved rifle companies on search-and-destroy missions. Attacks on isolated and vulnerable American units were usually short and violent and favored the North Vietnamese and Vietcong instigators. U.S. forces at fixed bases were not immune from attack; enemy shells frequently rained down from hidden emplacements, causing numerous casualties.

In March the NVA began to avoid combat and to pull back many of its forces over the border to avoid further destruction, and on April 5, 1967, Operation Sam Houston ended. The Americans listed a total of 733 enemy KIA, compared to 169 total combat deaths for the 4th.

The border and the sanctuary it afforded were among the enemy's greatest weapons. Because American troops were forbidden from crossing into and operating in Cambodia and Laos, NVA and VC troops could pull back across the border to regroup and resupply virtually unmolested. This added to the American frustration during Operation Sam Houston— and all through the war. General Peers complained that "the closer the engagements approach the SVN-Cambodian border, the greater opportunity he [the enemy] has to take advantage of its protective sanctuary." The NVA employed this tactic with special effect during Sam Houston, Peers reported, for "of the eleven major engagements of Operation Sam Houston, nine of them occurred within 5,000 meters of the Cambodian border." Second Lieutenant Charles S. Newman, who joined the 1st Battalion, 8th Infantry, recalled that the NVA "only wanted to fight on their terms, when they wanted to and where they wanted to. They'd come in and hit you, and then they'd retreat back across the border. It was like kids playing tag." And he added with understandable exaggeration, "They'd cross the border and stand there and thumb their noses at you."

American artillery was allowed to return fire from across the border, and it was not uncommon for a handful of enemy mortar rounds to be answered with hundreds of American shells. General Peers viewed such exchanges as compensation for his unit's frustration with the enemy sanctuaries.

Regardless of such official constraints, however, American units did occasionally stray into Cambodia and Laos—sometimes by accident, sometimes by design. Lt. Newman recalled that after the patrols of the 4th were foiled by the NVA, which was fading across the border, "we started changing the rules a little bit on them." As time passed the men began to "move the border," as Lt. Newman put it. "Any time you were in contact, or imminent contact was about to take place, you could cross the border. And lots of times we'd run teams across the border to observe troop movements and concentrations, so when they'd start to infiltrate into the Vietnam side we'd be waiting for them." But such tactics were at best improvised, and U.S. units had to respect the neutrality of Laos and Cambodia. Like several other American units, the 4th's only officially sanctioned cross-border operations came during the incursion into Cambodia in 1970.

Long hot summer

At the conclusion of Operation Sam Houston the division assumed positions closer to Camp Enari for the coming summer monsoons. The 1st Brigade established a base west of Pleiku, dubbed "Jackson Hole" after its commander, Colonel Charles A. Jackson, and set up a string of small bases along the border stretching from Plei Djereng to the Ia Drang Valley. To the east, behind this screen, the 2d Brigade prepared for offensive operations. From these points the brigades could monitor NVA infiltration routes along Highway 19 and through the Ia Drang Valley and guard the approaches to populated areas during the rainy season. These were the objectives of the new operation, christened Francis Marion, after the revolutionary war's "Swamp Fox," who outwitted British commanders with his hit-and-run guerrilla tactics.

The poncho-covered body of a fallen comrade lies on the field as 4th Division troops pursue VC into a forest near Plei Djereng, during Operation Sam Houston, March 18, 1967.

The men of the division's 4th Engineer Battalion and 937th Engineer Group raced against time to prepare the area of operations before the monsoons broke. They cut roads and trails, built bridges, and dug culverts to allow for smooth transportation. Though their efforts were largely successful, heavy rains and flooding during the coming months occasionally prevented resupply of units for as long as three days.

On this and other operations Peers and his brigade commanders relied on the scouts of long-range reconnaissance patrols, or LRRPs, for intelligence. Small teams of men were scattered throughout the area with the mission of observing rather than fighting. When a team encountered an enemy unit, it reported the position so it could be targeted for air strikes or attacked by infantry. Although Peers placed a high value on the assistance of his patrols, claiming later that every "major" 4th Infantry Division battle of 1967 was initiated by the warning given or action taken by a LRRP, it was the enemy who continued to dictate the circumstances of most firefights.

Combat was light during April, but reconnaissance patrols and LRRP teams operating southwest of Duc Co began to spot small enemy concentrations that seemed to be advance parties for a larger NVA force. Suspicions arose that a sizable NVA unit, having infiltrated the Ia Drang Valley before the 1st Brigade established its screen, now threatened the Special Forces camps at Duc Co and Plei Djereng and the 1st Brigade command post at Jackson Hole. American patrols began to pay special attention to the areas around their camps.

Company A of the 2d Battalion, 8th Infantry, was patrolling around the Ia Meur River near Duc Co on the morning of April 30 when just after nine o'clock the 2d Platoon spotted two NVA soldiers in the thick woods. The men gave chase and, unable to determine the exact location of the enemy, saturated the area with rifle and machine-gun fire. Meanwhile, the 1st Platoon spied thirty NVA and established an ambush site farther down the trail. The Americans waited until all of the enemy had entered the killing zone and then opened fire. Several NVA fell dead in the surprise attack, but others were able to withdraw down the trail, dragging their dead and wounded behind them.

Three platoons bore down on the NVA, but the enemy regrouped 200 meters away and began to return a blistering fire. Americans fell both from bullets and dehydration in the oppressive heat, and an LZ had to be cleared 150 meters away for medevac helicopters. Meanwhile, aircraft streaked overhead dropping cluster bombs and napalm on the enemy. By this time, however, both the Americans and North Vietnamese could barely make out each other's positions in the thick growth. The two sides could only fire away into the dark jungle. Finally at dusk the American company withdrew to its base. U.S. artillery continued to pound the area all night. By the next morning the enemy soldiers had either slipped away or been killed by the fire.

Heavy firefights erupted throughout the weeks ahead. The 1st Battalion, 8th Infantry, established a firebase west of Duc Co and sent its companies north to sweep toward the Chu Guongot Mountains by the border west of Highway 14B. Operating northwest of Duc Co on the morning of May 18, Bravo Company came across an NVA soldier on the trail ahead. The American point man fired and missed, and the NVA soldier disappeared. Minutes later three more NVA appeared. The Bravo platoons inched forward. Suddenly shots rang out. The NVA soldiers had been merely bait; cut off from the other platoons, Bravo's weapons platoon was caught in an ambush.

Inside the ambush area enemy fire picked off six men almost instantly. Platoon Sergeant Bruce A. Grandstaff ordered the rear of his unit forward but saw that one man was wounded and could not move. Grandstaff jumped from his cover and pulled the man to safety but was hit in the leg. He then popped a smoke grenade, hoping that helicopter gunships could pick out the company through the thick trees. When that seemed futile, he fired tracer rounds in the air and finally heard over his radio that he had been spotted from above.

A camouflaged enemy machine gun continued the carnage in the American ranks. Grandstaff pulled his radio operator to safety, then grabbed a handful of grenades, crawled close to the gun, and lobbed a few into the position, silencing the gun. Grandstaff was hit in the other leg and, bleeding profusely, managed to radio for artillery strikes within forty-five meters of his position. Still the NVA advanced. Grandstaff cried into the radio, "Bring it in twenty-five meters closer!" Shells, both North Vietnamese and American, whistled all around as the sergeant gasped into the radio: "We're being overrun. Place the artillery fire on top of me. I've only got eight men left." Moments later an enemy rocket exploded, killing Grandstaff.

The NVA overran the platoon and spent forty minutes stripping the dead bodies. Two American survivors were captured and bound but inexplicably left behind. Some men played dead, successfully enduring the kicks and jabs of the victors in hope that they would be spared.

When Alpha Company reached the ambush site the following day, it found only eight men alive, some unconscious. They probably owed their lives to the gallantry of Sergeant Grandstaff, who was later awarded a posthumous Medal of Honor. Twenty-nine men of Bravo Company were killed, and another was never found. A search uncovered 119 NVA bodies.

It was a tragic beginning to what became known as "Nine Days in May." During that long week, three battalions of the 4th Infantry Division, totaling more than 2,000 men, faced off against 1,500 troops of the 32d and 66th NVA regiments. On the night of May 20 waves of NVA regulars attacked the hilltop position of the 1st Battalion, 8th Infantry. Dispatched to reinforce them, the 3d Battalion, 12th Infantry, was attacked by a battalion of the 66th NVA

Strength in Reserve

Nowhere was the uncertainty of the American military commitment to the war in Vietnam more apparent than in the nation's use of its reserve forces. After the initial deployment of ground troops in 1965, the Johnson administration spent almost three years agonizing and debating before calling up the reserves and the National Guard. In the years after the war some military men claimed that the failure to mobilize these troops early in the war precluded any chance for victory.

Though he realized that America's previous major conflicts had been fought with help from reserves, Lyndon Johnson was unwilling to call up standby forces in 1965. To do so, the president reasoned, would serve notice to China and Russia that his nation was at war. The two powers then "would be forced into increasing aid" to North Vietnam, the president told the National Security Council on the eve of his announcement of more troop deployments on June 28, 1965. "For that reason I don't want to be overly dramatic and cause tensions."

Johnson also feared the domestic repercussions of a call-up, realizing that the mandatory declaration of a state of emergency or war would jeopardize the success of his Great Society domestic programs and perhaps result in hawks demanding that he take more drastic steps in Vietnam. "I think we can get our people to support us without having to be too provocative and warlike," he told the NSC.

Johnson's commander in Vietnam shared his sentiments, but for different reasons. Though he favored some "expression of national resolve," General Westmoreland believed that a call-up of reserves "should be made only when the enemy was near defeat and more American troops could assure it." The reserve trump card should be played only when the troops could serve for a short time for an imminent victory; otherwise, public support for the war could wane.

Though Secretary of Defense Robert McNamara also backed the president, this policy was not popular in other corridors at the Pentagon. The Joint Chiefs of Staff warned McNamara and President Johnson several times that the military was being overextended and recommended a call-up of the reserves. Each time their advice was rejected.

Many outside the military supposed that a call-up would have sped the expansion of American infantry forces in Vietnam and that the failure to do so resulted in the slow, piecemeal commitment of troops to the war. Actually, mobilization would not have meant more combat soldiers on the front lines. Reserve units were intended largely to provide experienced logistical and support troops to combat outfits. Only the deployment of more infantry units, more likely from the active ranks, would have put more fighting men in the field.

The Ready Reserve, composed of over 900,000 reservists and guardsmen most likely to be called, remained on the "inactive" rolls until January 1968, when events forced the White House to reconsider its opposition to a call-up. After North Korea's seizure of the USS *Pueblo,* the president finally called up reserve forces to demonstrate his resolve. On January 25 he promulgated an executive order activating 14,801 members of the Naval Reserve, Air Force Reserve, and Air National Guard. No Army or Marine units were called. Though the mobilization was not specifically for Vietnam, four Air National Guard tactical fighter squadrons eventually served there.

The Tet offensive and the realization that American military strength was stretched perilously thin finally convinced the president that a call-up of reserves for Vietnam service was in order. On April 11 newly installed Secretary of Defense Clark M. Clifford, announced the second—and last—reserve mobilization of the war. More than 24,500 men were activated from the reserve lists. Only 10,000 were bound for Vietnam; the rest would fill the ranks of the strategic reserve, the domestic force depleted by the continuing demands of the war. This time the Army Reserve and National Guard formed the bulk of the call, totaling 20,000 men in 76 units. By law they could only be deployed in units; individual postings were made from the Individual Ready Reserve (IRR), composed of unassigned troops such as Vietnam veterans with time left on their military obligations.

About 3,600 members of the IRR were called to fill out regular stateside forces and understrength reserve units.

The reservists reported for duty on May 13 but widespread shortages of both equipment and trained personnel delayed their deployment. The Army had estimated that it would require a maximum of eight weeks to bring a unit up to par, but for fifty-eight of the seventy-six units training time had to be extended to as long as twenty-eight weeks.

Some reservists were reluctant soldiers. Like their neighbors who fought the draft, some went to court to prevent the government from sending them to Vietnam. Men from at least nine reserve units filed suit in federal court, claiming that the president could only send them overseas in time of war or that because the 1966 act authorizing him to call up the reserves was passed after they enlisted, they were exempt from service.

One of the first groups to sue, the 113 members of the 1002d Supply and Service Company, an Ohio Army Reserve unit, found a sympathetic ear on the Supreme Court. In September 1968 Justice William O. Douglas granted a last-minute stay to the 1002d just as it was about to ship out to Vietnam. Douglas approved the appeals of at least three additional units, but the full court overruled his stays. The reserves were cleared to go to Vietnam.

Ten thousand men and women of the reserves, 7,600 from the Army Reserve and National Guard, the rest from the Naval and Air Force Reserves and National Guard, ultimately served in Vietnam, the last unit coming home by the end of 1969. By design, they performed mostly medical, supply, and other logistical and support roles. The only National Guard or reserve infantry unit to serve in Vietnam was Company D, 151st Infantry (Long-Range Patrol), from Indiana's 38th Infantry Division. Rear–echelon outfits ranged from North Carolina's 312th Evacuation Hospital at Chu Lai, one of the busiest medical evacuation hospitals in Vietnam, to the 448th Army Postal Unit from New York, which processed mail for 60,000 men in II Corps. The 1002d Supply and Service Company, which had fought its deployment to the Supreme Court, ended up at Camp Evans, north of Hue. Its task: to provide shower facilities and clean clothes for soldiers and man an ice cream factory.

Regiment. Ten Americans and at least seventy-nine North Vietnamese were killed. Four days later an estimated 100 NVA virtually surrounded Company B of the 3/12 with mortar and small-arms fire. Company C and helicopter gunships arrived to assist, and by late afternoon the obstinate enemy withdrew, leaving 37 dead. The Americans were drastically under strength and perilously low on ammunition and could not give chase. By the end of the "Nine Days" on May 26, seventy-one Americans had died in five major battles. More than 300 NVA dead were tallied.

Large-scale battles continued to rage over the next few months. On July 12 Companies B and C of the 1st Battalion, 12th Infantry, ran into "the better part of two battalions" of the 66th NVA Regiment in the hills north of the Ia Drang River. The Company B commander was mortally wounded by an enemy mortar and Company C was driven back to its base, but the battalion, reinforced by the arrival of Company A by helicopter, was able to establish two secure perimeters by nightfall as the fighting ebbed. The battalion commander later lamented that, as usual, "the choice of time and location for a sizable engagement in the Central Highlands basically rests with the NVA."

After Francis Marion ended in October, the 1st Brigade commander, Colonel Jackson, characterized the enemy's tactics as "the old sucker treatment": a handful of NVA soldiers would draw an eager American unit into a carefully planned and controlled ambush. The result would be a vicious firefight. "I can't overemphasize the violence," Jackson said. "The NVA was capable of fighting for a period of two to four hours. He always prepared the battlefield and had his mortars adjusted." Though the Americans were challenging the enemy on the battlefield, they were doing so at an enormous price.

Second generation

In August 1967 MACV devised what it hoped would be a solution to the confusing alignment of the 3d Brigades of the 4th and 25th Infantry Divisions. On August 11 the 3d Brigade of the 4th officially became the 3d of the 25th, and the 3d Brigade of the 25th joined the 4th. In one stroke the 2d Battalion, 12th Infantry, and 2d and 3d battalions, 22d Infantry, went over to the 25th Infantry Division, while the 1st Battalion, 14th Infantry, and 1st and 2d battalions, 35th Infantry, became part of the 4th Infantry Division. Some in the fiercely independent 3d Brigade of the 25th Division resented attachment to what some of them derisively called the "Sorry Fourth." But to most men in the field, the change of colors only formalized what had been standard operating procedure for a year.

Though MACV cleared up that problem, manpower shortages posed a greater difficulty. As the 4th marked its first anniversary in Vietnam, most of the soldiers who had arrived with the initial deployment of the division had either already rotated back to the United States or would

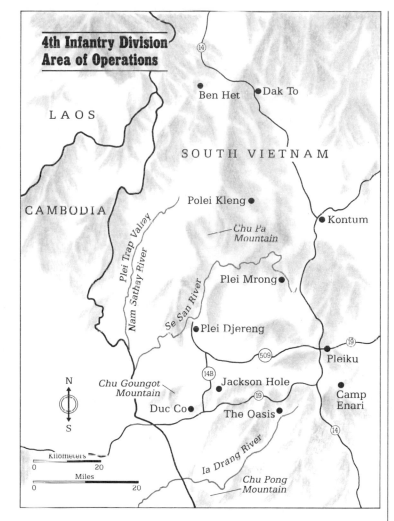

soon, in accordance with Army policy. Taking their place was a new generation of Ivy troops.

One of the unintended results was a weakening of the strength of many units. At the end of 1967 both the 1st and 2d brigades cited this as their greatest problem. "The personnel turbulence" of 1967, reported a battalion commander during the year, "had reduced the strength of line companies to less than 70 percent of the aspired 130 personnel in the field. Coupled with the turnover of small-unit leaders, commissioned and noncommissioned officers alike, the tactical experience of platoons and companies was drastically reduced." A fourth company was authorized for each battalion, but it was difficult to train these units while trying to maintain the combat readiness of the existing ones. In 1967, and throughout the entire war, the 4th Infantry Division and the rest of the Army were handicapped by the shuffling of men in and out of their ranks as each soldier finished his one-year tour.

As fighting in Pleiku waned, many NVA regiments pulled across the border or avoided battle, and for the most part the summer months were quiet. After the "pretty good scraps" in the Chu Pong Mountains, General Peers recalled, "the NVA just disappeared, and we never saw anything in strategic intelligence—we didn't see a damn thing and kept looking, kept our long-range patrols out."

Operation Francis Marion

In the spring of 1967, NVA troops moved into the hills around Duc Co, hoping to choke off American outposts near the Cambodian border. The 4th U.S. Infantry Division increased its patrols in the area, and scattered skirmishes in April gave way to the fierce firefights of May. Intense battles flared along the border throughout the summer.

Right. A rifleman of the 1st Battalion, 12th Infantry, takes cover after coming under enemy fire west of Pleiku, May 1967.

Fourth Division troops ride an armored personnel carrier through the jungle southwest of Pleiku in June 1967. Though APCs were available during Francis Marion, some rugged terrain could be traversed only on foot or by helicopter.

After a battle ninety kilometers west of Pleiku on May 25, 1967, a soldier breaks down from the strain and is comforted by a buddy. Francis Marion's "Nine Days in May" featured bloody battles along the border, as NVA regulars dug in and fought toe to toe with the Americans.

Soon signs of activity returned. The 173d Airborne Brigade and the 3d Brigade of the 1st Cavalry Division (Airmobile) confronted a determined enemy in Kontum Province fighting from well-hidden and fortified bunkers. It was apparent that a sizable NVA force was in the area. Consequently the 4th joined with other American units in Operation MacArthur. Launched on October 12, this operation resulted in one of the largest and most important battles of the war as American troops trudged through the rugged hills around Dak To.

In General Peers's initial deployment, the 3d Battalion, 8th Infantry, screened the border west of Dak To while the 1st Battalion, 12th Infantry, and 1st Battalion, 22d Infantry, conducted operations farther south in Darlac Province. Then from Special Forces and CIDG reconnaissance teams and "people sniffers"—unmanned devices designed to detect the presence of enemy forces—came alarming news: The NVA was pouring into the area in numbers greater than previously imagined. By the last week of October, at least three regiments of NVA regulars were poised to strike the Special Forces camp near Dak To.

Peers acted quickly. The 1st Brigade moved to Dak To in a massive airlift from Jackson Hole. The general requested a battalion of the 173d Airborne Brigade from General Westmoreland. The MACV commander, hoping for a climactic showdown, sent the entire brigade. By the first week of November the paratroopers of the 4th Battalion, 503d Infantry, were at Ben Het, near Dak To, under the operational control of the 1st Brigade of the 4th Infantry Division, and the rest of the 173d was on the way.

American and South Vietnamese units moved quickly into the hills to prevent the enemy from gaining the high ground. From the 4th Infantry Division, the 3d Battalion, 12th Infantry, and the 3d Battalion, 8th Infantry, were ordered to take the ridges to the south and west of the American camp. Both were supported by the 173d Brigade's firebase near Ben Het, straddling the Cambodian and Laotian borders. With the thick forest making it virtually impossible to clear landing zones, much of the maneuvering took place on foot.

On November 3, as Alpha and Bravo companies of the 3/12 tramped up the dense growth on Hill 724 along the ridge southwest of the base, enemy automatic-weapons fire erupted from above. The two sides exchanged fire for about forty minutes before the lead American troops realized that the enemy positions could be captured only at an extremely high cost. So the men of the two companies spread out on the side of the hill and settled in for a sleepless night. Enemy shells fell around their positions while U.S. planes rained napalm and bombs down on the NVA on the top of the hill. The battle of Dak To had begun.

Progress came slowly the next day. Any platoon that ventured out was fired upon by NVA rockets and mortars. Further air strikes could silence the enemy only momentarily. As soon as new patrols started their advance, the NVA drove them back. Finally, on the morning of November 5, their third day on the hill, the Americans, using the covering fire of machine guns and dumping grenades into bunkers, reached the summit.

From ridge to ridge the battalions trudged. The men called in intense air strikes on pockets of enemy resistance, then waited while the dense forest in front of them became a firestorm. Then they pushed on over the newly denuded landscape. Along the way they found hidden prizes in the countless enemy bunkers dug into the hills and mountainsides, including considerable quantities of uniforms, medical supplies, and ammunition.

It took another week of fighting on hills whose designations would ring in the ears of the veterans of the 4th—1,338, 1,262, 1,294—before the highlands to the south of Dak To were cleared. "As far as brutal fighting goes," General Peers told news correspondents on the scene, "I would say this is the worst we've had."

Meanwhile the 173d Airborne Brigade was engaged in heavy fighting southwest of Ben Het. Two of its battalions, supported by the 1st Battalion, 12th Infantry of the 4th Infantry Division, fought the most publicized battle of the operation, the one for Hill 875 that ended on Thanksgiving Day. After relinquishing that hill the battered NVA slipped back over the border, but victory had not come cheaply for the Americans. In the largest battle of the war up to then, 86 men of the 1st Brigade of the 4th Infantry Division died in combat. The 3d Battalion, 8th Infantry, suffered 46 KIA, while the 3d Battalion, 12th Infantry, lost 24. In the three brigades that participated in the operation—the 1st of the 4th Infantry Division, the 1st of the 1st Cavalry Division (Airmobile), and the 173d Airborne—a total of 283 men died at Dak To. More than 1,600 enemy bodies were counted, but the total NVA loss was thought to exceed 2,000.

"Indian Country"

When General Peers relinquished command of the Ivy Division in January 1968, his successor, Major General Charles P. Stone, faced an immediate challenge. An increase in skirmishes in his division's area of operations, as well as captured documents, indicated that the enemy was planning greater attacks in the near future, perhaps by the Tet holiday at the end of the month. Units of the 4th Infantry Division, especially those around Pleiku and Kontum, were placed on alert after enemy rockets hit Pleiku on January 20 and 27.

Though the Tet offensive began in the early morning hours of January 31 throughout most of South Vietnam, some attacks in the highlands began a day earlier, either by design or as a result of a communications breakdown

A UH-1B helicopter resupplies Company B, 1st Battalion, 8th Infantry, southwest of Dak To, December 1967. The Huey was essential to 4th Division troops manning far-flung outposts.

between distant Communist commanders. At 2:00 A.M. on January 30, Vietcong and NVA raiders seized government buildings in Kontum, including an ARVN base. Near Pleiku the enemy attacked the 4th Infantry Division compound, which had grown from a hamlet of tents and sandbags to a small town with its own concrete bunkers, a busy airstrip, and a swimming pool. The commandos freed hundreds of Vietcong prisoners in an assault on the provincial prison and set more than fifty buildings on fire.

The division quickly dispatched troops to quell the attack. At Kontum tanks of the 2d Squadron, 1st Cavalry, were joined by air cavalry troops of the 7th Squadron, 17th Cavalry, and troops of the 1st Battalion, 22d Infantry, with air support from the 4th Aviation Battalion. At Pleiku the 4th Engineer Battalion and the 1st Battalion, 69th Armor, the primary armored unit of the division, assisted ARVN troops in repulsing the attack. Within a week the enemy had been pushed back, leaving several hundred of its dead in both cities.

The threat to the population centers during the Tet attacks heightened American and South Vietnamese fears for the future of their civic action programs among the many montagnard tribes in the area. Though many villagers were unsympathetic to or, at best, ambivalent about the VC and NVA, they were no less distant to the Americans and ARVN and thus a target for wooing by both sides.

In an effort to win over and control the indigenous population of "Indian Country," as the men of the 4th Infantry Division called the highlands, MACV and the division had already instituted several civic action projects aimed at pacifying and gaining the loyalty of the montagnards. The division's "Good Neighbor" program sent civic action teams, usually composed of at least five Americans and one interpreter, into each hamlet in its area five times each week. One program provided vaccinations and distributed such scarce items as soap. Construction teams built shelters, sanitation facilities, and even larger structures such as meeting houses, for villagers' use.

Civic action programs expanded as the division deemed greater areas sufficiently secure for pacification. By mid-1967 as many as 15,000 civilians had been reached. Yet real success in the battle for the hearts and minds of the montagnards was usually slight. Mindful of possible VC reprisal, villagers were sometimes wary in their cooperation with the Americans. Local guerrillas or NVA soldiers occasionally attacked civic action teams in the field. Besides, American soldiers disliked pacification assignments because they counted for so little in promotion decisions. In any event, few of the men of the 4th Infantry Division were assigned to civic action as full-time duty.

In addition to the Good Neighbor program, the division took more drastic steps to ensure the safety and cooperation of the population by moving the people themselves. Under the aegis of the ARVN command and Pleiku Province chief, the 4th took part in Edap Enang, a term in the

Jarai dialect meaning "peace and security." The objective was to transfer more than 10,000 people from villages in contested areas in the highlands to more secure territory along Highway 19 West, closer to Pleiku City and within the divisional area of operations. Beginning in 1967, Ivy soldiers and vehicles helped transport thousands of Vietnamese to the Edap Enang center. The 2d Brigade alone helped transport by air and land 2,757 inhabitants of eighteen villages, along with their personal effects and livestock. This action was not unique to the II Corps area; joint GVN/MACV resettlement programs were common in areas continually threatened by the enemy.

Chase to the south—and north

As the emphasis on the protection of populated areas in order to facilitate pacification operations increased in 1968, General Stone became less inclined than Peers to commit large numbers of men to remote border areas to engage NVA units as they entered South Vietnam. Rather, he was willing to allow the NVA to move closer into the highlands, then deploy troops to their rear and cut off their escape routes. This strategy was designed to allow the division to trap the enemy in an area more advantageous for battle and to minimize losses.

Nevertheless, Stone's men confronted NVA troops in Kontum and Pleiku provinces throughout the year, with some battles taking place near the border. After a period of regrouping after Tet, the enemy attacked several American bases in April. Tenacious NVA regulars attacked a firebase of the 1st Battalion, 22d Infantry, west of Polei Kleng and were repulsed only after four days of bitter fighting. When other bases in this area and farther north near Dak To came under heavy rocket and mortar attack, Stone formed Task Force Mathews, composed of the 1st Brigade of the 4th Infantry Division and the 3d Brigade of the 101st Airborne Division to meet the challenge.

The soldiers swept through the area north of Ben Het in search of at least a full North Vietnamese division. The rough terrain made the going even more difficult, but with the support of B–52 strikes and artillery the task force rooted out pockets of NVA. By June scouts indicated that much of the NVA force had left Kontum Province. But within a month a greater enemy presence was detected in Darlac and Quang Duc provinces to the south, an area thus far relatively untouched by both the Americans and North Vietnamese.

General Stone sent his 2d Brigade 130 kilometers south from Pleiku to Ban Me Thuot, a city that had been quiet since Tet. From its hastily built base at the city's airfield, the brigade began operations with the 23d ARVN Infantry Division. The 1st Battalion, 22d Infantry, and 2d Battalion, 35th Infantry, screened the south and west of the city while the 1st Battalion, 12th Infantry, met the NVA in a series of small firefights to the north.

Men of the 3d Battalion, 8th Infantry, keep a sharp eye out for enemy troops after repelling an attack on their position west of Kontum, near the Cambodian border.

The NVA took advantage of the deployment of American and South Vietnamese troops around Ban Me Thuot to move sixty kilometers southwest to Duc Lap, the site of a Special Forces camp astride the Cambodian border. On August 23 they attacked the base and did not withdraw, even in the face of heavy American artillery and ground fire. The enemy's three-day stand at Duc Lap suggested that a larger battle was looming, so the 4th Battalion, 503d Infantry of the 173d Airborne Brigade was rushed south from the highlands to reinforce the American troops. Some NVA remained in the area, and contact with the Americans, organized into Task Force Spoiler, continued into October. By then it seemed that the threat to the area around Ban Me Thuot and Duc Lap had dissipated.

The chase continued as reports of the NVA's return to Kontum and Pleiku sent the Americans back north. Enemy units threatened lines of communication and outposts in the highlands, but action was light because much of the NVA force remained in Cambodia for most of the fall. Late in the year the new commander of the 4th Infantry Division, Major General Donn R. Pepke, took advantage of the lull to send infantry and engineers against NVA staging and supply areas in the Plei Trap Valley, along the border and the Dak Payou Valley southeast of Pleiku.

On December 22 an American, ARVN, and montagnard spoiling party named Task Force Winner swung into action in the Dak Payou Valley, otherwise known as "VC Valley" due to its long-standing domination by the enemy. The 3d Battalion, 12th Infantry, formed a blocking force along the Dak Payou River while the 3d Battalion, 8th Infantry, swept the valley floor. The mobile howitzers of the 6th Battalion, 29th Artillery, helped keep the enemy on the run, and combat was light and fleeting. Aside from water buffalo and chickens used by the enemy in their staging areas, the booty collected over four days included more substantial items such as new uniforms and equipment and huge rice stores. The number of enemy bodies found was not substantial, but General Pepke declared that the efforts of Task Force Winner "have severely hampered the enemy in his attempts to make VC Valley a safe haven."

Like General Stone, Pepke was aware of the limitations of what his division could now do. He saw his role as providing an "impenetrable protective screen" against NVA infiltration and large-scale offensives while ARVN forces established greater control in the II Corps area. The key to maintaining such a presence, Pepke realized, was economy of force, utilizing a minimum of troops along the border and concentrating the bulk near the population centers to help the GVN in its pacification efforts. Emphasis was on rapid deployment to trouble spots within the area by lighter, airmobile forces.

But the enemy was not very obliging. NVA troops massed in the "Triborder" area, where South Vietnam,

Laos, and Cambodia meet. Rocket attacks on the American Special Forces camp at Ben Het became heavier and more frequent in late February. On the foggy night of March 3–4, the enemy showed its muscle. A battalion of infantry attacked the base, supported by eight to ten Soviet-made PT76 tanks. The American tanks of the 1st Battalion, 69th Armor, knocked out two of the PT76s and then turned their guns on infantry positions. Enemy fire slackened as the NVA failed to enter the camp. At Ben Het the NVA used tanks for the first time in the highlands. It was the only occasion of the war in which American tanks countered a North Vietnamese armor attack.

There were scattered attacks on American firebases in the following months, but for the most part fighting in the highlands abated in 1969. The 4th Infantry Division, reported General Pepke, "returned to large-scale support of the pacification programs" and prepared for its inevitable redeployment to the United States.

Parting shots

That process began in the spring of 1970 as the 1st Battalion, 8th Infantry, the 1st Battalion, 35th Infantry, and the 1st Battalion, 69th Armor, returned home and the division's 3d Brigade was placed on inactive status. On April 15, 1970, Camp Enari was turned over to the South Vietnamese and the 4th Infantry Division moved east to Camp Radcliff at An Khe, the former base of the 1st Cavalry Division (Airmobile).

But the war was not yet over for the division. Before it left, the 4th got a chance to strike back at the source of one of its greatest frustrations—the NVA border sanctuaries. In May 1970, while American and South Vietnamese units were penetrating the Fishhook and Parrot's Beak in the controversial incursion into Cambodia, the 4th Infantry Division crossed the border into the Se San Basin west of Duc Co in a similar spoiling raid against enemy bases. Because of the relatively small size of the attack, however, it received less attention than the other forays.

The new division commander, Major General Glenn Walker, committed most of the 4th to the incursion. Five infantry battalions, plus the 3d Battalion, 506th Infantry from the 173d Airborne Brigade, were shifted closer to the border to participate in the operation, leaving only one infantry battalion, a cavalry squadron, and a Ranger company at An Khe. On May 5 the 4th sprang from its forward base at Plei Djereng. After devastating B–52 strikes softened the area, the American and South Vietnamese force airlifted across the border. "Hey, man," shouted one soldier over the roar of the helicopter blades, "this place doesn't look any different from Vietnam."

Chow time. Their weapons loaded and ready in case of attack, 4th Division soldiers line up for a meal at a fire support base near the Cambodian border in 1969.

Though the enemy had anticipated the invasion and moved some supplies and men deeper into Cambodia, substantial NVA opposition still greeted the American and South Vietnamese force. Blistering ground fire drove the helicopters of the 3/506 from their planned landing zone. After the 3d Battalion, 8th Infantry, had put sixty men on the ground, enemy fire shot down one helicopter and crippled two more before the whole unit could be dropped off. Heavy fire greeted other assaults, but the task force was eventually able to land, though sometimes at alternate sites.

On the ground, heavy fighting was rare. MACV had warned the division to avoid substantial losses and, according to one military historian, there was "a noted lack of division aggressiveness in following through with airmobile assaults if opposed by any ground fire." Like the Fishhook and Parrot's Beak raids, the sweeps through the Se San area revealed a sizable trove of materiel, including small weapons, rockets, mortars, even larger crew-served guns. Other finds were more striking. On May 8 the 1st Battalion, 22d Infantry, came upon a huge hospital complex containing X-ray equipment and a modern laboratory. Also uncovered the same day was a training site complete with a wooden mockup of a U.S. jet aircraft.

Unlike the incursion to the south, the Ivy Division's time in Cambodia was brief. On May 13, just a little over a week after entering Cambodia, the 4th began to pull out, leaving the area to ARVN troops. The raid over the border may have satisfied some in the division, but with the war winding down it was too little, too late.

The Cambodian operation marked the last significant operation for the 4th Infantry Division. In subsequent months Ivy patrols secured the area around An Khe. In November 1970 the 1st Battalion, 22d Infantry, the 1st Squadron, 10th Cavalry (Armored), and the 5th Battalion, 16th Artillery, were reassigned to other U.S. commands in Vietnam for further action. The colors of the battalions in the original 3d Brigade of the 25th Infantry Division units—the 1st Battalion, 14th Infantry, and the 2d Battalion, 35th Infantry—were returned to the Tropic Lightning Division headquarters in Hawaii. As they departed Cam Ranh Bay, more than 11,000 men still wore the Ivy Division patch, but their final destination was not their old home at Fort Lewis. The "Funky Fourth" was headed for Fort Carson, Colorado, where after combining its resources with the 5th Infantry Division (Mechanized) it became a mechanized division.

Thus the Ivy Division ended its four-year term in Vietnam. A total of eleven men of the Ivy Division received the Medal of Honor for their deeds there. Some 70,000 men had served in its ranks, and 16,844—more than one-fourth of that number—had been killed or wounded in action. Like thousands of men who served in Vietnam, many of them had been green recruits or draftees, but they had quickly become "regular Army" in the dark forests and remote mountains of "Indian Country."

The Road to Saigon

In December 1965, as most Hawaiians observed the anniversary of the Japanese attack on Pearl Harbor, thousands of soldiers at Schofield Barracks on the central island of Oahu, headquarters of the 25th Infantry Division, girded themselves once more for war. General William Westmoreland had issued an urgent call for more troops. The 25th responded.

A direct descendant of the old Hawaiian Division, the 25th had distinguished itself in action throughout the Pacific basin since its formation in 1941. In 1955 the Army designated the division as the primary reaction force in that ocean. In fulfilling this role the division established the Hawaiian Jungle and Guerrilla Warfare Center to train its members for an Asian war. Now, after ten years of preparation, that training was to be put to the test.

In fact, by 1965 more than 2,200 soldiers from the 25th had already seen duty in Vietnam as helicopter crewmen flying in support of the South Vietnamese. In August of that year, Company C, 65th Engineer Battalion, landed in Vietnam to help build a U.S.

base at Cam Ranh Bay. On December 23, as part of Operation Bluelight, the 4,000 men of the 25th's 3d Brigade, with more than 9,000 tons of equipment and supplies, boarded Air Force C–133 Cargomasters and C–141 Starlighters bound for Pleiku Province in the central highlands of Vietnam.

As the 3d Brigade landed in Vietnam, the two remaining brigades hurriedly prepared for their own deployment. Responding to Gen. Westmoreland's request to speed up the process, the Dependents' Assistance Center in Hawaii worked around-the-clock to aid the soldiers arriving from across the island and the mainland preparing for the division's impending departure. The 2d Brigade arrived in Vietnam on January 25, followed three months later by the 1st Brigade on April 29, completing the deployment five months ahead of schedule.

The area selected for the 25th's home—Cu Chi—lay thirty kilometers northwest of Saigon, astride the major land and water routes into the capital city—the Saigon River and Highway 1, which connected Saigon with Cambodia. Cu Chi was one of several bases established by Westmoreland in a protective ring around Saigon. The major task of the 25th was to block infiltration of enemy troops crossing the Cambodian border from the Ho Chi Minh Trail within striking distance of the capital city.

Long under VC control, the surrounding area contained several important enemy strongholds: the Ho Bo and Bo Loi woods and the Iron Triangle, which one U.S. general described as "a dagger pointing at Saigon." As recently as August 1965, the VC had staged victory parades through the center of Cu Chi. The 25th's commander, Major General Frederick C. Weyand, calculated that the base would "act as a sort of lightning rod for the enemy."

The tunnels of Cu Chi

On January 25, 1966, a convoy of 635 vehicles carrying the men and supplies of the 25th's 2d Brigade arrived at Cu Chi. Less than a week later, on February 2, the VC attacked. Suddenly appearing inside the perimeter in an area just cleared by men of the 1st Battalion, 5th Mechanized Infantry, the VC fired several rounds into the camp, touching off a series of explosions in the base ammunition dump, then disappeared as quickly as they had come. More distressing than the attack itself was its source. The VC had infiltrated unnoticed from underground. "They've been below us all the time," exclaimed the unit's executive officer, Major John Y. S. Chang, adding, "We've got to blast every single hole."

In locating the 25th's base on the site of an old abandoned peanut farm, Weyand noted, "It was the one place that was above the water table, where we could put trucks and tanks without having them sink out of sight during the monsoon season." Dry land could support tunnels just as easily as tanks, and it was for this reason that the VC had also chosen the sight to dig their tunnel system. Unbeknown to the Americans, the tunnel complex was begun nearly a quarter of a century before the arrival of the 25th and had served the VC against the Japanese, the French, the Diem regime, and now it was serving them in their fight against the Americans. By setting up at Cu Chi, the 25th, according to General Ellis W. Williamson, commander of the 173d Airborne Brigade and later of the 25th, "had bivouac'd on a volcano." For the men of the 25th it was "Hell's Half Acre."

The complex of tunnels was uncovered in January 1966 by the 1st Infantry Division and the 173d Airborne Brigade during Operation Crimp. Limited efforts to destroy them proved ineffective. American officials had recognized neither the scope nor the importance of the tunnels that provided the enemy with not only a place to hide but also a place to sleep, to plan, to train, to store food and weapons—and a place from which he could fight. Within the narrow confines of the tunnels, the VC effectively neutralized America's great firepower and logistical advantage above ground.

As the attacks upon the base continued, the 25th determined to solve the problem. "We realized that there were tunnels," recalled Weyand. "And gradually we realized the extent of them. Now, as that realization dawned, we dealt with the problem as best we could." Weyand first called upon the newly formed "tunnel rat" squad of the 1st Infantry Division to help train his men to fight this underground war. Eventually, he also opened the Tunnels, Mines and Booby-Traps School to train members of the 25th. Located on the western side of the Cu Chi base, the school included more than 150 meters of captured VC tunnels that the division maintained for training purposes.

Destroying the rest of the tunnels proved much more difficult than first imagined. Booby traps, trap doors that blunted attempts to gas or flood the tunnels, rock-hard laterite clay that resisted explosives, an enemy who had spent a lifetime fighting and living in the underground, and simply the sheer size of the tunnel complex (which covered more than 240 kilometers) all combined to thwart U.S. clearing efforts. To destroy them would have required a commitment of manpower and time that the 25th, like most other U.S. units, was unwilling to make. Too many more appealing targets presented themselves above ground, targets the division had been trained and equipped to handle. Riding through the nearby Bo Loi Woods at the end of 1966, a captain of the 1/5 Mechanized Infantry noticed that they had not even begun to clear out the tunnel system in that area. "Some day we'll have to go in and give it a thorough house cleaning." However, he added, "none of us are pining away for that day."

25th Infantry Division

Arrived Vietnam: March 28, 1966   **Departed Vietnam:** December 8, 1970

Unit Headquarters

Cu Chi   *March 1966–Dec. 1970*

Commanding Officers

Maj. Gen. Frederick C. Weyand *Jan. 1966*	Maj. Gen. Fillmore K. Mearns *Aug. 1967*	Maj. Gen. Harris W. Hollis *Sept. 1969*
Maj. Gen. John C. F. Tillson III *March 1967*	Maj. Gen. Ellis W. Williamson *Aug. 1968*	Maj. Gen. Edward Bautz, Jr. *April 1970*

Major Subordinate Units

1st Brigade (2/14, 4/9, 4 [mech]/23)	2/9 Artillery	125th Signal Battalion
2d Brigade (1/27, 2/27, 1 [mech]/5)	7/11 Artillery	725th Maintenance Battalion
3d Brigade* (1/14, 1/35, 2/35)	3/13 Artillery	25th Administration Company
3d Brigade** (2/12, 2 [mech]/22, 3/22)	2/77 Artillery	25th Military Police Company
2/34 Armor**	6/77 Artilllery	372d Army Security Agency Company
1/69 Armor*	1st Support Battalion	9th Chemical Detachment
3d Squadron, 4th Cavalry (Armored)	2d Support Battalion	25th Military Intelligence Company
Company F, 50th Infantry	3d Support Battalion	18th Military History Detachment
Company F, 75th Infantry	25th Medical Battalion	15th Public Information Detachment
25th Aviation Battalion	25th Supply & Transport Battalion	20th Public Information Detachment
1/8 Artillery	65th Engineer Battalion	

4,547 KIA	31,161 WIA	21 Medals of Honor
(Casualty figures are "Vietnam Era.")		

*Transferred to the 4th Infantry Division, August 1967.   **Arrived from the 4th Infantry Division, August 1967.

By year's end, the 25th did clear and secure the tunnel system directly below their base, resorting in several instances to the crude but effective means of leveling an area with plows and bulldozers. However, this did not put an end to attacks on the base. Denied access to these tunnels, the VC simply expanded and improved their tunnel system around the base. Called the "Belt," this complex of tunnels allowed the VC to observe and fire upon the base with relative impunity.

While the VC waged their war from underground, above ground the 25th shifted into high gear, greatly expanding the size of its operations. Inevitably, larger operations led to more intense and bloodier engagements. In October 1966, the 25th participated in Operation Attleboro, which grew into a multidivisional operation aimed at the Communist strongholds in War Zone C. On November 3, as Attleboro moved into its second phase, the 1st Battalion, 27th Infantry (the Wolfhounds), air assaulted into a landing zone near the Cambodian border. The Wolfhounds moved quickly to set up a blocking position and trap a VC force flushed out by two battalions of the 196th Light Infantry Brigade—the 4th Battalion, 31st Infantry, and the 3d Battalion, 21st Infantry.

From his command helicopter flying overhead, the 1/27's commander, Major Guy S. Meloy III of College Station, Texas, watched his Company B land without mishap. "Nothing happened," he recalled, "so I went ahead and put my Charlie Company in up in the northwest, holding Alpha Company in reserve. Pretty soon, Charlie Company was in one hell of a fight." Company C had landed on top of a reconnaissance company of the 9th VC Division. After

exchanging fire for several hours the enemy quietly withdrew, allowing Meloy to land his remaining forces and establish a night position.

After a night of inconclusive enemy probes and U.S. artillery responses, Meloy and his command moved out to attempt to trap the VC. Companies B and C of the 2d Battalion, 1st Infantry, which had arrived the previous night, pushed east, while the 4/31 drove down from the south and Meloy and his five companies headed northeast.

On all sides, the extremely dense jungle limited visibility. In some locations the troops could see less than ten meters off the trail. It was a perfect site to ambush the inexperienced American troops. "One moment it was as quiet as can be and the next instant it was like a Fort Benning Mad Minute," Meloy said. From three sides, at some points less than twenty meters away, the VC unleashed a fearsome volley of automatic-weapons fire.

Diving to the ground, Meloy reached for the radio, shouting orders to his men to pull back into a defensive position. Company C, however, was cut off from the others, pinned down by the savage fire. Meloy called for artillery strikes, some as close as twenty-five meters to his men. The shrapnel shredded trees above the U.S. soldiers. The firing continued unabated. "Rounds everywhere," Meloy recalled. "Ten, twelve inch trees were being cut down by bullets."

The enemy next pounded Meloy's force with a barrage of 60MM mortar fire. One shell exploded near Meloy, wounding him in the elbow and back. Another landed less than a foot from his side. It was a dud. On the left flank the mortar fire inflicted the heaviest casualties, so Meloy

Tunnel Rats

The 25th Infantry Division's tunnel rats had one of the more arduous duties in the Vietnam conflict—clearing the miles of Vietcong tunnels that riddled Cu Chi District northwest of Saigon. Armed with pistols, flashlights, compasses, and telephones, tunnel rat teams of six to ten men explored the enemy's underground mazes, never quite sure what they would find. They braved mines, booby traps, bats, and scorpions and often came face to face with waiting Vietcong. Their mission was never complete as the Vietcong continually expanded the tunnel network. It was a hot, dirty, and dangerous job.

Left. A tunnel rat takes a final glance up before going underground. Below. Tunnel rats of Company A, 1st Battalion, 5th Infantry (Mechanized), inspect grenades, magazines, and automatic weapons unearthed in a VC tunnel in September 1966.

called for Companies B and C of the 2/1 to support him. However, a second VC force stopped them short of his position. Then, after five hours of fierce fighting and without warning, the VC shifted tactics.

"I heard them let out a whole bunch of whooping and hollering and screaming and then there was about 100 of them coming at us through the undergrowth," a sergeant from the 1/27 said. Rising up en masse, the VC attacked the trapped soldiers in a human wave. "There were so many of them," the sergeant said, "so close together, they could have held hands with the men on either side of them as they charged us."

Meloy, whose father had witnessed similar charges as a commander in Korea, and his men stood fast. The troops stopped the charge less than ten meters from their perimeter. Fifteen minutes later a second wave attempted to sweep over the position but once again the line held; an hour later the U.S. forces rebuffed a third charge.

Throughout this fierce fighting, Company C remained isolated from the other units. Several times Meloy tried to link up—"I tried the direct route, I tried going a three-quarter circle route the other way and I tried again at night"—but he could not break through. "It was bad in there," said Captain Robert F. Foley, who led the battalion's company on one rescue attempt. "When we moved quickly, we would stumble into the lanes of machine-gun fire. If we moved slowly, the snipers would go after us, picking us off one by one." Foley and another member of his company, Staff Sergeant John F. Baker, both later received the Medal of Honor for their efforts during the battle.

When Company C lost its company commander, one of its platoon leaders, and a squad leader, Meloy reached a young radioman, PFC William Wallace, at the other end of the radio. Although he later admitted he was "scared out of his wits," Wallace held his composure enough to take control of the battered company and carry out Meloy's orders.

Unable to free the company, Meloy gambled that the VC had not yet pinpointed its location. He ordered Wallace to stay hidden. "Hold your fire whatever you do, regardless of how many times you're probed." Again and again the VC probed the area with fire, inflicting heavy casualties on the company. Each time, Wallace requested permission to fire but Meloy refused. "It was fantastic," Wallace said. "At times there would be drumfire of enemy bullets spurting in on us. How were we to know this was not the main enemy assault, an attempt to overrun us? But the men held their fire. I don't know where they got the will power."

When day finally dawned, the enemy still had not located Company C. The gamble had paid off. With the aid of several additional companies, Meloy rescued the beleaguered unit and pulled out his battered force. In all, they had survived six frontal assaults in less than thirty hours of combat.

Despite the setback suffered by Meloy and his battalion, Operation Attleboro was judged a success, accounting for more than 1,100 enemy killed and 1,130 tons of rice, 3,340 pounds of cement, and 1,614 rounds of ammunition captured or destroyed. Although begun as a brigade-size search-and-destroy mission, the operation expanded quickly to division strength. Eventually more than 22,000 U.S. and allied soldiers took part. Attleboro signaled an important development in U.S. strategy. As Lieutenant General Bernard W. Rogers pointed out, it "introduced the large-scale, multiorganization operation to the war, albeit as an accident." The next time such large forces were used in an operation it was not an accident and once again the 25th played a vital role.

The big-unit war

Operations Cedar Falls and Junction City, conducted from January through March 1967, provided vivid examples of Gen. Westmoreland's adoption of big-unit warfare. The first preplanned, multidivisional operations of the war, they marked a turning point in U.S. strategy from shoring up ARVN's position toward offensive operations. Both operations attacked the enemy in its strongholds, Cedar Falls in the Iron Triangle and Junction City in War Zone C.

In Junction City, the largest operation of the war to that time, the 25th returned to the sight of its battle during Attleboro. The first month of operations yielded impressive amounts of captured equipment, but the enemy was difficult to find. On March 19, the 3d Battalion, 22d Infantry, and the 2d Battalion, 77th Artillery, prepared to air assault into War Zone C. The 3/22 was part of the 3d Brigade, 4th Infantry Division, which was then under the 25th's operational control. Later that August it would be formally transferred to the division as the 4th and 25th swapped third brigades. In midmorning three flights of helicopters airlifted the 3/22 and the 2/77 into an oval clearing near the abandoned village of Suoi Tre to establish Fire Support Base Gold. The enemy greeted them with exploding mines. Four electrically detonated charges destroyed three UH-1Ds and damaged three more. The blasts also killed ten soldiers and wounded eighteen. After this initial success, the VC, as they had during Attleboro, withdrew, allowing the Americans to secure the firebase.

The next morning, the 2d Battalion, 12th Infantry, having joined the 3/22 the previous afternoon, pushed out to the west to join the 2d Battalion, 34th Armor, in a sweep of the area. By sending the 2/12 out on its own, Colonel Marshall Garth, commander of the 3d Brigade, 4th Division, hoped to lure the 272d VC Regiment, operating in the vicinity, to attack the base. That afternoon, Garth spotted a force of thirty to forty VC moving east toward Gold. From his command helicopter, he warned the base to prepare for an attack and ordered the separate infantry and armor columns to support the base.

Operation Attleboro

Operation Attleboro was the initial field test for the U.S. Army's recently devised search-and-destroy mission. Aimed at rooting out North Vietnamese and Vietcong forces west of the Michelin plantation in Tay Ninh Province, it began as a battalion-size operation in September 1966. Because of stiff enemy resistance, however, Operation Attleboro drew in more and more troops until in November more than 22,000 U.S. and allied soldiers were involved, including battalions of the 25th Infantry Division. The success of the three-month struggle led to the adoption of a new approach for U.S. forces—large-scale, multidivisional search-and-destroy operations.

Above. As soldiers from the 25th Infantry Division confer, a helicopter carrying reinforcements approaches a clearing during Operation Attleboro. Right. Men of a weapons platoon head into battle against the North Vietnamese on November 5, 1966, at the height of Operation Attleboro.

Left. Men of the 1st Battalion, 27th Infantry, 25th Infantry Division, look down at a North Vietnamese soldier killed as he emerged from a spider hole. Below. Major Guy S. Meloy, wounded commander of the 1st Battalion, 27th Infantry, directs his men during Operation Attleboro, November 1966.

Upon receiving Garth's warning, Lieutenant Colonel John A. Bender, a veteran of World War II and Korea and now commander of the 3/22, and Lieutenant Colonel Jack Vessey, a future chairman of the JCS, then commander of the 2/77, pushed their men at FSB Gold to complete the base's defenses before nightfall, a task they had been working on steadily since landing there the day before. Vessey had even drilled his artillery crews in infantry tactics in case the base was overrun.

Through the long night, the soldiers tensed for the attack. At 4:30, just before dawn, a forward patrol led by Specialist 4th Class Virgil M. Ledford reported movement in its area. For two hours the patrol waited. Finally at 6:30, as the men prepared to return to base, they discovered that the VC had entirely surrounded their position. Cut off from FSB Gold, Ledford ordered seven of his men to run for safety while he and three others covered their retreat.

At the first shot, the earth erupted in a fury of gunfire. Automatic-weapons fire, RPGs, and 75MM recoilless rifle shells ripped through the air while more than 650 mortar rounds rained down upon the firebase. The first mortar rounds pounded the ammunition dumps and the command posts, especially the artillery CP, so conspicuous with its assortment of antennas.

Ledford and his three remaining men were killed in the first charge as the VC rushed toward the base. The others, who had run for safety, also were overtaken by the onrushing enemy but found cover in hastily dug foxholes where they remained for the duration of the battle.

For the next four hours the VC force, estimated at more than 2,500 men, pushed the perimeter of the base inexorably inward. The base faced its most serious challenge from the northeast and southeast. During the initial assault the enemy penetrated the perimeter of Company B, 3/22. A group of artillerymen cleared the area momentarily, but a second wave of attackers pushed them back leaving Company B surrounded. A newly arrived forward air controller flying overhead quickly called in artillery and air strikes on the eastern tree line in an attempt to relieve some of the pressure on Company B.

As FSB Gold struggled to withstand the attack, Col. Garth ordered the 2/12 and 2/34 Armor to rush to the base's defense. The infantry faced a stiff march of more than 1,500 meters through bamboo thickets and heavy underbrush. The armor also found its progress stymied by the steep-banked Suoi Samat River. Garth ordered them across the river even "if you have to fill it [the river] up with your own vehicles and drive across them." Eventually, they crossed the river by plowing dirt into it at the ford.

With help still some distance away, the VC tightened their grip on the base. Using the tactics of fire and maneuver so familiar to the U.S. soldiers staring out from within the firebase, the determined, disciplined VC quickly and efficiently surrounded and overwhelmed one position after another. Their advance was a "story book picture of well-trained, well-equipped soldiers," Lt. Col. Bender observed. Soon, the entire northeastern, eastern, and southeastern portions of the perimeter had to be drawn in as the U.S. forces retreated to a second line of defense.

As the enemy closed in, the artillery leveled its guns and fired round after round of deadly beehive shells into the onrushing foe. These shells, containing more than 8,000 tiny fléchettes, showered the attackers with a deadly hail of steel. When they had exhausted their supply of beehives, the artillerymen substituted high-explosive rounds.

Numerous supporting artillery and air strikes also pounded the enemy, some shells falling within fifty meters of U.S. positions. Still, the VC forged ahead. Specialist 4th Class Samuel Townsend, a twenty-one-year-old draftee from Detroit, hurled grenades at enemy positions now less than thirty meters away. Specialist 4th Class Richard Hazel literally ran into a VC who had wormed his way into the perimeter. "I bumped into him," the surprised soldier said. Unarmed at that moment, Hazel resorted to the simplest means to defend himself. "There were no fancy punches, I just knocked him down." Before the enemy soldier could fire his own weapon, a nearby artilleryman shot him.

By midmorning, the enemy was on the verge of overrunning the defenders. Ammunition was desperately low: Many were down to their last grenade and clip of bullets. The one remaining quad .50-caliber machine gun had burned out all four barrels during the fight, and eleven of the battery's eighteen howitzers lay silenced by enemy fire. Most of those still operating were using parts cannibalized from other damaged weapons. One gun crew resorted to squinting down the bore of the gun to aim after its gun sight had been shot off. They were now firing at targets less than seventy-five meters away, aiming at small tussocks of earth to detonate their shells. "They'd fall down or be chopped to pieces," said Specialist Fourth Class James Morales of the attackers, "but more kept coming. You're so busy you don't know what you're doing. But I prayed, and God was here with us. He came and helped us."

Just as the enemy seemed about to overwhelm the base, help arrived. "It was just like the 10 o'clock show on TV. The U.S. Cavalry came riding to the rescue," said the grateful battalion commander, Lt. Col. Bender, afterward. Only it was the infantry and armor, not horses. Just after nine o'clock, soldiers from the 2/12 charged in from the south. Linking up with Company B, they quickly pushed the enemy back outside the original perimeter. The infantry had traveled more than a kilometer through dense jungle in less than two hours. "We knew you were in trouble," a private first class later told Bender, "and we never stopped running to get here." Ten minutes later, the 2/34 Armor crashed through the underbrush. Sweeping northwest along the tree line, guns blazing, they routed the surprised VC. By nine-thirty, the base was secured and mopping-up operations began.

On the battlefield, U.S. forces found 647 enemy dead and estimated that 200 more had been carried away during the battle. A VC who surrendered revealed that the attacking force, the 272d VC Main Force Regiment, had suffered more than 65 percent casualties. In defense of the base, air support had flown thirty-one sorties, delivering thirty-four tons of ordnance, while supporting artillery had fired 1,744 rounds. The base's own artillery had fired 2,240 rounds of 105MM ammunition, including forty beehive shells. The defenders had paid a high price, however. Thirty-one had been killed and another 187 wounded, 92 of whom had to be evacuated. Westmoreland called the battle "a major victory of the Vietnam War," and the unit later received a Presidential Unit Citation for its actions.

Into the monsoon

In the months following Junction City, the VC returned to guerrilla tactics, temporarily disbanding their larger units in favor of smaller squads. To counter this, the 25th also reduced the size of its operations, cutting back to battalion-

Soldiers of the 25th Infantry Division on a "search and snatch" mission in Hau Nghia Province hold a VC suspect as they wait for a helicopter to lift them out.

and company-size patrols. And, as the monsoon rains rendered the roads nearly impassable to the 25th's heavy tanks and APCs, Weyand also made greater use of helicopters to ferry the division's troops over the rain-soaked countryside.

In particular, the division employed a very effective air assault tactic called the Eagle Flight. Developed in 1964 by Special Forces advisers for the South Vietnamese, Eagle Flight took off at prearranged times, then assaulted into randomly selected landing zones. If no enemy contact developed, the troops could be lifted out and deposited at a second or third LZ. Although the lack of artillery fire prior to landing could result in an enemy ambush at the LZ, it also meant that the VC would not be alerted to the approach of the U.S. troops. A variation of the Eagle Flight—the Blitz—called for numerous simultaneous landings to prevent the enemy from massing at a single LZ.

Troops of the 4th Battalion, 23d Infantry, 25th Infantry Division, work their way down the eastern face of Nui Ba Den during a sweep of the mountain in 1969.

The lull in fighting also allowed the division to develop its civic action programs such as MEDCAP, County Fairs, Helping Hand, and others. At the same time, the division increased its efforts to train and equip the local ARVN and Regional and Popular forces. One very successful part of this effort was the Combined Reconnaissance and Intelligence Platoon (CRIP). Made up of half of the 2/27 Reconnaissance Platoon and the ARVN Hau Nghia Province Intelligence Platoon, the CRIP could react much more quickly and effectively to intelligence than most other larger, separate U.S. or South Vietnamese forces.

With the return of the dry weather, the enemy once again adopted the tactics of large-scale warfare. In December, enemy forces twice attacked 25th Division forces in large numbers during Operation Yellowstone in War Zone C. These attacks, however, proved to be only a prelude to the countrywide Tet offensive. When, beginning on January 31, 1968, the VC attacked targets all across South Vietnam, the 25th rushed to defend Saigon. At Tan Son Nhut Air Base outside the capital, the 3d Squadron, 4th Cavalry, joined by the 1st and 2d Wolfhounds and the 1/5

Mechanized Infantry, thwarted several furious attacks by VC forces. Other units from the 2d Brigade also moved westward, to Hoc Mon, first to prevent infiltration into the city and then later, after the initial offensive had been defeated, to block the enemy's retreat. There the brigade also conducted extensive riverine operations along the water routes in and out of Saigon.

The 25th served in the Saigon area during a second enemy offensive in May and into the summer monsoon season. In July, intelligence reported a third offensive scheduled for later that month or early August. Intelligence officers, however, debated the target for this new offensive. MACV planners in Saigon insisted that the capital would once again be the enemy's primary goal. However, intelligence officers of the 25th's 1st Brigade, stationed at Tay Ninh City, argued that the city would be the target. MACV held to its theory and refused requests by the 1st Brigade's new commander, Colonel Duquesne (Duke) Wolf, for additional troops and equipment to meet the threat at Tay Ninh.

A graduate of West Point, Wolf had assumed command of the 1st Brigade on August 5. His assessment of his new command's capabilities revealed a great shortage of manpower and air support. The response to his initial request, however, had been clear and emphatic—no reinforcements would be forthcoming and he was not to make any further requests. This left the under-strength 1st Brigade to man an area 800 square kilometers larger than the state of Delaware, an area previously covered by two full-strength brigades. The brigade had to defend seven U.S. bases and more than 320,000 civilians against two enemy divisions, the VC's 5th and 9th and a separate VC regiment, the 88th.

To contend with his manpower shortage, Col. Wolf followed the plan developed by his predecessor, Colonel Freemont B. Hodson. Deploying most of his combat forces in a defensive ring around Tay Ninh City, he conducted extensive reconnaissance-in-force operations during the day and strung his forces in ambush positions along likely infiltration routes during the night. In this way he hoped to engage the enemy before they reached the city. If any VC/NVA troops did breach this perimeter and enter the city, the task of defense then fell to the Regional and Popular forces stationed at Tay Ninh.

The air support shortage proved a more difficult problem to overcome. Lack of air transportation meant Wolf had to rely upon truck convoys to resupply his troops. This in turn required assigning valuable men and materiel to keep open the main supply route into Tay Ninh, Highway 26. He assigned his mechanized forces to patrol Highway 26 by day, returning them to the firebases at night.

Despite MACV's predictions, Wolf continued to proceed with his plans for defending Tay Ninh against an enemy offensive. The argument was settled on August 17 when troops from the 1st Brigade encountered a large enemy force east of Tay Ninh. At 10:00 P.M. the 2/27 Wolfhounds, occupying a series of ambush positions strung in an arc—called a "trip wire" formation—between FSB Buell II and FSB Rawlins, surprised an enemy battalion heading toward the city. Employing heavy artillery and air support, they routed the opposing force after two hours of battle.

Even as these first attackers retreated, others struck at U.S. positions around the city. At 1:30 A.M. three battalions of the 273d VC/NVA Regiment and 5th VC/NVA Division attacked FSB Buell II. Half an hour later another force attacked the communications facility atop nearby Nui Ba Den, the Mountain of the Black Virgin.

At both bases, the enemy hurled themselves boldly upon the heavily defended U.S. positions. At FSB Buell II a thunderous rocket and mortar attack preceded an assault by waves of enemy soldiers. However, the base's own artillery, tanks, APCs, machine guns, and automatic weapons, together with supporting artillery and air strikes, decimated the Communist ranks even before they could reach the base's perimeter. A reported 105 enemy soldiers died attacking the base, many literally torn apart by the U.S. fire. "The battlefield was strewn with carnage instead of bodies," Wolf noted. American losses amounted to one soldier killed and 26 wounded.

Atop Nui Ba Den, the defenders faced a much stiffer challenge. Rising more than 900 meters above the valley floor, Nui Ba Den dominated the countryside. Its extensive honeycomb of caves had long been used by the VC as a base camp but now the U.S. held the mountain, establishing a communications station at its peak, the essential link in the province's communications network.

With thick clouds and a driving forty-five-mile-per-hour wind covering its approach, a reinforced VC company assaulted the outpost in a six-pronged attack. Armed with AK47s, RPGs, grenades, and satchel charges, the attackers breached the defense along the southern perimeter, occupying several bunkers near the helipad before the defenders could drive them off. Although the VC force left behind fifteen dead and more than 100 unexploded satchel charges, they destroyed one generator, temporarily disrupting the flow of communications, and killed five U.S. soldiers while wounding another twenty-three.

Under cover of the attacks on Buell II and Nui Ba Den, two VC battalions slipped through the defensive ring around Tay Ninh and attacked an RF compound and district headquarters in the southeastern sector of the city. Hoping to avoid the political repercussions sure to follow the destruction of any large section of the city, the 1st Brigade leaders opted not to use heavy artillery and air strikes to dislodge the enemy. Instead, they adopted a plan to combine the Vietnamese and U.S. forces in a hammer

While howitzers based at Tay Ninh shell Vietcong positions on Nui Ba Den, armored personnel carriers of the 4th Battalion, 23d Infantry, circle the base of the mountain.

and anvil operation in which the Vietnamese infantry and mechanized forces acted as the hammer and the U.S. 2/34 Armor and 4/23 Mechanized Infantry served as the anvil.

Unfortunately the hammer never materialized. After the U.S. forces fought their way into position, they waited in vain for the South Vietnamese to appear. The district chief balked at the last moment and refused to send his forces through the city, protesting that he had to keep them to protect his own headquarters.

"This refusal of South Vietnamese military commanders to do their share of the fighting became a frequent occurrence during this campaign," Wolf later complained. The problem arose again several days later when the commander of an ARVN Airborne Brigade refused to take part in combat around the city and, according to Wolf, "astonished the 1st Brigade by insisting that he conduct an attack in another province some forty kilometers south of Tay Ninh City." One South Vietnamese unit, the 51st ARVN Ranger Battalion, did acquit itself well in the fighting. However, several U.S. officers felt that the general reluctance of the South Vietnamese to fight greatly hampered the already under-manned 1st Brigade's efforts.

The following day, when the district chief finally allowed his forces to advance upon enemy positions, they found that the enemy had fled. In its wake, the VC/NVA force left four blocks of burnt-out buildings. However, it had failed in its primary purpose of occupying the city.

Over the next several weeks U.S. and VC/NVA forces clashed repeatedly, both around the city and firebases and, in particular, along Highway 26 and the nearby Ben Cui rubber plantation, a major infiltration route. However, the 1st Brigade denied the enemy any further opportunities to reach the city. When the offensive ended on September 20, the enemy forces had suffered more than 2,500 dead while the 25th's casualties numbered 370 KIA and 755 wounded. South Vietnamese forces counted 137 KIA and another 138 wounded during the offensive.

Although enemy attacks slackened momentarily following the battle for Tay Ninh, this month-long offensive signaled a period of increased enemy activity lasting until the second attack on Tay Ninh in June 1969. To Major General Ellis W. Williamson, the 25th's new commander, this meant a reconsideration of his unit's role. Pacification efforts and attacks upon the local VC infrastructure now took a back seat to battling Main Force VC/NVA units.

Williamson's observations during the battle for Tay Ninh, the first action during his tour as the division's commander, also prompted him to rethink the 25th's tactical approach to the war, particularly its use of the firebase. Recognizing that the firebase attracted concentrated enemy forces, Williamson perceived it to be not just a defen-

Bunkers ring the 25th Infantry Division's redesigned FSB Sedgwick at Cu Chi. To increase efficiency, the division's firebases were made smaller and circular in 1968.

sive but an offensive position. The construction of fire-bases along Communist infiltration routes, he argued, would lure the enemy into the open. He could then attack them with the division's formidable firepower. In this way, he would engage the enemy on his terms, not its.

To accomplish this, Williamson first had to change the physical configuration of the firebase. He altered its overall shape from elliptical to circular and then reduced the base in size so that it could be manned by a single rifle company. These adjustments allowed for more efficient defense and more rapid construction.

In addition to changing the structure of the firebase, Williamson also developed the concept of "Force Fed Fire Support." Operating on the principle that at any one time there would be only one major contact within the division's area, (an assumption that proved generally correct) all of the division's fire support was made available to the commander in that battle. "In any significant contact," Williamson wrote, "the Division Tactical Operations Center will dispatch a Forward Air Controller, a helicopter fire team, a load of tactical CS gas, and a flame bath helicopter with an immediate napalm capability. The ground commander is expected to employ these assets along with his organic weapons and all available artillery support in a coordinated, continuous attack on the enemy position so that the enemy force is eliminated in the shortest possible

time." This followed Williamson's overriding dictum of using bullets not bodies to fight a battle. By making effective use of the firepower available to him, he could inflict the greatest number of casualties upon the enemy while minimizing his own.

The first test of Williamson's new tactics came in December 1968. On the eighteenth, Companies B and C, 9th Infantry, 1st Brigade, air assaulted into a clearing fourteen kilometers south of Tay Ninh City along a major infiltration route through the nearby Angel's Wing section of Cambodia. In a single day, Company A, 65th Engineers, transformed 186,000 pounds of building materials hauled in by twenty-seven helicopter sorties into a well-fortified position dubbed Patrol Base Mole City. Three days later, the enemy attacked.

Shortly after midnight on December 22, soldiers of the 272d Regiment, 9th VC/NVA Division, unleashed a barrage of 75MM recoilless rifle, mortar, and RPG fire upon the firebase. "The mortars were coming in so fast you would swear that they were automatic," recalled Private First Class Walter Schmiel of Company B. Soon, the sharp cracks of hundreds of AK47s added a deadly counterpoint

---

As their transport helicopters withdraw, soldiers of the 2d Battalion, 14th Infantry, 25th Infantry Division, prepare to approach a Vietcong wood-line position on August 20, 1969.

to the sounds of the exploding mortars as the enemy rose up to assault the base. "Tracers, ours, theirs, were going everywhere," said First Lieutenant Wilbur D. Saulters, a platoon leader for Company B. "After a few minutes we got our artillery coming to the front of Charlie Company and not long after that gunships and air strikes. We had all the help in the world we could get."

While the battle raged around the base, several hundred meters to the east Sergeant José Olea and his patrol found themselves surrounded by the attacking force. "We were so far outnumbered that we hoped they wouldn't see us, but one of the last ones noticed something and started to bring his AK around in our direction," Olea said. "Then we opened up on them with grenades and pretty soon there were grenades falling all over the place." Three men in Olea's patrol were killed and seven others wounded but they survived the night, and next morning a medevac lifted them to safety.

Despite the heavy firepower used on the enemy, including artillery support and air strikes by helicopter and AC-47 Spooky gunships, the VC/NVA momentarily breached the perimeter in several locations before American infantrymen drove them back. At dawn the enemy withdrew, leaving the soldiers of the 25th in control of the field. Behind them they left 103 dead. Drag marks and blood trails indicated another possible 120 enemy dead. Losses to the two U.S. companies stood at 17 dead and 34 wounded.

Mole City proved to be only the warm-up for a series of battles that tested the defense of Williamson's new firebases. Late in February 1969, the VC/NVA repeated their 1968 Tet offensive on a smaller scale. Locating his bases in exposed positions along the Cambodian border, Williamson hoped to entice the enemy to attack these apparently isolated bases. When they attacked, the VC/NVA had to fight on Williamson's terms, and the fighting could be kept away from population centers.

On the border

The attacks began at 1:00 A.M. on the morning of February 23. In the midst of a series of countrywide attacks, the VC/NVA attacked Patrol Base Diamond I, located little more than two kilometers from the Cambodian border. The 2/27 Wolfhounds manned the base. As at Mole City, the enemy began the attack with a heavy mortar barrage followed by sapper attacks on the perimeter and, finally, the charge. Once again, the attackers breached the perimeter despite the heavy fire directed by the defenders. Manning his bunker along the edge of the base, platoon Sergeant Gonzales A. Marquez suddenly found himself face to face with an NVA soldier. "I shoved my M16 into his chest and pulled the trigger," he recalled. As the enemy swarmed over the U.S. position, the artillery lowered their guns and began firing pointblank into the attacking force.

"It was just like a firefight," said Specialist 4th Class John Jasinski, "only we were using howitzers."

After ten hours of battle, the attacking force withdrew. On the battlefield the following day, the Wolfhounds found 129 enemy bodies. The defenders had little time to relax, however. Two days later, the enemy attacked again but this time the charge stalled far short of the perimeter. After another night of futile probes, the VC/NVA forces retreated, this time leaving behind 78 dead.

Over the next three weeks, the Wolfhounds twice repeated the same tactics they had followed at Diamond I: at Diamond II on April 5 and at Diamond III on April 15. Each time, the enemy responded to the construction of the new firebases by attacking in force. And each time, the tremendous firepower of the U.S. forces repulsed the attack, inflicting heavy casualties on the enemy. At one point during the attack on Diamond III, in addition to the weapons stationed on the base, the U.S. commander had helicopter gunships strafing the enemy along the northwest perimeter, planes attacking to the south, and artillery firing from several different locations.

The final round of fighting along the border occurred ten days later at Patrol Base Frontier City. On April 24, Companies A and C, 4th Battalion, 9th Infantry, accompanied by engineer units constructed Frontier City on a site in the same area as the Diamonds, less than three kilometers from the Cambodian border. Completed in less than nine hours, the base included triple rows of concertina wire, covered bunkers, two 105MM howitzers, several hundred claymore mines and trip flares, and a twenty-foot, prefabricated observation tower. Bulldozers also cleared fields of fire nearly 100 meters from the perimeter.

The following night, just after ten o'clock, radar and starlight scopes detected a number of soldiers closing on the base. The defenders called in air and artillery strikes but the enemy pressed ahead. At midnight, the NVA attacked. Preceded by mortar and recoilless rifle fire, the attackers charged the base firing as they ran.

Sapper squads, carrying bangalore torpedoes and satchel charges with which they would try to blow a hole through the wall of wire surrounding the base, presented the greatest threat. Heavy fire from .50-caliber machine guns and M16s held them at bay at most points. But in one area several sappers wriggled through the wire and claymore mines to the edge of the first line of bunkers before pointblank fire from the two howitzers stopped them.

With the failure of the sapper attack, the base brought to bear its expertly coordinated supporting fire. Standing atop the observation tower, Major Harry L. Ray and 1st Lieutenant Kenneth Montoya directed air and artillery strikes with unerring accuracy even as RPG and automatic-weapons fire whistled past them in their exposed position. "So many small arms' tracers were bouncing off the tower," said Specialist 4th Class Melvin Lingle, "that it looked like a giant Fourth of July sparkler."

When dawn arrived, the enemy had fled. Although the defenders suffered only one wounded, 214 enemy bodies littered the battlefield. For Gen. Williamson, Frontier City provided the final vindication of his new tactics. In all, the series of attacks upon the Diamonds and Frontier City accounted for more than 700 enemy killed, while U.S. forces incurred less than 50 dead.

Williamson's system of efficient air and artillery support continued to serve the division well through the summer, especially during a June attack on Tay Ninh City where the defenders of Firebase Crook killed more than 400 enemy troops while losing only a single soldier. However, as 1969 drew to a close, the enemy, having suffered substantial losses during the previous twelve months, abandoned large-scale operations and returned to guerrilla warfare. Its Main Force units were broken down into small sapper squads. Major General Harris Hollis, who assumed command of the 25th in September, noted that enemy forces in the division's area steadily dwindled from a high of 18,000 in January 1969 to less than 4,000 in January 1970.

To counter the enemy's new tactics, Hollis opted for what he called a "light war," shifting the division's emphasis from conventional, large-unit operations to small-unit reconnaissance. Under his direction, the 25th adopted a technique developed by Lieutenant General Julian Ewell for the 9th Infantry Division in the Mekong Delta. Dubbed "jitterbugging," this technique, much like the Eagle Flight, called for repeated airmobile insertions into a particular area. If contact was made, the commander could reinforce with additional troops to seal the area and then call in air and artillery strikes to defeat the enemy with a minimum of U.S. casualties. Hollis, who had seen this tactic used effectively during a previous tour as commander of the 9th, employed it with similar results in the 25th's area.

Hollis also greatly expanded the 25th's night operations. Starting in January 1970, the 25th conducted more than half of its offensive operations at night, generating over 70 percent of the division's contacts with the enemy. A significant number of these contacts developed out of Bushmaster ambushes. These company-size operations called for the insertion of troops into an area just prior to sundown. Resting through the last hours before dark, the company then dispersed and set up a number of smaller ambushes throughout the area. The next morning they gathered at specified locations where they spent the day hiding and resting until the following night when they set up a different set of ambushes. On the second morning they were finally taken out and returned to base. These night ambushes and increased airmobile assaults enabled the division to maintain a low casualty ratio. During Hollis's period as commander, the 25th averaged thirty-four enemy killed or captured to every U.S. soldier killed.

Reflecting the Army's emphasis on pacification during this period, Hollis stepped up division efforts to train and develop an ARVN division (the 25th) that operated in his area. Under the Dong Tien "Progress Together" program, the number of combined U.S./Vietnamese operations increased dramatically. In January alone, the allies conducted 1,520 company-size combined operations. Several units even shared the same firebase. The 25th also allowed the Vietnamese to make greater use of U.S. air power. By February 1970, U.S. aircraft supported Vietnamese operations nearly 30 percent of the time; this percentage increased as assaults by the 25th decreased.

The Vietnamization program, however, was not an unqualified success. Major General Edward Bautz, Jr., who assumed command of the 25th in March 1970, noted that despite the increased number of combined operations, the vast majority were planned and commanded by U.S. leaders with U.S. forces providing "the preponderance of combat power in the operations." Furthermore, when the Vietnamese did command their own forces, the U.S. and Vietnamese units operated more as separate though coordinated forces rather than as a single, combined unit.

The last lap

The invasion of Cambodia was the 25th's last major offensive operation of the war. After patrolling the South Vietnamese side of the border for the first week of the operation, the 25th at last received permission on May 6 to cross the border. During its two months in Cambodia, the 25th took part in three major operations. The most important of these attempted to locate and destroy the Central Office for South Vietnam (COSVN), the headquarters of the Communist party in South Vietnam. Operating to the north of the Dog's Face area of Cambodia, the men of the 4/9 and 2/27 uncovered a large training and headquarters complex on May 9. Lieutenant General Michael S. Davison, commander of all U.S. forces in Cambodia, later identified this as "a piece of COSVN."

While contacts with the enemy remained light throughout the invasion, the 25th uncovered enormous quantities of enemy equipment, supplies, and buildings. General Bautz viewed the operation as very successful from a tactical standpoint. Upon the division's return to South Vietnam, it found the enemy presence reduced to where even small units could operate with relative impunity.

Bautz and others viewed the incursion into Cambodia as a final effort to secure South Vietnam before U.S. forces redeployed and to give ARVN time to complete the process of Vietnamization. In the period immediately following the invasion, however, the 25th saw not a reduction but an expansion of its responsibilities. As the 9th Infantry Division, the 199th Infantry Brigade, and the 1st Infantry Division returned to the U.S., part or all of their areas of responsibility fell to the 25th. In addition, the 3d Brigade, 9th Infantry Division, came under the 25th's control before it followed its parent division home.

With his forces stretched to the limit, Bautz placed a

promium on mobility, particularly ground mobility. MACV solved his problem in part by placing the 11th Armored Cavalry Regiment under his operational control. In conjunction with the 25th's own three mechanized battalions and its tank battalion, Bautz now commanded an essentially mechanized, highly mobile force. Bautz further improved the division's mobility by eschewing large, static bases in favor of smaller, temporary bases that he moved constantly. This freed a number of infantry units from the task of base security and also confused the enemy as to the day-to-day location of U.S. forces.

Aware of the division's impending departure, Bautz also stepped up the training of the Vietnamese forces in his area, particularly the RF/PF units. Initially he employed Mobile Training Teams that trained local Regional and Popular units throughout the 25th's area. Later, when it became obvious that a more in-depth training effort was needed, he organized the Dedicated Company Program. Under this program, the small, mobile training teams were replaced by an entire U.S. company that located with an RF/PF force and operated with the Vietnamese until they were trained sufficiently.

The 25th's training programs came to an abrupt halt in late 1970 when MACV issued orders for the division to prepare to return to Hawaii. Bautz had known that the 25th was slated for redeployment but he had expected a much later date. MACV, however, viewing its dwindling force level, chose to retain the more mobile 1st Air Cavalry Division rather than the 25th. In December, the division ended all operations and planned for its departure. Just as it had hurried to deploy to Vietnam five years earlier, the 25th now scrambled to meet the deadline for its return home. By month's end both the 1st and the 3d brigades had returned to Hawaii. The 2d Brigade, however, remained in Vietnam for another four months before completing the division's redeployment in April 1971.

During its tour in Vietnam, the division had taken part in some of the stiffest fighting of the war. A total of 34,484 soldiers from the division were either wounded or killed in action, almost seven times the number of Tropic Lightning casualties in World War II and nearly three times the 13,685 casualties from Korea. But now, a little more than five years after arriving in Vietnam, the division could rest. The 25th had come home.

Men of the 3d Squadron, 4th Cavalry, 25th Infantry Division, unleash cannon, machine guns, and M16s on the enemy in Mimot District during the invasion of Cambodia, May 1970.

In the Field With the 25th

Without a virtual army of civilian photographers following the American soldiers wherever they fought in Vietnam, the war could never have been brought home as vividly as it was. To capture on film poignant moments of war, the photographers had to travel with the soldiers for days, even weeks, at a time, often undergoing the same rigors as the men they covered.

One of the many photographers to accompany American units in the field was Bunyo Ishikawa, a Japanese freelance photojournalist, whose work appears here for the first time in a Western publication. His experience of the war was typical of most dedicated photographers: He not only came away with many dramatic images of men at war, but he also learned firsthand the realities of warfare.

One of the units that was usually just a short helicopter ride away from Ishikawa's temporary home in Saigon was the 25th Infantry Division, and the photographer visited them several times. Typically, he would live with the men for a week, patrolling for six days and resting for one at the Tropic Lightning Cu Chi base. The patrols were anxiety-ridden because of the many mines and booby traps planted by the VC around Cu Chi. Once he was saved from certain death when a soldier stopped him from walking across a trip wire in the nick of time.

Combat was terrrifying. "You couldn't see around you," Ishikawa remembered. "You didn't know where to go, what to do." One enemy ambush in the Ho Bo Woods in 1967 was especially harrowing. "There were dense woods all around and you couldn't see more than three meters in any direction," he said. "We knew there were VC out there but you couldn't see them. Before I knew it they started throwing hand grenades. We all lay down in a circle, facing out with our legs touching. I tried to take pictures but it was too frightening to pick up the camera. Gunfire was all around, and leaves and branches kept falling all over us." Ishikawa overcame his fear and took the picture on page 93 of a company commander calling battalion headquarters as enemy fire pinned down his men.

Most of the time Ishikawa spent with the men was relatively quiet. "From the soldier's point of view," he remembered, "it was better if there were no battles to fight." When the men dug in at camps in the field, the young photographer listened to their conversations in the idle hours: frequent reminiscences of girls back home and favorite foods that they missed.

Walking on patrol, wondering if the enemy was near and a battle imminent, the men were anxious, even afraid, but they and Ishikawa seemed to reassure each other. He felt safe because the soldiers carried guns, and they in turn felt that his camera kept them from danger. "In fact, they seemed to feel that with me along, things, at least on the day I was with them, would be OK."

Returning from action against the enemy, soldiers of the 25th Infantry Division trudge through a swamp in Tay Ninh Province in February 1967.

The enemy's use of Cambodia as a sanctuary led to an increased emphasis on American operations in Tay Ninh Province, which lay along the border northwest of Saigon. Here soldiers of the 25th Infantry Division head out from an LZ near the border in 1967 as a UH-1 helicopter pulls away.

Above. *Soldiers of the 25th Infantry Division carry the bloody corpse of a comrade killed during a firefight in the Ho Bo Woods in 1968.*

Right. *As he and his men come under fire in the dense foliage of the Ho Bo Woods in 1967, a 25th company commander calls his battalion headquarters for assistance.*

170840

93

Above. With American helmets neatly arranged nearby, a 25th Infantry Division soldier mans a 155MM howitzer in the Parrot's Beak inside Cambodia in May 1970.

Left. Men of the 25th Infantry Division uncover part of the huge weapons and ammunition cache found near Mimot, Cambodia, during the American incursion in June 1970.

Army Combat Uniforms

Rifleman, 1965

A rifleman of the 1st Infantry Division carries an M14 rifle at the ready as he prepares to fill his polyethylene water canteen, one of the many plastic items used by the Army in Vietnam. His field utility shirt and trousers reflect the early military attire issued to many troops arriving in Vietnam. He wears the traditional white name tape and gold-black "US Army" insignia above his shirt pock- ets. As tropical clothing supplies in- creased, hot–weather apparel ("jungle fatigues") replaced these field utility gar- ments. Likewise, the demands of combat soon mandated the general demise of white undershirts and full-color insignia items. New tropical combat boots de- signed for wet climates and reinforced against punji stake injuries were issued instead of the all–leather combat boot worn here. Even the M14 rifle quickly dis- appeared as the M16 rifle became avail- able for general issue. This soldier also wears the new insignia of private first class (E-3), which was introduced in April 1965 and became official that September. At the time the rank was also known as lance corporal because Army publications and recruiting journals of that period so designated the novel E-3 stripes.

Illustration by Donna J. Neary

25th Infantry Division

Tunnel rat, 1966

Tunnel rats in Vietnam utilized a bewildering array of equipment depending on individual fancy and the availability of specialized tools. Most soldiers engaged in tunnel exploration and destruction were infantrymen or engineers whose military gear came from standard items adopted for this unusual task. This soldier, an American Indian combat engineer, loads his 9MM automatic pistol as he prepares to enter a newly uncovered Vietcong tunnel complex in War Zone C. He wears a phone headset connected to a long length of wire (played out from the spool) for communications to his comrades aboveground.

He wears a minimum of clothing to enhance his agility at slithering through narrow tunnel obstructions and keeps his flashlight handy. This tunnel expert carries the Frank and Warren, Inc., survival ax, issued by the Army as the Type IV survival tool kit. It is used both for tunnel digging and enlarging work as well as for emergency fighting. This versatile implement is worn in a quick-release fashion on his belt; its cloth protective cover lays on the ground.

Illustration by Donna J. Neary

173d Airborne Brigade

Paratrooper, 1967

A paratrooper of the 503d Infantry (Airborne), patrols with his twenty-round M16 rifle ammunition magazines taped "back to back" for ease in fast reloading, enabling him to unleash a suppressive burst of nearly continuous fire in a surprise encounter. This trooper wears the silver metal parachutist badge with gold jump star on his helmet camouflage band, signifying his participation in the brigade's combat parachute assault during Operation Junction City, the only large American combat jump of the Vietnam War. He has not yet sewn this additional award onto his cloth parachutist badge, seen displayed underneath the combat infantryman's badge on the left breast of his hot–weather coat. He carries an M18 antipersonnel claymore mine bag over his personal effects pack. A smoke grenade has been fitted to his upper field pack suspenders, and fragmentation grenades are attached to the front ammunition pouches. He wears the locally produced subdued 173d Airborne Brigade shoulder sleeve insignia on his left sleeve. The difference between this subdued brigade insignia and the full-color patch (*above*) is striking.

Illustration by Donna J. Neary

9th Infantry Division

Riverine sniper, 1968

A veteran sniper of the 9th Infantry Division attached to the Mobile Riverine Force holds an XM21 sniper M14 rifle with sionics noise suppressor as he receives information concerning helicopter sightings of enemy locations through his PRR-9 lightweight helmet radio. The radio transmitter is attached to his shirt pocket. He would normally turn off the set when occupying an ambush position. He wears a multitude of insignia on his tailored camouflaged clothing, issued to American forces in Vietnam under the Mutual Defense Assistance Pact and known as MDAP contract tiger stripes.

His ranger status is displayed by the yellow ranger tab worn on his left shoulder above the locally produced subdued 9th Infantry Division insignia, as well as an earlier Vietnamese Ranger qualification badge above his name tape. The elite 9th Infantry Division Recondo badge is worn on the right pocket, and his metal staff sergeant rank is pinned on the collar. He wears ammunition pouches and grenades on his pistol belt as well as the collapsible two-quart water canteen.

Illustration by Donna J. Neary

4th Infantry Division

Grenadier, 1967

This 4th Infantry Division soldier advances over fallen deadwood in Vietnam's western highlands. He wears hot–weather jungle fatigues with tropical combat boots and carries spare ammunition in his M79 grenade carrier vest. The vest front is made of nylon duck, but nylon mesh composes its shoulders and back to increase ventilation. The vest, with its twenty-four grenade pockets, becomes very heavy when loaded. The grenadier carries the M79 grenade launcher, a distinctive Vietnam-era weapon popularly known as the thump gun, in the "break-open" position with a round chambered. In combat the grenadier quickly snaps the weapon shut and begins firing 40MM grenade rounds to flush enemy snipers out of dense jungle foliage and to reach areas beyond the range of hand-thrown grenades. This grenadier wears on his right wrist a Montagnard bracelet, usually reserved for Special Forces working with these mountain people but also earned by other combatants directly supporting the remote tribal hill warriors of western Vietnam. Many 4th Infantry Division soldiers were honored by the hill people with this bracelet.

Illustration by Donna J. Neary

199th Infantry Brigade

Medical specialist, 1968

A combat medic of the 199th Infantry Brigade holds the bottle from a field intravenous injection set during the treatment of a casualty in Tet offensive fighting around Saigon. The protective medical emblems authorized by the Geneva Convention were usually not worn by American medics in Vietnam, since early experiences in the war demonstrated that enemy guerrillas actually singled out Red Cross arm bands and other devices in selecting targets. Most medics simply wore their jungle fatigues without any special markings.

Medics were still recognized on the battlefield by their unique equipment, the most prominent being the heavy medical pack worn here. This medic has attached plastic canteens to the pack's supporting straps with metal snap links. He also wears an Army-issue towel around his neck and keeps an emergency medical text handy in his helmet camouflage band. Another plastic medical reference card is just visible protruding from a side pocket in the medical pack. Like many medics in Vietnam, this one carries no weapons of self-defense, allowing him to pack extra medical supplies.

Illustration by Donna J. Neary

11th Armored Cavalry

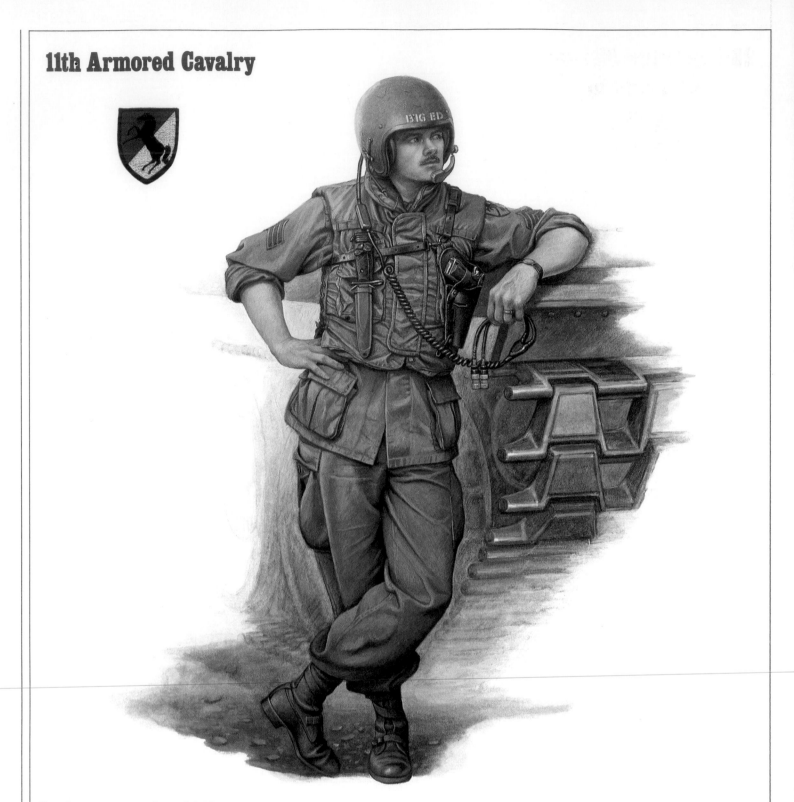

Tank commander, 1970

This sergeant of the 11th Armored Cavalry (Regiment) in Vietnam, pauses momentarily beside his M551 Sheridan armored assault vehicle during the Cambodian invasion of May 1970. He wears the armored vehicle crewman's helmet with a built-in communication system. He protects himself from shrapnel with body armor over his hot–weather clothing. The .45-caliber automatic pistol and shoulder holster, along with an M14 bayonet and scabbard, hang over his protective vest.

He also wears the favorite footwear of many armor troops: commercially produced, storm–welted tanker boots with double-wrap leather straps and reinforced stitching, ideal for work around mechanized vehicles. He wears Vietnam-made subdued cloth sergeant chevrons on his sleeves, although by 1970 smaller, subdued, pin-on enlisted grade insignia was the preferred manner of displaying rank on combat uniforms.

Illustration by Donna J. Neary

23d Infantry Division (Americal)

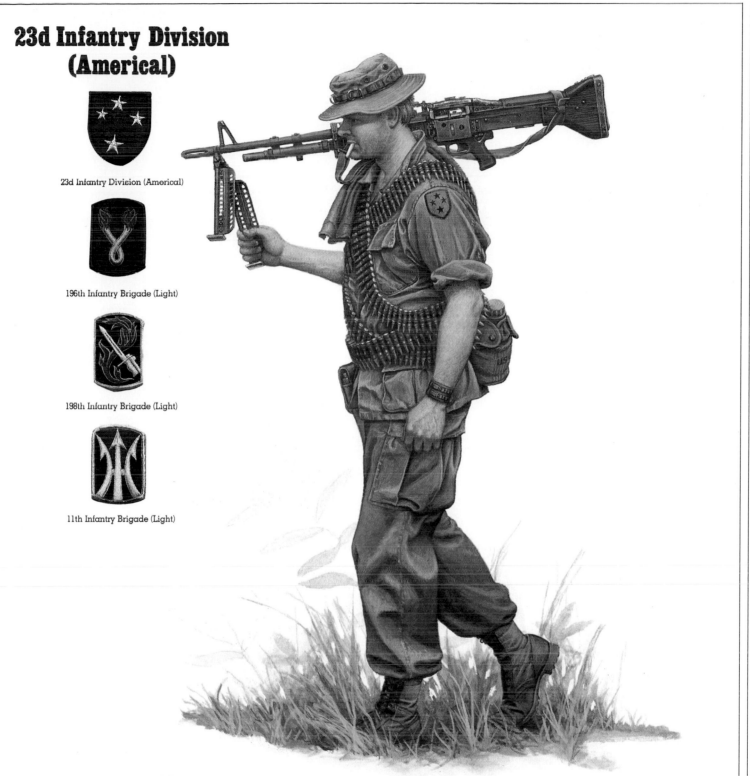

23d Infantry Division (Americal)

196th Infantry Brigade (Light)

198th Infantry Brigade (Light)

11th Infantry Brigade (Light)

Machine gunner, 1969

This soldier of the 23d Infantry Division (Americal) advances across a field in 1969, balancing his M60 machine gun on his shoulder by holding its extended bipod. An olive-drab towel is used to cushion the weapon. He wears the tropical combat uniform with boots and the popular tropical hat—known by the servicemen in Vietnam as the "bush" or "boonie" hat—instead of the heavier helmet. In typical fashion he has personalized his hat with grenade rings. He carries ammunition belts wrapped around his tunic, a common practice that was offically frowned upon because it tended to make ammunition dirty or wet, resulting in a higher number of misfires. Other than his weapon and ammunition, he is lightly equipped, carrying only a canteen and a .45–caliber pistol, shown barely extending in front of his right hip. Rapid helicopter supply often allowed front-line troops to dispense with heavy packs, increasing their ability to pursue the elusive Vietcong.

Illustration by Donna J. Neary

Defending the Capital

The United States Army had already been at war for a year when on April 8, 1966, Colonel George D. Rehkoph at the U.S. Army Infantry School, Fort Benning, Georgia, received orders to form a separate new infantry brigade. Though the directive set no specific timetable beyond the customary six-month training cycle, it was clear from the outset that the Army wanted the unit, designated the 199th Infantry Brigade (Light), to achieve combat-ready status as quickly as possible. Also unstated, yet equally apparent, was that the 199th would eventually be deployed to Vietnam, where the mutual buildup of American and North Vietnamese regular army forces continued unabated.

To fill the ranks of the fledgling brigade, raw recruits were rushed in from training centers across the U.S., while many of the field grade officers and NCOs came from Army outposts in Europe. Even so, by the time the unit was formally activated on June 1, manpower shortages still plagued the brigade at every level, with one infantry battalion—the 3d Bat-

chers. By then the men knew they would be leaving for Vietnam before the year was out, with the bulk of the brigade scheduled to ship out in late November. Once the troops were on their way, a 280-man advance party headed by the unit's newly appointed commander, Brigadier General Charles W. Ryder, flew ahead to prepare for the brigade's arrival.

On December 10 the first shipload of Redcatchers docked at Vung Tau, followed two days later by the rest of the brigade. From there the men moved by truck to a tent encampment on the northern edge of the sprawling American military complex at Long Binh, where the 199th would eventually establish its main base. Even though much of the brigade's equipment was still in transit, before the end of the week the 199th was declared fully operational and was assigned a permanent mission: the defense of Saigon.

Fairfax/Rang Dong

After establishing a forward command post at Cat Lai, eleven kilometers east of the South Vietnamese capital, the brigade launched its first major operation on January 12, 1967. Code-named Fairfax/Rang Dong, the campaign brought together the 199th and the 5th ARVN Ranger Group for a year-long pacification effort that foreshadowed the Vietnamization program of later years. The South Vietnamese troops were issued M16s and American rations, instructed in the use of artillery and aerial fire support, and then paired with comparably sized elements of the 199th down to the company level. Under the terms of this arrangement, called "double force," operations ranging from village searches to night ambushes were to be conducted jointly, with the Rangers shouldering a growing share of responsibility as time wore on.

Designed to quell criticism of ARVN's lackluster performance and at the same time advance the GVN's "revolutionary development" program, Fairfax/Rang Dong met with mixed reviews from the very start. While high-ranking U.S. and South Vietnamese officials tended to be upbeat about the experiment, many of the American soldiers involved in the operation offered a more pessimistic appraisal. "We're supposed to work jointly with these guys," one major with the 199th stated at the time, "and I have tried—God, how I've tried, to have them take some of the initiative in planning. It's resulted, though, in our intelligence, our planning, our pushing. They're awfully passive, and I just wonder what's going to happen when they have to take over." Some officers complained bitterly about the unprofessionalism of the ARVN troops, including their tendency to intermingle while on patrol, their penchant for three-hour siestas, and their almost total lack of fire discipline, as evidenced by the case of several Rangers who reportedly began shooting down coconuts in the middle of a firefight. Differences of language and culture complicated matters. "They had to adapt to our food, our

Helicopters of the 199th Light Infantry Brigade drop U.S. soldiers and ARVN Rangers twenty-five kilometers southwest of Saigon during Operation Fairfax/Rang Dong, August 1967.

talion, 7th Infantry—at less than half its authorized strength. Rehkoph, who headed the Department of Brigade and Battalion Operations, nevertheless pressed forward with the task of organizing, drilling, and equipping the men, drawing on the experiences of returning Vietnam veterans to prepare them for what lay ahead. "We were fortunate enough to be right there at the infantry school," the colonel recalled, "where they were getting all the hot tactical information that was being developed in Vietnam." In addition to utilizing the Air Mobility School at Benning to practice helicopter assault techniques, Rehkoph instituted a grueling program of around-the-clock field exercises to familiarize the soldiers with the rigors of continuous combat operations.

In September, after completing the small-unit phase of training, the 199th moved to Camp Shelby, Mississippi, to conduct additional tests at the battalion and brigade level. There the troops donned the unit's newly designed shoulder patch—a flaming spear embedded in a blue-and-white shield—and brashly assumed the nickname Redcat-

---

Preceding page. *Men of Company B, 4th Battalion, 12th Infantry, 199th Light Infantry Brigade, carry a wounded buddy to safety, Thu Duc District, October 14, 1967.*

199th Infantry Brigade (Sep.) (Light)

Arrived Vietnam: December 10, 1966   **Departed Vietnam:** October 11, 1970

Unit Headquarters

Long Binh/Cat Lai *Dec. 1966–Dec. 1967*	Long Binh/Duc Hoa *May 1968–July 1969*	Long Binh/Gia Ray *July 1970–Oct. 1970*
Bien Hoa *Jan. 1968–April 1968*	Xuan Loc *Aug. 1969–June 1970*	

Commanding Officers

Brig. Gen. Charles W. Ryder, Jr. *Dec. 1966*	Brig. Gen. Franklin M. Davis, Jr. *May 1968*	Brig. Gen. William R. Bond *Nov. 1969*
Brig. Gen. John F. Freund *March 1967*	Col. Frederic E. Davison *Aug. 1968*	Col. Robert W. Selton *April 1970*
Brig. Gen. Robert C. Forbes *Sept. 1967*	Brig. Gen. Warren K. Bennett *May 1969*	Col. Joseph E. Collins *July 1970*

Major Subordinate Units

2d Battalion, 3d Infantry	Company F, 51st Infantry	313th Signal Company
3d Battalion, 7th Infantry	Company M, 75th Infantry	152d Military Police Platoon
4th Battalion, 12th Infantry	3d Squadron, 11th Armored Cavalry	44th Military History Detachment
5th Battalion, 12th Infantry	7th Support Battalion	503d Chemical Detachment
2d Battalion, 40th Artillery	179th Military Intelligence Detachment	856th Army Security Agency Detachment
D Troop, 17th Cavalry (Armored)	87th Engineer Company	40th Public Information Detachment

754 KIA	4,679 WIA	4 Medals of Honor
(Casualty figures are "Vietnam Era.")		

dominant way of doing things," one captain noted. "I'm sure they also had to get used to our kidding around, our backslapping, our shouting. You know, they intensely dislike someone who shouts. I'm sure there was more than one time when they said, 'Those crazy Americans.' "

In part these problems could be attributed to the dual nature of the task assigned to the 199th Infantry Brigade. Ordered to root the Vietcong out of densely populated areas while simultaneously preparing the South Vietnamese to take over the war, the Redcatchers at times became frustrated by their inability to carry out either mission to completion. As one company commander put it, "The concept of a joint command with the Vietnamese sounds good, but the way it works out is I wind up commanding two companies: one American and one Vietnamese. You can't stop the war to start training people, and that's what this boils down to."

Under the umbrella of Fairfax/Rang Dong, the 199th spent most of 1967 patrolling the villages and hamlets around Saigon, dispensing medical aid and food to the local population, and searching for signs of enemy activity. The brigade also made several forays into the swamp-ridden Rung Sat Special Zone, where it joined elements of the 9th Infantry Division and the U.S. Navy in a series of riverine operations. For the most part contact with the enemy was light and sporadic, however, as the Vietcong chose to elude rather than to confront the Americans. When action did erupt, it typically took the form of a brief, intense firefight triggered by accident or ambush.

Such was the case with the brigade's first significant engagement on January 21, 1967, nine days after Fairfax/Rang Dong began. The lead platoon of Company A, 4th Battalion, 12th Infantry, was moving through an open field near the town of Thu Duc when it suddenly came under heavy fire from a well-entrenched VC force. PFC Herbert E. Frenzell, concealed in a tree line on the edge of the ambush site, immediately opened fire to cover the platoon's retreat. After everyone had pulled back, Frenzell withdrew from his position, only to be shot and killed as he attempted to rejoin the men he had saved. Specialist 4th Class Billy C. Jones then left his own cover, crawled through the mud, and braved the enemy's fire to retrieve Frenzell's body. During the next two hours Jones dragged his fallen comrade through thick jungle growth and hazardous swamps until he reached a suitable landing zone. After placing Frenzell on a medevac helicopter, Jones himself was killed while rushing to the aid of another wounded soldier. In recognition of the bravery displayed by Frenzell and Jones, the first two soldiers of the 199th killed in action, the brigade's main base camp at Long Binh was subsequently named in their honor.

Aside from a two-day engagement on May 14 and 15 that netted twelve VC killed, the months that followed were relatively quiet as the brigade pressed on with its pacification duties and swept the countryside for enemy supply caches. Forced to measure their achievements in terms of bunkers destroyed, weapons seized, and villages "secured," the soldiers of the 199th grew increasingly discouraged with both the lethargic pace and limited results of Fairfax/Rang Dong. Ranking U.S. and South Vietnamese officials, however, continued to trumpet the operation as a successful test case. During a four-day visit to Vietnam in early July, Defense Secretary Robert McNamara, vowing to hold future U.S. troop deployment "to a minimum," advocated further integration of American and South Vietnamese forces along the lines of the 199th and 5th ARVN Rangers. Brigadier General John F. Freund, who had taken command of the 199th on March 1, echoed the

official view. "By all logic this entire plan should never have worked," Freund told reporters in early August. "Not only is it working, it's working beautifully."

Several days later, on August 7, Freund was seriously wounded when Company E of the 4th Battalion, 12th Infantry, and the 30th ARVN Ranger Battalion jointly air assaulted into an ambush in the Hoc Mon District north of Saigon. Entrenched in bunkers and spider holes around the landing zone, a company of the 2d VC Local Force Battalion unleashed a torrent of small-arms and weapons fire, destroying two helicopters and damaging seventeen. Among those hit was the command helicopter of Gen. Freund, which was attempting to pick up two wounded soldiers. After Freund was evacuated, reinforcements moved in and spent the next six days clearing out the forty-man enemy force.

When it became clear that Freund would not be able to return to duty because of his wounds, Brigadier General Robert C. Forbes was named his successor. Convinced that Fairfax/Rang Dong had run its course and that ARVN had become "too dependent on us," Forbes immediately began lobbying to dissolve the long-standing relationship between the 199th and the 5th ARVN Rangers. "We ought to get the hell out of this business," he remembered saying at the time, "and move out into War Zone D, and into a little more action." Under mounting pressure to demonstrate ARVN's ability to fight on its own, MACV agreed. Though the separation of the 199th and the Rangers would not become official until December, on September 24, 1967, the brigade received authorization to conduct independent operations.

In the weeks that followed, the pace of action steadily picked up, culminating in the bloodiest battle of the year for the soldiers of the 199th Light Infantry Brigade. It began on the morning of December 6, when two platoons from Company A, 4th Battalion, 12th Infantry, stumbled into a Vietcong base camp near Phuoc Lac in Long Khanh Province, fifty-five kilometers northeast of Saigon. Engulfed by intense fire from a battalion-size enemy force, the 4th Battalion "Warriors" of the 12th Infantry hugged the ground and called for reinforcements. A short time later Company A of the 3d Battalion, 7th Infantry, arrived on the scene, backed by a mechanized platoon from Troop D of the 17th Cavalry. Throughout the day and into the night the battle raged on. By the time it was over, twenty-one Redcatchers lay dead and seventy-four were wounded, compared with sixty-seven VC killed.

American losses would have been even higher had it not been for the courageous actions of Captain Angelo J. Liteky, the battalion chaplain. Despite painful wounds in his neck and foot, Liteky repeatedly exposed himself to

Soldiers of Company C, of the 4/12, patrol the dense, booby-trap-laced jungle near Cat Lai during Operation Fairfax/Rang Dong, February 1967.

General Frederic E. Davison

"I can think of no man," announced General Creighton W. Abrams on September 15, 1968, "who has worked harder or who deserves the promotion to general officer more than General Davison." With these words, the commander of United States forces in Vietnam pinned a star on Frederic E. Davison, making him a brigadier general. During the small ceremony at Binh Chanh, Davison officially assumed command of the 199th Light Infantry Brigade and became only the third black general officer in United States history.

General Davison's promotion came during a bitter period of racial tension among troops in Vietnam. The assassination of Dr. Martin Luther King, Jr., in April 1968 had marked a turning point for many black enlisted men who increasingly perceived Vietnam as an exploitative white man's war tearing them away from the civil rights struggle at home. Contributing to this sentiment were draft rates that had remained proportionally higher for blacks than for whites throughout the war, while the number of black officers hovered below 3 percent. Although the Armed Forces had been officially desegregated since the early 1950s, many blacks continued to feel the burden of discrimination in Vietnam.

The long, distinguished career of General Frederic E. Davison offered an example to many that such obstacles could be overcome. After graduating from Howard University in 1938, Davison completed his ROTC training and was commissioned a second lieutenant the following year. During World War II, he rose to the rank of major while serving as a machine-gun platoon leader and later led an all-black heavy-weapons company. Davison and his men deeply resented the Army's segregationist policies, he recalled, "because we didn't feel we were given the true opportunity to show our capabilities. On the other hand, we tried to prove that even under these handicaps, the job could be done."

After the war, Davison took the Advanced Infantry Course at Fort Benning, Georgia, and then served at Eighth Army Headquarters in Korea. When he returned to the United States, he was chosen to attend the Command and General Staff College in Fort Leavenworth, Kansas. Soon afterward Davison became the first black to attend the Army War College in Carlisle, Pennsylvania, and in 1963 earned a master's degree in international affairs from George Washington University. Then in 1967, Davison volunteered for duty in Vietnam.

Initially assigned to the 199th as a deputy commander, Davison skillfully led the brigade in its defense of Saigon during the Tet offensive, virtually ensuring himself a promotion to the unit's commanding general. Proud of what he felt was "probably the finest brigade in the Army," General Davison remained committed to the men of his unit. He made a point of speaking with troops in the field daily, and each Sunday visited the brigade's wounded. He quickly gained a reputation as a caring, concerned leader.

"It's in the field where you really learn what's going on," Davison always believed.

During his command of the 199th, the general continued to fight for racial equality in the Army. "In this brigade," he declared, "I'm not going to put up with black power, or white power, or yellow power, or red power." Despite racial problems, Davison remained optimistic about changes taking place in the Army. "I believe the opportunity is there," he insisted. "It isn't equal yet, but it's equalizing." Yet General Davison also understood that for his men, the great equalizer was too often the reality of combat. "On the battlefields there is no black and white," he noted, "and everyone's blood runs red when he's hit."

Brigadier General Davison (left) confers with an ARVN captain and U.S. advisers in October 1968, a month after assuming command of the 199th Infantry Division.

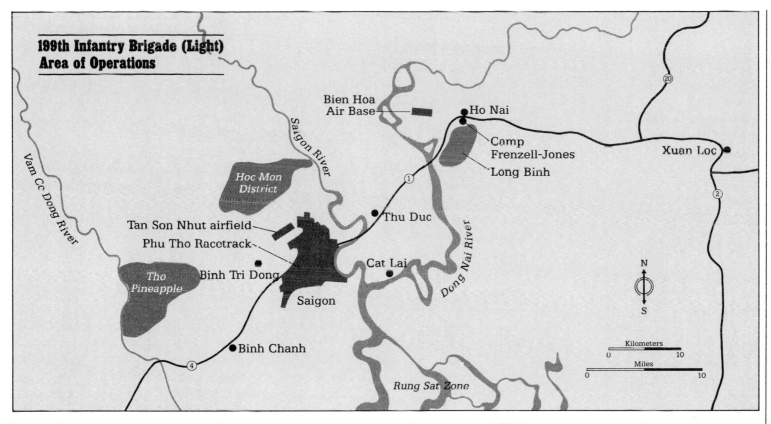

199th Infantry Brigade (Light) Area of Operations

hostile fire in order to evacuate the wounded, administer last rites to the dying, and guide medevac helicopters in and out of the area. Moving upright across the battlefield and at times placing himself directly between the enemy and the wounded men, the Catholic priest dragged more than twenty soldiers to safety during the course of the engagement. "As everyone crawled and ran during the battle, Chaplain Liteky walked through the woods with the shrapnel and bullets cutting down trees all around him," recalled First Lieutenant Wayne Morris, who received a Distinguished Service Cross for his role in the action. "He would not take cover and I never saw him try to protect himself."

Liteky himself later tried to minimize his heroism. "I'm just as scared as they are when we go into an area where we think there is going to be a firefight," he told a reporter from the brigade newspaper. "But I believe that the men like to have a chaplain along. I really admire those men and want to do anything I can for them, and that's why I get out every time I can." In recognition of his inspired leadership, Father Liteky later received the Medal of Honor, the first member of the 199th Light Infantry Brigade (Light) and only the fifth chaplain in U.S. history to receive the nation's highest commendation for valor.

As the year came to a close, the 199th officially relinquished responsibility for the defense of Saigon to the 5th ARVN Ranger Group and shifted its attention to security operations in and around the Bien Hoa-Long Binh complex. By placing the South Vietnamese in charge of their own capital, General Westmoreland hoped at once to reduce the visibility of the U.S. presence and to demonstrate the

willingness of ARVN to carry a larger burden of the war effort. As events would soon show, however, the decision could hardly have been more ill-timed. By late December 1967 Vietcong forces throughout the Saigon area were already moving into position for a major thrust against the capital, part of the 1968 Tet offensive.

The battle of Saigon

Signs of the impending enemy offensive did not go unnoticed. By mid-January 1968 the brigade's 179th Military Intelligence Detachment had gathered a variety of evidence indicating that something big was under way, and by January 28 the unit's analysts were convinced that the attacks would come during the Tet holiday cease-fire. Informed of these findings, Colonel Frederic E. Davison, acting commander of the 199th while Gen. Forbes was on leave, immediately prepared for the worst. In addition to increasing night surveillance and tightening security around the brigade base camp, Davison repositioned his maneuver battalions closer to the Bien Hoa-Long Binh complex in an effort to preempt the enemy's plans.

At 3:00 A.M. on January 31, an intense barrage of 122MM rockets and mortar fire slammed into Long Binh, signaling the onset of the anticipated enemy attack. Striking out of the village of Ho Nai across Highway 1, elements of the 275th VC Regiment attempted to penetrate the northern perimeter of Camp Frenzell-Jones but were beaten back by a force that included riflemen from the 199th's 7th Support Battalion. Two platoons of the 4th Battalion, 12th Infantry, supported by a platoon of armored cavalry assault vehicles (ACAVs) from Troop D, 17th Cavalry, then launched a counterattack, meeting up with the enemy at a hilltop cemetery just north of Ho Nai. Entrenched in shallow ditches among the graves, the VC fought furiously but could not hold out for long in the face of the Americans' vastly superior firepower. Throughout the night helicopter gunships from the 3d Squadron, 17th Cavalry, and the 105MM guns of the 2d Battalion, 40th Artillery, hammered the enemy relentlessly until the few remaining survivors finally broke and ran. Another large enemy force met with a similar fate as it prepared to stage an attack from a dense jungle area northwest of Long Binh. Surrounded by U.S. infantry and armor, the VC had no choice but to hole up in their bunkers as artillery, air strikes, and aerial rocket fire were brought to bear with devastating effect.

By first light, as the intensity of the fighting diminished, the only serious problem confronting the defenders of Long Binh was the ammunition dump. During the night VC sappers had penetrated the huge storage facility and planted satchel charges on a number of its pads. Although Army ordnance disposal teams managed to detach most of the demolition packages before they detonated, at 7:00 A.M. four ammunition bunkers exploded, rocking the entire Long Binh compound.

In the meantime, Company A of the 3d Battalion, 7th Infantry, raced toward Cholon, the densely populated Chinese district of Saigon, with orders to retake the Phu Tho racetrack from the 6th VC Local Force Battalion. Accompanied by eight ACAVs from Troop D, 17th Cavalry, the "Cotton Balers" moved to within six blocks of the racetrack before they were halted by a heavy barrage of rocket-propelled grenades and automatic weapons fire. Firing from rooftops and buildings along the street, the VC hit the lead vehicle, killing a cavalry platoon leader and two crewmen. The cavalrymen countered by blasting the enemy positions with recoilless rifle fire, while helicopter gunships swooped down and unleashed their rockets and miniguns. The infantrymen then dismounted and swept the boulevard, engaging the VC in ferocious house-to-house combat.

Pressing forward through the enemy's intense fire as well as throngs of fleeing civilians, the column had advanced four more city blocks by one o'clock in the afternoon. By then the Vietcong had already begun to withdraw into the racetrack under the cover of heavy-weapons emplacements located in the spectator stands. Met by a withering torrent of machine-gun fire and grenades as they attempted to storm the track, the men of Alpha Company fell back, regrouped, and decided to mount a second assault from the southeast. As helicopter gunships and recoilless rifles pounded the VC positions, the weary infantrymen charged forward, firing their weapons. Convinced that they could not hold out, the soldiers of the 6th VC Local Force Battalion scattered and fled, and by 4:30 P.M. the Phu Tho racetrack was declared secure.

Shortly after nightfall, Companies B and C of the 3d Battalion, 7th Infantry, were airlifted in, accompanied by Col. Davison. After setting up a battalion forward command post under the racetrack's concrete grandstand, Davison began mapping out a counteroffensive plan to clear out any remaining pockets of enemy resistance. Reinforced by the arrival of two companies from the 9th Infantry Division's mechanized 5th Battalion, 60th Infantry, and the 33d ARVN Ranger Battalion, the 3/7 cautiously moved out into the surrounding streets on the morning of February 1. During the next few days fighting in the vicinity of the racetrack periodically erupted, then died down, as the combined force systematically "mopped up" the area.

At the insistence of President Thieu, all American troops were withdrawn from Saigon on February 4 so that ARVN forces could complete the clearing operation on their own. Five days later, however, the South Vietnamese high command requested that the 3d Battalion, 7th Infantry, return to the Phu Tho racetrack in response to a fresh upsurge of enemy activity throughout the Cholon district. Sporadic fighting continued until February 12, when men of the 199th stormed the Phu Lam communal temple, which had served as the main Vietcong command post for the area. Though the battalion initially believed it had found and killed General Tran Do, the commander of all VC forces in Saigon, a subsequent check of his fingerprints revealed otherwise.

As the Tet offensive sputtered out, the 199th Infantry Brigade (Light) returned to its customary areas of operation: The 2d Battalion, 3d Infantry, patrolled the southwestern outskirts of Saigon while the 3d Battalion, 7th Infantry, and the 4th Battalion, 12th Infantry, combed the jungles and forest northeast of Long Binh. On April 8 the brigade joined with every other allied unit in III Corps Tactical Zone to inaugurate Operation Toan Thang (Certain Victory), a counteroffensive campaign designed to prevent future attacks on the South Vietnamese capital. Bolstered by the addition of the recently arrived 5th Battalion, 12th Infantry, the brigade initially moved into southern War Zone D and later took up positions south and west of Saigon.

Though the first few weeks of Toan Thang generated only occasional contact with enemy forces, heavy fighting resumed in early May with the onset of the Communists' "mini-Tet" offensive. The brigade's first significant encounter occurred on the morning of May 6, when elements of the 272d VC Regiment unsuccessfully attempted to overrun a base camp manned by Companies C and D of the 4th Battalion, 12th Infantry. Later that night, another enemy battalion charged into the perimeter of the main battalion base camp four kilometers west of Saigon. Battered by

Soldiers of Company A of the 3/7 and D Troop, 17th Cavalry, rest outside the recaptured Phu Tho racetrack in Saigon after bitter street fighting through Cholon, January 31, 1968.

heavy automatic weapons, air strikes, and pointblank howitzer fire, the enemy force reeled and scattered in confusion, leaving nearly 100 dead.

On the afternoon of May 7, elements of the 3d Battalion, 7th Infantry, joined Bravo Company of the 4/12 and Troop D, 17th Cavalry, in an effort to dislodge a well-entrenched VC battalion from the village of Binh Tri Dong, three kilometers west of Saigon. Intense combat raged throughout the day as the Americans repeatedly attempted, but failed, to penetrate the hamlet. Aided by eleven air strikes and a steady rain of artillery fire, the men resumed their assaults the following day but again were unable to enter the village. Finally, on May 9, the enemy's resistance slackened, allowing a five-company force to sweep through Binh Tri Dong behind a shield of armored assault vehicles, bringing the battle to a close. A sweep of the village and surrounding area revealed more than 100 enemy dead,

identified as members of the 273d VC Regiment.

That same day, Company D of the 4th Battalion, 12th Infantry, ambushed a 200-man NVA/VC force attempting to slip through the brigade screen en route to Saigon. Halted by automatic-weapons fire and command-detonated claymore mines, the enemy troops ran south, directly into Company C of the 4/12 at the battalion base camp. Again the NVA/VC rebounded, this time into positions manned by Alpha Company of the 3d Battalion, 7th Infantry. In the meantime Army helicopter light-fire teams and Air Force C-47 Spooky gunships swept in and raked the trapped enemy from above. By morning 135 enemy troops had been killed and 18 captured, while brigade casualties were officially recorded as "minimal."

During the next few days the intensity of the fighting temporarily slackened. Then, on the night of May 12, a reconnaissance platoon from Company E, 2d Battalion, 3d

Infantry, intercepted another sizable VC force attempting to withdraw from Saigon. The soldiers immediately called for air strikes and artillery, as the enemy fled into an abandoned factory less than a kilometer from the brigade's forward command post. The following morning three companies of the 2/3 arrived on the scene along with Company A of the 5th Battalion, 12th Infantry, and Company B of the 4th Battalion, 12th Infantry. Heavy combat raged into the next day until the enemy, later identified as elements of the 271st, 272d, and 273d VC regiments, finally broke contact and dispersed.

The brigade's last major engagement of the "mini-Tet" campaign took place on May 14, when the 6th VC Local Force Battalion launched simultaneous attacks on three company-size outposts of the 2d Battalion, 3d Infantry, and another manned by elements of the 5th Battalion, 12th Infantry. In each case the enemy troops were beaten back before they could penetrate the wire, although one contingent managed to get within grenade range of positions held by Company D of the 2/3. "They crawled up behind dikes and rice paddies around us," the company commander reported. "With the heavy rain, we didn't see them until they were twenty meters from the perimeter and had started firing. The men let go with all we had and held them." An hour and a half later, the Delta Company commander called for the 2d Battalion, 40th Artillery, to place fires "360 degrees around us." The ensuing barrage broke the attack.

As the enemy offensive gradually ran out of steam, the 2d Battalion, 3d Infantry, the 3d Battalion, 7th Infantry, and

Members of the 2d Battalion, 3d Infantry, lead suspected Vietcong toward the battalion basecamp south of Saigon for interrogation, March 1968.

the 5th Battalion, 12th Infantry, returned to Camp Frenzell-Jones, then moved out to conduct a series of search-and-destroy missions north and northeast of Long Binh. The 4th Battalion, 12th Infantry, meanwhile, continued to operate along the western approaches to Saigon, working in conjunction with ARVN units to clear the area of enemy stragglers.

The Pineapple

In late June 1968 the brigade resumed its defensive mission west of Saigon, this time plunging into the unfamiliar territory of the Pineapple—an area of expansive rice fields, treacherous swamps, and steamy fruit groves that had long served as a sanctuary for Communist forces infiltrating from Cambodia. Under the command of Brigadier General Franklin M. Davis, Jr., who had taken over the brigade on May 10, the 199th set up a fire support base at Horseshoe Bend on the Vam Co Dong River and then set out in search of the enemy. Working under a relentless tropical sun, their gear perpetually wet yet their throats parched, the Redcatchers found the assignment tedious, thankless, and frustrating. It was also dangerous. For while contact with enemy troops was rare, casualties caused by mines and booby traps were all too common. The searches and sweeps nevertheless continued throughout the summer, resulting in the discovery and destruction of hundreds of enemy bunkers and cache sites.

More of the same followed after newly promoted Brigadier General Frederic E. Davison assumed command of the 199th on September 1 (see sidebar, page 110). The third black general officer in the history of the United States Armed Forces, Davison inherited the brigade's colors when it became clear that Gen. Davis, wounded during a riverine operation in early August (the second 199th commander wounded in the space of a year), could not return to duty. Fittingly enough, among Davison's first responsibilities as brigade commander was to accept a Valorous

Smoke billows as a soldier of Company B, 4th Battalion, 12th Infantry, fires upon the VC with his 90MM recoilless rifle in Binh Tri Dong village on May 7, 1968.

Unit Award for the unit's performance during the Tet offensive, a campaign in which Davison himself had played a crucial role.

On September 18 the brigade made its biggest find to date when a group of soldiers stumbled upon a huge enemy storage depot in the southeastern sector of the Pineapple. Surrounded by a network of freshly placed booby traps, the complex contained vast amounts of equipment, ammunition, and weaponry—all neatly stored in fifty-five-gallon drums. In addition, the brigade found three sophisticated field hospitals and more than 200 bunkers.

The remaining months of the year were relatively uneventful, as the Redcatchers continued to crisscross the western outskirts of Saigon in search of enemy fortifications and cache sites. In early 1969, however, the pace of action picked up again as NVA and VC forces attempted to move into position for another major spring offensive. Among the year's first casualties was Colonel Jeffrey G. Smith, acting commander of the 199th in the absence of Gen. Davison. Smith's helicopter was hit and forced down during a rescue mission on January 6. The third brigade commander to be wounded in action, Smith was attempting to aid the survivors of a downed AH-1G Cobra gunship when automatic-weapons fire tore through his command helicopter, wounding him in the shoulder and leg and forcing him to return to a nearby firebase.

Three weeks later, on January 27, two companies of the 3d Battalion, 7th Infantry, supported by two companies from the 9th Infantry Division, trapped a 100-man enemy force fifteen kilometers north of Tan An near the Cambodian Parrot's Beak. Later joined by elements of the 4th and 5th Battalions, 12th Infantry, the combined American force slugged it out with the enemy for three days until the NVA/VC, having lost nearly half their men, retreated across the Cambodian border.

With the approach of the Tet 1969 Lunar New Year holiday in February, there was a temporary lull in the fighting throughout the Saigon area. The Redcatchers of the 199th nonetheless maintained a vigilant posture throughout the official "cease-fire" period, remembering all too well the events of the previous year. As a result, when the enemy's long-anticipated Spring offensive broke on February 23, the brigade was well positioned to respond. Though the magnitude and intensity of the 1969 attacks bore little resemblance to the cataclysm of 1968, brigade forces once again had to drive a combined NVA/VC force from Ho Nai Village to forestall an assault on the Long Binh compound.

Counteroffensive operations during the post-Tet period were conducted in tandem with a major new pacification effort designed to neutralize the Vietcong infrastructure throughout the brigade's area of responsibility. The central feature of the campaign was a series of five large cordon-and-search missions, code-named Strangler and Caesar,

A radio telephone operator of Company C, 2d Battalion, 3rd Infantry, tries to hear his orders during a firefight south of Saigon, in September 1968.

involving the 199th, the 5th ARVN Ranger Group, the South Vietnamese National Police Field Force, and several Regional Force units. In each case the area surrounding a targeted village was first sealed off by regular U.S. and ARVN forces to prevent enemy forces from escaping. Regional Forces then moved in and undertook detailed searches of each hamlet, while police units rounded up the local inhabitants and brought them to a tent encampment that served as a combined holding and interrogation center. After undergoing questioning by members of the brigade's 179th Military Intelligence Detachment, the villagers either received government-issued identity cards or were turned over to South Vietnamese authorities as VC suspects. During the processing, which in some instances lasted a full week, brigade civil affairs teams provided food and entertainment, while medical and dental teams treated hundreds of patients. South Vietnamese propaganda units and cultural drama troupes were also on hand to rally support for the GVN. By the time the Strangler-Caesar series came to an end in late May, 24,000 men, women, and children had been interviewed and issued new identification papers. Two hundred and forty-nine others had been identified either as members of the Vietcong infrastructure or as VC troops.

In June 1969 the brigade closed down its firebase at Horseshoe Bend and moved its center of operations to Long Khanh Province, a sparsely populated region of sprawling rubber plantations and dense virgin jungle northeast of Saigon. Under the command of Gen. Davison's successor, Brigadier General Warren K. Bennett, the brigade established a forward headquarters at the Blackhorse base camp of the 11th Armored Cavalry Regiment near the provincial capital of Xuan Loc. The 2d Battalion, 3d Infantry, also moved into Blackhorse, while each of the other battalions either took over recently vacated firebases or hacked new camps out of the jungle. The 4th Battalion, 12th Infantry, after replacing elements of the 1st Cavalry Division (Airmobile) at Fire Support Base Joy northeast of Xuan Loc, later set up shop at Fire Support Base Nancy in Dinh Quan. The 5th Battalion, 12th Infantry, meanwhile constructed FSB Libby along Route 20 northwest of the province capital. In September the 3d Battalion, 7th Infantry, after spending the summer under the operational control of the 3d Brigade, 9th Infantry Division, built FSB Mace east of Xuan Loc.

Under the auspices of MACV's new Vietnamization program, formally called Dong Thien (Progress Together), the brigade found itself working closely from the start with ARVN units in the area. Operating under an arrangement called "counter-parting," in which each of the brigade's battalions was paired with a regiment of the 18th ARVN Division, the 199th once again took up the threefold task of pacifying the local population, rooting out the enemy, and preparing ARVN to fight on its own. Throughout the summer and into the fall the combined U.S./ARVN forces combed the countryside for enemy bunkers and supply caches, set up ambushes, and searched contested villages for evidence of VC activity. Though the region was known to be a haunt of the 33d NVA Regiment and the 274th VC Regiment, where uniformed soldiers had at times been spotted walking nonchalantly through open fields, contact with the enemy proved frustratingly elusive. When the Redcatchers and their ARVN counterparts plunged into the uninhabited northern reaches of the province, they found ample evidence of the enemy's presence—including several battalion-size base camps—but rarely any sign of enemy troops.

The lack of battlefield action gradually led to a shift in emphasis from combined field operations to a variety of training programs designed to upgrade South Vietnamese forces throughout Long Khanh Province. At the brigade level, the 199th organized a ten-man Mobile Training Team to instruct ARVN officers and soldiers in skills ranging from simple weapon maintenance to airmobile tactics, convoy counterambush techniques, land navigation, and demolition. At the battalion level, training programs for Regional and Popular Force units were instituted under such acronyms as HUT (Hamlet Upgrading Team), LIFT (Local Improvement of Forces Team), and SAM (Stamina, Accuracy, and Marksmanship). While the success of these efforts varied widely, all were designed with a single end in view: to ready the South Vietnamese for the eventual withdrawal of all U.S. combat troops.

The final year

In early 1970 the brigade once again set out in search of the 33d NVA Regiment, driving across the border of Long Khanh into Binh Tuy Province. A series of squad- and platoon-size actions followed, as the enemy this time chose to defend its sanctuaries rather than surrender them to the intruding Americans. The most savage encounter of the campaign occurred on the night of January 31, when an NVA company attacked a platoon from Company C, 4th Battalion, 12th Infantry, killing two men and wounding twenty-six. Pinned down by intense small-arms and automatic-weapons fire, and unable to call in supporting fires because of a damaged radio, the unit might have been annihilated had it not been for the bravery of Sergeant Richard A. Penry. One of only three men to emerge unscathed from the battle, Penry three times crawled outside the defensive perimeter to retrieve and reassemble pieces of the radio. Once communications were reestablished, artillery and air strikes were called in to break the attack. For his actions Penry became the thirteenth member of the brigade to receive the Distinguished Service Cross for valor on the battlefields of Vietnam.

Two months later, on April 1, a column of tracked vehicles from Troop D, 17th Cavalry, tripped into an ambush near the town of Vo Xu. A brief firefight ensued, after which brigade commander Brigadier General William R. Bond, who had taken command in December 1969, arrived on the scene to inspect the enemy dead and to determine their unit. As the search party began to move out, a sniper's bullet found its mark, killing General Bond, bringing the number of 199th commanders wounded or killed to five. He was replaced by Colonel Joseph E. Collins.

In early May the 5th Battalion, 12th Infantry, joined Operation Toan Thang #43, the combined U.S./ARVN incursion into Cambodia, under the operational control of the 1st Cavalry Division (Airmobile). Held back at Song Be during the first two weeks of the campaign, the Warriors finally crossed the border on May 12 and moved into Landing Zone Brown, a combat patrol base three kilometers inside the Fishhook region of Cambodia. The battalion had barely settled in when, at three o'clock in the morning, an intense barrage of mortar fire slammed inside the perimeter, heralding the onset of an NVA ground assault. With only a single 81MM mortar providing fire support, the men of Companies B and C fought off the attackers until dawn, when a series of air strikes finally broke the attack. Fifty enemy bodies were later found and buried in a mass grave, while American casualties were very light—only one killed and seven wounded.

The next day Company B set out to patrol the surrounding area and promptly stumbled upon an NVA bunker complex. "We walked in and got trapped for quite a while," recalled Sergeant Ronald Orem. "Then a track unit from the 11th Armored Cavalry Regiment came down, and we moved out with them. On the way out the NVA sprang an ambush, and that was when we really got shot up. There were twenty-four men in my platoon. By the time we returned to LZ Brown the next afternoon I had fourteen."

In the weeks that followed, the 5/12 continued to operate inside Cambodian territory, combing the Fishhook for enemy base camps and supply caches. Though battalion patrols came under sniper fire with annoying regularity and occasionally became embroiled in brief firefights, it soon became apparent that most NVA units had fled the area in advance of the allied onslaught. The battalion nevertheless succeeded in uncovering and destroying large quantities of NVA war materiel, including nine jeeps, more than a thousand mortar rounds, nearly 300,000 AK47 rifle rounds, and several crew-served weapons. "What really hit us was the sheer amount of material the enemy had," Sgt. Orem remembered. "We had no idea just how vast their resources were."

In accordance with the June 30 deadline for the withdrawal of all U.S. troops from Cambodian soil, the 5th Battalion, 12th Infantry, returned to Camp Frenzell-Jones on June 25. During the next few months the incidence of contact with enemy forces steadily dwindled, as the brigade adopted an increasingly defensive posture and prepared to "stand down." On September 15, 1970, the 2d Battalion, 40th Artillery, fired its last rounds at a ceremony at Fire Support Base Silver, 110 kilometers northeast of Saigon. Three years and ten months after it first arrived in country, the Redcatchers' mission was over. A month later, the 199th Infantry Brigade (Light)—a unit specifically created for the Vietnam War—was formally deactivated at Fort Benning, Georgia.

"Redcatchers" wade through a canal near a pineapple plantation in search of Vietcong west of Saigon during the post-Tet counteroffensive in March 1969.

Tracks in the Jungle

Even as the American military committed more heavy equipment, such as helicopters and airplanes, to the growing war in Vietnam, the number of tanks and other armored vehicles dispatched by late 1965 remained relatively low. Many senior armor officers viewed the situation in Vietnam as an anomalous conflict best fought with regular infantry. In Saigon, General William Westmoreland declared, "Except for a few coastal areas, most notably in the I Corps area, Vietnam is no place for either tank or mechanized infantry units." He and the Pentagon had nightmares of American armor immobilized in a morass of paddies, jungles, and mountains, evoking memories of the earlier failure of French armor.

While it had some basis in fact, the army's position was also somewhat oversimplified. French armor had been effective in Indochina but was hampered by a paucity of vehicles thinly deployed throughout the war zone. ARVN units, advised by Americans for almost a decade, had been equipped

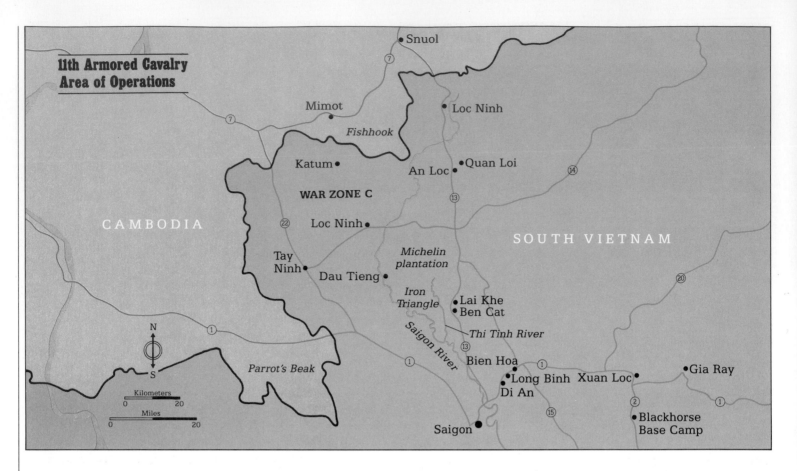

Snuol

Mimot

Loc Ninh

Fishhook

Katum

An Loc • Quan Loi

WAR ZONE C

CAMBODIA

Loc Ninh

SOUTH VIETNAM

Tay Ninh • Dau Tieng

Michelin plantation

Iron Triangle

Lai Khe
Ben Cat

Thi Tinh River

Saigon River

Bien Hoa

Long Binh Xuan Loc • Gia Ray
Di An

N
S

Parrot's Beak

Kilometers
0   20
Miles
0   20

Saigon

Blackhorse Base Camp

---

with tanks and armored personnel carriers (APCs) for several years and had achieved some success against the Vietcong. The U.S. Marines brought tanks to Vietnam as part of their combat units and were employing them in I Corps. Based on these experiences, some American officers began to feel that there was indeed a place for more armor in the American arsenal in Vietnam.

But their declarations aroused little interest. When the 1st Infantry Division went to Vietnam in the fall of 1965, its two tank battalions were stripped of equipment and its two mechanized infantry battalions "dismounted," their APCs eliminated. Its single divisional cavalry squadron brought a limited number of M48 Patton tanks and M113 APCs. The pleas of the division's commander, Major General Jonathan O. Seaman, for more armor support were denied.

The 1st Infantry Division's cavalry squadron operated well in support of troops, and Seaman continued to push his case to Westmoreland. His prospects were no doubt boosted by the performance of his division's APCs in repelling a VC attack at Ap Bau Bang on November 11 and 12, 1965, and by generally favorable reports on the achievements of ARVN armor by American advisers.

By early 1966 MACV was willing to utilize a few armored units, though on a trial basis. When Gen. Westmoreland sent for the 25th Infantry Division, it arrived with its APCs

and tanks. In addition, Westmoreland requested the deployment of the first full tank and mechanized regiment to Vietnam, the 11th Armored Cavalry.* It was the largest armored unit to serve in the war.

Changing horses

Unlike most other former U.S. horse cavalry regiments, the 11th Cavalry did not get its spurs on the western plains during the Indian wars of the nineteenth century. In fact, it was not formed until 1901 at Fort Meyer, Virginia. Its campaigns were often unconventional. It fought in the Philippines and Cuba, quelling insurrections after the Spanish-American War, and took part in General John Pershing's punitive raid into Mexico against the bandit Pancho Villa from March 1916 to February 1917.

The regiment did not serve in World War I and was still a horse unit when World War II began. The old cavalry regiment was officially deactivated in 1942, but its immediate descendant, the 11th Cavalry Group (Mechanized), saw service as an armored unit in Holland and Germany over the next two years. After the war the 11th Armored Cavalry was reactivated to instruct armored units fighting in the Korean War. Then, after service with NATO forces, it was assigned to Fort Meade, Maryland, in 1964.

Preceding page. *Tanks of the 11th Armored Cavalry leave Cambodia on June 29, 1970, after eight weeks of operations against enemy sanctuaries across the border.*

---

*Army regulations after World War II dropped the use of the word "regiment" in designating units. The official name of the regiment thus became simply the 11th Armored Cavalry, but in Vietnam the use of "regiment" and the abbreviation "11th ACR" was widespread.

11th Armored Cavalry

Arrived Vietnam: September 8, 1966   **Departed Vietnam:** March 5, 1971

Unit Headquarters

Bien Hoa *Sept.–Nov. 1966*	Lai Khe *Feb. 1969*	Bien Hoa *Oct. 1969–June 1970*
Long Binh *Dec. 1966–Feb. 1967*	Long Giao *Mar.–Sept. 1969*	Di An *July 1970–March 1971*
Xuan Loc *March 1967–Jan. 1969*		

Commanding Officers

Col. William W. Cobb *Sept. 1966*	Col. Charles R. Gorder *March 1968*	Col. Donn A. Starry *Dec. 1969*
Col. Roy W. Farley *May 1967*	Col. George S. Patton *July 1968*	Col. John L. Gerrity *June 1970*
Col. Jack MacFarlane *Dec. 1967*	Col. James H. Leach *April 1969*	Col. Wallace H. Nutting *Dec. 1970*
Col. Leonard D. Holder *March 1968*		

Major Subordinate Units

1st Squadron (A, B, & C Troops, Company D)	3d Squadron (I, K, & L Troops, Company M)	919th Engineer Company
2d Squadron (E, F, & G Troops, Company H)	Air Cavalry Troop	37th Medical Company

728 KIA	5,761 WIA	3 Medals of Honor
(Casualty figures are "Vietnam Era.")		

The Blackhorse Regiment, so called because of the rearing horse on its official patch, was not at full strength at the time of its official summons to Vietnam service in March 1966. Almost 1,000 newly assigned recruits were still training at Fort Meade, and the second squadron (of the usual three) had been activated only within the past year. Training was scattered to nearby camps because the rapid deployment of so many Army units had made facilities scarce.

The regiment's organization remained standard. It consisted of three squadrons, each having three troops (the equivalents of infantry companies) and a tank company. But before the regiment could head for Vietnam, the Army altered its equipment to satisfy continued reservations about armor's usefulness there. The mainstay of the regiment, the M48 Patton tank, the Army's medium tank, was replaced in each of the regiment's nine organic troops by the M113 APC, twenty-eight of which were given to each troop. Each squadron retained its seventeen M48s. Weighing only twelve tons and capable of carrying twelve men, the aluminum APC was believed to offer greater mobility and speed in the thick vegetation of Vietnam. With the addition of such features as gun shields and two M60 7.62MM machine guns to its standard .50-caliber machine gun, the M113 became known as the armored cavalry assault vehicle, or ACAV, in Vietnam.

Thus the 11th ACR was stripped of some of its firepower and modified to become more like a mechanized infantry unit. The number of tanks in the regiment was cut from 132 to 51, while the total of M113s swelled from 83 to 320. At the same time, the Army boosted the authorized strength of the regiment by over 600 to 3,672 officers and enlisted men, a reflection not only of the increased logistical needs of its vehicles but also of a greater emphasis on mounted infantry operations.

Transport ships bearing the men and equipment of the regiment arrived at Vung Tau in September 1966, and the troopers settled into temporary quarters at the Long Binh staging area, north of Saigon. Over 100 commissioned and noncommissioned officers went into the field to observe combat operations of the 1st and 25th infantry divisions. There a sergeant from C Troop received the regiment's first Vietnam award, a Purple Heart.

With armor still on trial in Vietnam, MACV directed the 11th ACR, for the time being at least, to provide security for the roads and highways in the Saigon area, especially along Highway 1. For this task, as well as most subsequent operations, the regiment was usually placed under the operational control of another unit. In fact, the regimental commander often retained control only of his own headquarters group and assorted support troops while his other men were conducting operations under units such as the 1st, 9th, or 25th infantry divisions or the 1st Cavalry Division (Airmobile).

Action for the squadrons through October was scattered. The 3d Squadron and the 919th Engineer Company were the first units to make contact with the enemy and inflict casualties, during Operation Hickory. They assisted in the cordoning of an area east of Saigon and in the discovery of numerous tunnels and bunkers in the area of Phu Hoa. Meanwhile, other elements of the regiment provided security along the roads around Bien Hoa and Long Binh.

The regiment remained without a permanent base camp until October, when on the twentieth vehicles of the 1st Squadron rumbled west to Xuan Loc, then turned south. The troopers surrounded and searched villages after sunrise and engineers cleared an area along Route 2 near Long Giao, nineteen kilometers south of Xuan Loc. This became the Blackhorse Camp, serving as the base for local

operations. At first, operations were limited to clearing and securing Highway 1 from Bien Hoa to Xuan Loc and Highway 2 south to the base camp, but soon Blackhorse tanks and ACAVs began to move off the roads and throughout the largely flat jungle and grassland in search of the enemy.

On and off the road

On roads all over Vietnam, the gravest danger to American convoys was ambush. As the 11th ACR started operations in III Corps, it had to watch for the enemy hiding in dense growth alongside the roads and develop tactics that would maintain traffic over these dangerous routes. One common counterambush technique was road-running, in which a convoy raced overland past possible enemy positions, too fast to provide a clear target. In a long procession, however, the disabling of just one or two vehicles could trap several in a killing zone, allowing the enemy to inflict heavy casualties.

On the morning of November 21, 1966, nine armored personnel carriers from C Troop were ambushed by two Vietcong battalions while escorting fifty trucks along Highway 1 from Long Binh to the 11th ACR's Blackhorse Camp. The lead vehicles pushed through the ambush site, but the ferocious enemy fire halted and trapped the center and rear groups.

The convoy commander, First Lieutenant Neil Keltner, quickly radioed for reinforcements, then ordered his driver to turn the vehicle around and move back to the ambush site to assist his halted men. The ACAV moved up and down the column, firing at the enemy in the high grass and rubber trees as it went. Helicopter gunships swooped in to unleash fire on the hidden enemy positions, and within thirty minutes the relief party arrived from the base camp. The guerrillas withdrew, but the squadron commander, Lieutenant Colonel Martin D. Howell, decided to keep his party in the area overnight to indicate to local villagers that it held the battlefield. ACAV guns covered either side of the road as the armored vehicles camped for the night. In the day's fighting thirty Vietcong soldiers were killed while seven Americans lost their lives. Six vehicles were damaged.

Less than two weeks later, in the late afternoon of December 2, an enemy force ambushed a B Troop convoy of three ACAVs, two M48A3 tanks, and a pair of two-and-a-half ton trucks on Highway 1. While traveling from the base camp to an engineer rock quarry site south of Gia Ray, deadly rocket-propelled grenades (RPGs) and recoilless rifle rounds began to land. Lieutenant Will Radosevich radioed his convoy to keep moving and ordered the

Weary soldiers rest atop an 11th Armored Cavalry ACAV while on patrol in the jungle near Loc Ninh, on the Cambodian border, in November 1968.

crews, "Odd vehicles fire right, even left." The guns of the vehicles slued in either direction and raked the rubber trees as enemy bullets bounced off their armor.

At the same time, the convoy radioed the base camp that it was under attack. Within five minutes the rest of B Troop had mounted up and was on its way to the ambush site, followed quickly by the rest of the 1st Squadron. The first relief vehicles met the battered convoy one and a half kilometers from the base camp, and the bolstered force reentered the enemy killing zone. By-passing a burning vehicle, the tanks blazed away with 90MM canister shot, high-explosive "quick" charges, and machine-gun fire, while ACAVs followed close behind and helicopters and jets fired from overhead. Several Vietcong fled from the woods and were mowed down by American fire.

The tanks and ACAVs sealed off the area as Col. Howell coordinated artillery strikes from his helicopter. Several vehicles formed a herringbone, a formation in which they angled in alternate directions to fire off the road. Again the squadron remained overnight, as artillery and air strikes peppered the area. The next day searchers counted 101 enemy dead; the only American fatality was a sergeant shot and killed while evacuating his crippled ACAV.

The success on the actions of November 21 and December 2 encouraged Blackhorse commanders, and counterambush techniques developed during those weeks became standard operating procedure for the regiment. The cavalrymen first used their firepower to fight clear of the ambush zone, then regrouped with reinforcements to seal and reenter the area and engage the enemy aggressively. This tactic allowed maximum use of the superior firepower of armored guns and avoided potentially dangerous static defense positions.

In early 1967 the case for armor was further strengthened by the release of an Army study that concluded that the potential for armored mobility over Vietnamese terrain was greater than had been previously believed. Compiling maps of "go" and "no-go" areas, the study group declared that tanks could travel over 61 percent of the terrain in the dry season and 46 percent during the rainy monsoons. APCs could operate in 65 percent of the area year-round. The study, entitled "Mechanized and Armored Combat Operations in Vietnam," showed that armor could be as effective off Vietnam's few roads as on them and signified its final acceptance in Vietnam. MACV then requested more tank and APC units as part of its subsequent buildup.

Having cut its teeth on road security and now assured of a greater role in future combat, whether on or off the road, the 11th ACR participated in five operations ranging over six provinces under three different commands in the first half of 1967. The first major operation of the year was Cedar Falls, the multidivisional drive into the Iron Triangle. The task force of fifty-four bulldozers and tanks with sharp Rome plows cleared more than twenty-three square kilometers of growth as cavalry vehicles of the 2d and 3d squadrons of the 11th ACR and infantrymen swept through the area. The enemy avoided contact, but numerous underground bunkers and caches were uncovered.

After Cedar Falls ended on January 25, the 11th ACR also participated in Operation Junction City. At daybreak on February 23, men of the Blackhorse left their fire support base at the southern tip of the area of operations in War Zone C. As had been the case in Cedar Falls, fighting was sporadic in the jungle, but the cavalry troops were on the lookout for any mines or booby traps that could disrupt the entire march. The danger was not just on the ground. The enemy had learned to suspend grenades from the trees, detonated by contact with radio antennas or troops riding on top of the ACAVs.

The infantry and armor found enemy bunkers and underground camps as they advanced. Reaching the northern line of the multidivisional force's horseshoe formation, the column pivoted to the west and continued its sweep. There the Vietcong was more inclined to stop and fight, so fighting grew heavier, though the 11th Armored Cavalry was engaged in no major action.

In the second phase of Junction City, the regiment was under the control of the 1st Infantry Division and assigned the tasks of clearing and securing a stretch of Highway 13 and running convoys between Lai Khe and Quan Loi. On six occasions Blackhorse troops came under small-arms fire, and three times ACAVs were damaged by RPGs or recoilless rifle fire. Meanwhile, the regimental psychological operations (psyops) team took advantage of its location in a populated area, distributing over 300,000 propaganda leaflets designed to win over the guerrillas with such slogans as "Your Family Needs You," "Ralliers Are Treated Well," and "Death If You Stay with the VC."

The importance of Highway 13 during the war was not lost on the American command nor on the 11th Armored Cavalry. Because it afforded the main access to the outlying cities of An Loc, Quan Loi, and Loc Ninh, all located near the Cambodian border, holding the road was essential to securing the border against NVA infiltration into those population centers. The enemy realized this and constantly mined and established ambush positions along the highway to restrict access. As a road security unit, the 11th ACR was charged with keeping Highway 13 open during much of its term in Vietnam.

Because it was impossible to post men all along the road, the regiment utilized a tactic that became known as a "thunder run." Armored columns of both tanks and ACAVs would race along the road firing harassment and interdiction (H&I) fire into suspected enemy areas along the route in an effort to deny the enemy the opportunity to ready an ambush or plant a mine. Such mobile saturation became a useful tool along heavily traveled thoroughfares, especially Highway 13, which the Americans called "Thunder Road."

Closer to home

In April 1967 the newly formed Task Force Oregon, based at Chu Lai in I Corps, appealed for cavalry reinforcement. MACV responded by ordering the 2d Squadron of the 11th Armored Cavalry north, and on April 22 the squadron departed for Chu Lai.

The loss of one-third of its infantry strength left the regiment handicapped for operations in the coming months. Standard operating procedure called for one squadron to remain at Blackhorse Camp as a security force while the other two went into the field. Now continued security requirements meant a smaller force was available for field operations. So for the time being the regiment remained close to its base, working on small operations in Long Khanh Province, including road security. Regimental clearing teams cut up to 100 meters of growth on either side of major routes to prevent sniper attacks and ambushes. Search-and-destroy and cordon-and-search operations

Men of C Troop, 11th Armored Cavalry, pause on a trail while the point man checks out possible enemy bunkers during Operation Junction City, March 1967.

continued, assisted by foot soldiers of the 18th ARVN Infantry Division.

After the 2d Squadron returned from the north in October, the 11th ACR continued to assert itself in III Corps. Particularly crucial in Long Khanh Province was an ongoing pacification program that in addition to offensive operations also involved MEDCAP and DENTCAP visits to villages. Such occasions were a prime example of the Americans "carrying a rose in the mailed fist," not only encouraging personal contact with the local population but also displaying the regiment's powerful vehicles to the countryside.

The outbreak of the Tet offensive in the early morning hours of January 31, 1968, found most of the 11th Armored-Cavalry at Loc Ninh, miles away from its base camp. The regimental commander, Colonel Roy W. Farley, was ordered to the Long Binh-Bien Hoa area to defend the huge American complex there. The Blackhorse regiment mounted up and raced over 100 kilometers in eight hours, arriving and encircling the area by 9:00 P.M.

The next day L Troop of the 3d Squadron and the 2d Battalion, 506th Infantry, swept into the populated area next to the Bien Hoa air base. Five hundred Vietcong fought stubbornly as the Americans moved from house to house to flush them out. At the end of the afternoon thirty-six Vietcong lay dead along with nine Americans killed, one of them from L Troop.

The bulk of the regiment remained in the area for the rest of February, under the operational control of various units assigned to mop up enemy resistance in the capital area. But of greater interest to the commanders of the 11th ACR than the action around Saigon was the dramatic news from I Corps that soon reached the capital. The North Vietnamese had used PT76 tanks to overrun the Special Forces camp at Lang Vei, near Khe Sanh, on the night of February 6-7. Until then the North Vietnamese had not used armor in the war. Obviously they were now capable of bringing their formidable Soviet-made vehicles to bear in the conflict.

North Vietnamese and American armor, however, clashed only twice in the entire war, both times fleetingly. In 1968, as NVA soldiers were washing a PT76 tank in the Ben Hai River in the DMZ, a U.S. Marine tank fired and disabled it. American F-4s subsequently reduced it to scrap. And in March 1969, NVA armor attacked a Special Forces camp at Ben Het and was driven off by the fire of Company H, 1st Battalion, 69th Armor of the 4th Infantry Division. But large-scale tank battles, reminiscent of World War II, never materialized, and the 11th ACR never met an opposing tank force. Only after U.S. ground combat forces had left the war did the NVA make extensive use of its armor inside South Vietnam, and its tanks ultimately spearheaded the climactic drive into Saigon in April 1975.

In early 1969 the arsenal of the 11th Armored Cavalry, and of all armored units in Vietnam, was strengthened by the delivery of a new armored reconnaissance vehicle. Though not classified as a tank, the M551 Sheridan was one in all but name. With its aluminum body it weighed only fifteen tons, about one third the weight of the M48. Its chief advantage was its superior armament, including a main 152MM gun capable of firing both guided missiles and HEAT (high-explosive antitank) rounds. However, since guided missiles were not considered necessary, they were never shipped to Vietnam. Ten years in development, the Sheridan promised to be the ultimate light armored weapon. One Pentagon official proudly dubbed it "the Rolls Royce of tanks," though it was in fact built by the Cadillac division of General Motors.

Unfortunately, it quickly became apparent that there were major flaws in the vehicle. In January 1969 sixty-four arrived in Vietnam and were given to two cavalry units—the 3d Squadron, 4th Cavalry attached to the 25th Infantry Division, and the 1st Squadron, 11th Armored Cavalry—for combat testing. Armor veterans found the tank's thin underbelly too vulnerable to mines and RPGs, and concerns arose that the ammunition used by the main gun might explode inside the tank. These fears were tragically realized on February 15, when a Sheridan of the 4th Cavalry was torn apart by a mine that ignited the ammunition and killed the driver.

Other problems also came to light. Dust and humidity caused short circuits and failures of the electrical system. Ammunition spillages and fires were a constant danger. The first official report on the vehicle cited 16 major equipment failures, 123 circuit failures, 41 weapons misfires, 140 ammunition ruptures, 25 engine replacements, and continual failure of the main gun.

The Army insisted that the vehicle had no more bugs than any other new weapons system. Despite its problems, the Sheridan was in Vietnam to stay. Besides, few could deny that when operating properly, it afforded impressive firepower and mobility, though it would only rarely be used to its full capability. More were shipped to Asia, and by late 1970 there were over 200 Sheridans in Vietnam. In the 11th Armored Cavalry, Sheridans replaced ACAVs in the scout sections, increasing their firepower.

In time the Army made some changes in the Sheridan to enhance the safety of the men, using carbon dioxide cartridges that blasted jets of air into the breech of the gun to clear noxious and flammable fumes and, in an effort to increase mine protection, lining the tanks' bellies with an additional 1,000 pounds of armor. In addition, the men in the field customized their vehicles, carrying smaller amounts of ammunition and adding sandbags to the armor. But some problems persisted. Despite the added weight, the Sheridan was still inferior to the heavier M48 for "jungle-busting." In addition, the heavier loads put greater strain on engines and caused more breakdowns.

Piling it on

The commander of the 11th Armored Cavalry when the first Sheridans arrived was eager to give the vehicles a chance to perform in upcoming operations. Aside from having extensive armor experience, he also bore one of the most famous names in the history of tank warfare.

Colonel George Smith Patton, the son of the renowned general and the fourth in his family to bear that name, had compiled an impressive record on his way to becoming a respected commander in his own right. A 1946 West Point graduate, he was on the staff of the Army Armor School when war broke out in Korea. He asked for and received a combat assignment as commander of a tank company. In January 1968, after serving in armor posts in Europe and the United States as well as various Army staff assign-

Thunder Road

Highway 13, the road running from Saigon through Loc Ninh, was the crucial link between the capital and the cities and towns close to the Cambodian border. It was essential that the men and vehicles of the 11th Armored Cavalry keep the highway open, either by escorting convoys through possible ambush positions or by going off the road to flush out pockets of enemy troops. On this operation in May 1967, tanks of the 3d Squadron of the 11th ACR made an assault into the suspected headquarters of the 101st NVA Regiment, which had been harassing American and South Vietnamese convoys along the highway.

From the command post halfway between An Loc and Saigon, Blackhorse M48s plunged into the jungle. The going was slow in the heat and mud, but the "jungle-busting" and firing capability of the tanks—aided by the backs and sweat of American infantrymen—cleared the jungle around Highway 13.

An M48A3 tank from the 3d Squadron slogs through a narrow, muddy creek in search of the enemy near Highway 13.

Left. *A tank bogs down in mud, requiring the muscle of the troopers to get it out.* Below. *During the operation, a 155mm howitzer fires into the jungle from the 3d Squadron command post.* Right. *The 11th ACR's chief objective: to keep the busy artery to An Loc and Loc Ninh open.*

ments, Patton arrived in Saigon to assume a staff position with U.S. Army, Vietnam. Six months later he was given command of the 11th Armored Cavalry.

Like "Old Blood and Guts," Patton was a colorful character known and feared for his aggressiveness. "I do like to see the arms and legs fly," he was once quoted as saying. And also like his father, Patton had a clear idea of the great firepower and mobility of armor and the ways to bring it to bear upon the enemy. Tactical success, Patton reasoned, "can only be gained through a combination of variety in operations, imaginative concepts or plans and bold execution." This final concept was crucial, Patton stressed, for audacity was the key. "Armor soldiers are trained to be bold and aggressive, to take calculated risks," Patton insisted later. "When we were overcautious, we often either got embarrassed and took unnecessary losses or got nothing." To encourage bold actions, Patton formed a regimental body known as the VIB Committee,

---

A sign at the headquarters of the 2d Squadron, 11th Armored Cavalry, at Dau Tieng in 1968 reminds the men of the Blackhorse Regiment's new motto.

for variety, imagination, and boldness. Its participants considered various tactical possibilities such as further air cavalry and even riverine operations. Patton proudly reported, "No idea, no solution, is discarded out of hand regardless of how unorthodox it may at first appear."

The key tactical manifestation of Patton's approach was known as "pile-on," a blanket term for the process that began with the dogged gathering of reliable intelligence and culminated in the aggressive engagement and violent destruction of the enemy. When contact was made, "a ready reaction force of rifle, armored cavalry, or tank elements piled on," Patton explained. "Forces were then literally thrown together on a fragmentary basis in order to overpower, encircle and destroy the located enemy."

Though pile-on was by 1969 a common procedure in the American tactical repertoire, Patton received credit for its refinement for armor. As much as anyone, Patton knew that the now-established mobility of his vehicles gave the cavalry the ability to bring its firepower to bear upon the enemy in virtually any situation. Blackhorse Regiment reconnaissance units in the bush or regimental air cavalry Pink teams would draw fire or fix enemy positions, then give way to the 11th's aero rifle platoon or APCs that would expand the fight for maximum effect and devastation. Any unit not in contact was considered to be in reserve, able to engage the enemy at a moment's notice. The Blackhorse's motto, "Allons," was joined by another: "Find the Bastards—Then Pile On."

Along the border

The Sheridan and Patton's aggressive strategy both had their greatest tests in the hotly contested areas between Saigon and the Cambodian border, an area long known as a staging and battle area for NVA troops. Blackhorse armor was especially important in keeping routes along the border open, permitting greater movement of U.S. and ARVN troops and interdiction of enemy infiltration. In March 1969, the 1st Infantry Division, which had operational control of most of the 11th Armored Cavalry during Patton's nine-month tenure, received intelligence reports of enemy infiltration from the Loc Ninh area toward Saigon. An NVA division, totaling 5,000 men, was located in the area of the Michelin rubber plantation, near Dau Tieng.

On March 15 the 11th Armored Cavalry was ordered to prepare to move to Dau Tieng. The area of operations would include the environs of the Michelin plantation, but the plantation itself was off-limits. Early on the morning of March 17, with the old cavalry call of "Scouts out!" the aero scout platoon was airborne. Operation Atlas Wedge had begun.

It quickly became apparent that there was a large enemy force in the plantation itself. Scout aircraft and forward air controllers observed large groups of NVA below, many of whom made no attempt to hide. Standard procedure dictated that 1st Infantry Division headquarters be asked for permission to fire into the plantation; the call was quickly made. Patton recalled the ninety minutes of waiting for approval as "the longest one and a half hours of my life." Finally clearance came over the radio. For the rest of the day Blackhorse air cavalry and 1st Infantry Division gunships, assisted by Air Force fighter bombers, made repeated strikes against enemy positions.

That night troops and vehicles of the 1st and 3d squadrons assembled on Highway 13 at the eastern edge of the plantation. On the afternoon of March 18, they moved from FSB Holiday Inn into the marshy rubber plantation along a swath cut by regimental Rome plows. Within an hour RPG and small-arms fire plowed through the trees, and both units reported enemy contact. The troopers quickly established landing zones to medevac their wounded, then settled in for the night. The next day, more firefights raged throughout the dense forest as infantry and armor stormed through to root out the enemy. Though the dry, ninety-degree weather was suited for tracked movement, the terrain, covered by low vegetation and cut by several streams, hindered mobility. In the dense growth, Blackhorse vehicles encountered numerous NVA bunkers, many uncovered by American B-52 strikes. Four days into the operation, the defenders of one bunker complex proved especially obstinate. They disabled four tanks of the 3d Squadron with RPGs before the squadron commander, Lieutenant Colonel Lee D. Duke, jumped onto the remaining tank, ordered his APCs to line up beside him, and led a charge against the firing enemy. Overrunning the bunkers, Duke wheeled and swept through again until the enemy was silenced. Seventy-five of the eighty-nine NVA killed that day fell in this action; three Americans lost their lives.

The next day fresh troops of the 1st Squadron took over in the area of operations, while the 3d Squadron retired to FSB Doc. The soldiers thrashed around the area, looking for more bunkers as enemy contact abated. Since only three light observation helicopters were available, larger and slower Hueys were pressed into reconnaissance duty. By this time, however, what remained of the enemy force had withdrawn from the rubber plantation. On March 24, after a week of fighting, Operation Atlas Wedge ended.

Colonel Patton was encouraged by the "combined use of TAC air, Army aviation, armor and infantry" and considered Atlas Wedge the most successful pile-on operation of his Blackhorse command. Also encouraging was the performance of the Sheridan. Patton later remarked that the HEAT round was especially useful for "bunker-busting." The vehicle, he declared, "gives us more gunpower, improves night fighting capability, and is able to keep up with the ACAVs more effectively than the medium tank."

American forces were not about to give up the initiative in the areas close to the border. Less than a month after

Colonel George S. Patton, commander of the 11th Armored Cavalry, in 1968. Comparisons with his legendary father followed him throughout his career.

Atlas Wedge, the 11th ACR deployed to Tay Ninh for Operation Montana Raider, a combined action by the regiment and the 1st Cavalry Division (Airmobile) against an enemy rear service and supply area in War Zone C.

Colonel James H. Leach, who had succeeded Col. Patton as Blackhorse commander on April 6, only three days before the alert for the new operation, huddled with 1st Air Cav commander Major General George Forsythe to devise a ruse to make the enemy believe the operation was targeted against another area farther to the northwest. Air cavalry units flew over the dummy area of operations, and a fake operational order was drafted and deliberately misplaced in hopes that it would fall into enemy hands. The 1st and 2d squadrons of the 11th ACR moved out to complete the feint. Suddenly they turned to link with cavalry units west of Dau Tieng for the operation.

On April 13 the vehicles swept east into the target area, heavy M48s leading the way due to their jungle-busting

The M551 Sheridan Armored Reconnaissance Assault Vehicle rolls into action in Cambodia, 1970. The crew has nicknamed the main gun "Peace Pipe," which is written on the barrel.

strength. Over the next week contact was sometimes heavy against a well-entrenched enemy. Artillery and B-52 strikes were often needed, and American forces once had to pull back after tracer fire ignited dry bamboo. But the vehicles stayed in the jungle, resupplied only by air.

Intelligence reports indicated that the enemy had withdrawn closer to the border, so the 11th ACR pulled out to move north. On April 22, after a two-day stand-down for maintenance, the regiment closed its Dau Tieng command post and raced north along Highway 13 to Quan Loi, a 149-kilometer drive of about twelve hours. Lieutenant Colonel James Dozier, operations officer of the regiment, characterized Phase II of Montana Raider, a series of short clashes with the NVA, as "a repetition of Phase I. The enemy was there, we found him and destroyed his supplies and facilities."

By the end of the thirty-two-day operation, the vehicles of the 11th Armored Cavalry had covered 1,280 kilometers. Regardless of the tactical successes of Montana Raider, the distances covered highlighted some obstacles that had frustrated armor officers almost since the beginning of the war. The strains of mobile combat had been taking their toll on the regiment's support system, taxing it almost to the breaking point.

Since the beginning of the war, the enemy's use of mines had presented a difficult obstacle, especially to armor. In the six-month period from November 1968 to May 1969, mines accounted for 73 percent of all tank losses and 77 percent of APC losses. In the next six-month period the 11th Armored Cavalry encountered over 1,100 mines in the northern III Corps area; only 60 percent were detected in advance, while the other 40 percent damaged 352 vehicles. In addition, concealed explosives caused a large percentage of the regiment's casualties.

To avoid mines or to minimize their devastation, the 11th ACR devised several precautions. By 1969 diesel engines had replaced the more incendiary gasoline motors on tanks and APCs. So that no one soldier would be overly exposed to risk, the job of driver, the most dangerous due to its seating position in a vehicle, was rotated among crew members. Though APCs were designed to hold up to twelve men, troops usually rode on top of them, preferring to take their chances with enemy fire rather than cabin shrapnel, and in doing so avoided the oppressive cabin heat. Belly armor kits and sandbags may have saved lives and boosted crew confidence, one armor colonel observed later, but "did not solve the mine problem." Armored units were given heavy mine rollers, mounted on the front of tanks to detonate mines without damage, but they did not work well in the field, especially in the jungle and along sandy beaches. Eventually most units shunned the roller because of the drag caused by its great weight.

The damage caused by mines was exacerbated by maintenance and supply problems. "Logistical tail wags tactical dog," Colonel Leach moaned in the Montana Raider after-action report. He wrote, "Mines, RPGs and maintenance failures make sustained operations for longer than 10 days almost impossible." Colonel Donn A. Starry, who succeeded Leach as commander of the 11th Armored Cavalry in December 1969, wrote, "Most armored units found the U.S. Army supply and maintenance system to be less than satisfactory at every level." Specifically, there was a lack of adequate maintenance facilities in major areas, due perhaps to the American decision to increase its manpower commitment "at the expense of the logistical base." Sufficient spare parts and qualified people to install them were frequently lacking, especially for the Sheridan. Vehicles often had to be sent great distances for repairs. To make matters worse, heavy recovery vehicles, in effect armored tow trucks, were in short supply, and commanders had to devise unique ways of retrieving and transporting their disabled vehicles when they were, in fact, salvageable.

As a result, many units raided their damaged or worn-out vehicles for parts. Tracks, wheels, guns, and other items from damaged vehicles became prime targets for repairs. During his command in 1969 and 1970, Colonel Starry noted that his regiment's supply network provided only half of its needs, cannibalism of vehicles the rest.

Over the border

However it kept its vehicles rolling, the 11th Armored Cavalry needed to have them at peak efficiency in the spring of 1970, for it was destined to take part in one of the most controversial operations of the war. The incursion into Cambodia, the invasion of North Vietnamese sanctuaries and supply depots in that country, was for many military men a prime example of the usefulness and swiftness of armored columns in Southeast Asia and the closest approximation to classical applications of armor honed in previous wars.

On April 27, after conducting interdiction and security missions near the border in the preceding months, the Blackhorse Regiment was ordered to prepare for the drive into Cambodia. Task Force Shoemaker, led by Brigadier General Robert Shoemaker, 1st Cavalry Division assistant commander, was composed of the 11th ACR and elements of the 1st Cavalry Division, two additional battalions of American armor and mechanized infantry, and two brigades of ARVN troops. The drive into the Fishhook, the narrow swath of land thrusting into South Vietnam, would come on the heels of an ARVN drive into the Parrot's Beak, 160 kilometers to the south.

Thursday night, April 30, the 2d and 3d squadrons of the 11th ACR were at their two firebases west of An Loc, South I and II, poised for the attack into the Fishhook the next day. For the time being the 1st Squadron was to remain at a firebase in South Vietnam. The plan called for the column to cross the border and hook up with the 3d ARVN Airborne Brigade, which had been sent deeper into Cambodia to act as a blocking force in a pincer movement intended to trap the North Vietnamese. One senior American officer described the operation as "pure blitzkrieg, like something from a World War II Panzer Division's book of tactics."

Next morning, May 1, American forces waited while B-52s bombed enemy positions just over the border. Finally just after 7:00 A.M. as the preparatory strikes ended, the Blackhorse vehicles rumbled three kilometers to the border, Col. Starry and the 2d Squadron leading the way with the 3d Squadron close behind. They moved in a narrow column because maneuver room was limited and this formation allowed for greater flexibility.

Even before the lead elements crossed the border, the enemy struck. At 8:55 A.M., Company H was hit by RPG fire and the tanks and ACAVs fell in line to fight back. The troopers called for air strikes and took shelter while shrapnel from the bombs bounced off their vehicles. The strikes routed the enemy and the column resumed its advance. Just after ten o'clock the first armored vehicles rolled through the stream that marked the Cambodian border.

North of the border the country opened up into terrain that was flat and clear, interrupted occasionally by stretches of jungle. It was from one of these patches that the lead armored vehicles picked up the first ground fire. While the 2d Squadron returned the fire, the 3d Squadron, whose progress had been slowed by enemy mines, continued on the eastern flank.

Late in the afternoon, the 2d Squadron again took the lead, and the combined force came upon a battalion-size enemy force entrenched in a bunker complex. As NVA fire erupted from the wood line, the 3d Squadron swung around to the enemy flank and the regimental air cavalry covered the rear and other possible withdrawal routes. The fighting lasted an hour. Col. Starry later recalled that it "looked like the Fourth of July." During the firefight two Blackhorse troopers, Private First Class Paul M. Dailey and Specialist Fourth Class Keith S. Arneson, were killed by RPG fire—the first Americans to die on the Cambodian operation. Fifty-two NVA also lay dead.

The two squadrons continued their drive north for the linkup with the ARVN forces planned for the next day. The well-worn trail was not swept for mines, on the assumption (which proved correct) that a route used by the enemy would not be booby-trapped. That night the rains began to fall, signaling the beginning of the summer monsoon season. Speed had become all the more important.

On May 3 the 11th Armored Cavalry and the ARVN task force met south of Route 7, the main highway, and mounted a widespread search for enemy supplies. The amounts uncovered that day were suggestive of other huge caches, but the 11th ACR was suddenly pulled from the search by an urgent order at 7:15 that evening. The regiment was to pass through the ARVN lines and advance to the village of Snuol, where a large depot and enemy force was said to be located. Speed was essential: Snuol was to be taken within forty-eight hours.

By next afternoon the armored vehicles had cut through to Route 7 and started up the asphalt road, once again with the 2d Squadron in the lead while the 3d Squadron maintained road security behind it. The men on top of the vehicles were especially wary of possible enemy fire from the deep jungle and lines of rubber trees along the road.

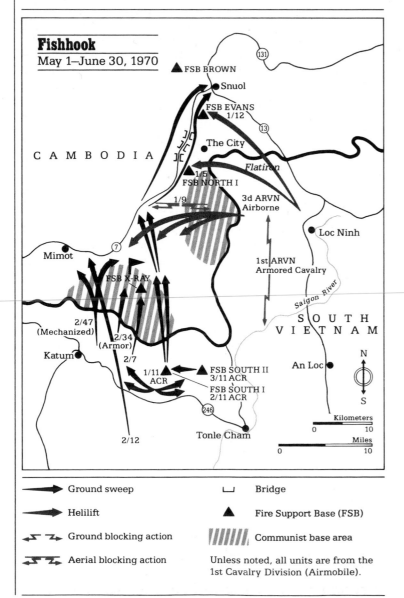

Fishhook
May 1–June 30, 1970

Ground sweep — Bridge
Helilift — Fire Support Base (FSB)
Ground blocking action — Communist base area
Aerial blocking action — Unless noted, all units are from the 1st Cavalry Division (Airmobile).

Air cavalry scouts reported that the enemy had knocked out three bridges along the route, so armored vehicle launched bridges (AVLBs) carried by the regiment would be put to use. Speeding up to sixty-five kilometers an hour, the lead vehicles reached the first of the destroyed bridges within a few hours. Men quickly laid down an AVLB and the vehicles crossed. By now his regiment was strung out along sixty kilometers of road, so Col. Starry decided to consolidate for the second crossing. The rear vehicles of the 2d and 3d squadrons sped along Route 7 through the night. Soldiers riding the tanks and ACAVs were surprised and pleased to see some villagers smiling and waving and handing them pineapples as they passed through.

Another AVLB replaced the second damaged bridge on May 5, and the column continued north to Snuol. Scouts reported that an AVLB would not be sufficient to cross the third site, so regimental engineers were ordered to airlift a heavier bridge ahead of the 2d Squadron. When the lead ACAVs arrived late in the morning, however, the huge CH-54 helicopter and ground crew had made little progress in erecting the bridge. Col. Starry grew impatient and flew to the site to scout possible places for a crossing. Setting out on foot with a sergeant and trailed by a vehicle lugging an AVLB, Starry tried several locations before settling on a site 150 meters to the west of the old bridge. The AVLB was placed and G Troop and the rest of the two squadrons rolled gingerly across.

About four kilometers south of Snuol, the armored cavalry halted and pulled off the road. Plans called for the 2d Squadron to swing left and form in a line to the east while the 3d Squadron readied an attack from the west. The 2d Squadron's G & E troops followed Company H to a point west of the city's airstrip, the location of several enemy antiaircraft guns. As the vehicles moved across the airstrip, RPG and small-arms fire broke out. The tanks turned and let loose with canister fire, and the thousands of pellets silenced the enemy positions. E Troop advanced nearer to the city's marketplace and drew additional RPG fire. The vehicles herringboned and returned the fire. Shortly thereafter American mortars started "walking" into enemy positions. The troop withdrew so that Air Force fighter-bombers could strafe the area, then returned with the tanks of Company H. After knocking out several small pockets of enemy resistance, the vehicles returned to their defensive positions to spend the night. Armored vehicles and helicopter gunships continually pounded the city. By nightfall the southern portion of the city was virtually obliterated and 138 enemy troops lay dead. Among the sixteen American wounded was Col. Starry, who was struck with shrapnel from an enemy grenade. Another soldier was wounded when a U.S. Cobra pilot accidentally fired on 2d Squadron vehicles.

Next morning, May 6, forty-eight hours after the order to take Snuol, the 11th Armored Cavalry entered the city in force and launched search operations. There was little left to examine. The American firepower had reduced many of the buildings to smoking rubble, while scattered fires still burned. Most of the enemy had either died or fled, but the American soldiers, largely unfamiliar with searches in populated areas, moved cautiously from building to building. In the ethereal haze, the tension of the men turned to giddiness. Some collected souvenirs such as articles of clothing and whatever they could find in the stores, even bottles of 7-Up. One trooper rode a commandeered motorcyle up and down the street. The commanders quickly forbade the looting, but the men were ordered to continue to search for any enemy material such as documents, uniforms, or arms. The sweep uncovered tank ammunition, a wealth of spare automobile parts, and a large motor pool.

With the fall of Snuol the regiment returned to its more common role of seeking out enemy positions in the jungle. The 2d and 3d squadrons began reconnaissance-in-force missions around the city and continued to uncover sizable enemy supply caches. On May 9 the 1st Squadron, which had remained in South Vietnam, was finally ordered into Cambodia to search the area around Mimot in rubber plantations southwest of Snuol. On May 21 it moved to the Snuol area to assist in operations there. American helicopters and trucks continued to ferry prodigious amounts of enemy supplies from the area, including arms, uniforms, and training manuals.

To the south, ARVN units were having a more difficult time. The thick jungle and continued enemy harassment had virtually paralyzed clearing efforts in early June, so the 11th ACR was dispatched to assist. The 1st Squadron moved out with two land-clearing companies, the 60th and 984th, and soon Rome plows were cleaving the dense forest in the ARVN area of operations. The 3d Squadron also moved south to keep Route 7 open, while the 2d Squadron straddled the border along Route 13 between Snuol and Loc Ninh.

Though they arrived in Cambodia later than their counterparts, the men of the 1st Squadron quickly made up for the lost time. The enemy had initially laid low while the Americans rooted out their supply caches, but now they became more daring in their attacks. Minings and ambushes increased, and 1st Squadron troops took fire almost daily. One morning five separate elements were engaged at the same time. C Troop reported contact seven times in one day. Methodical searching continued. By June 24 the Army reported that more than 1,600 acres of jungle had been cleared and over 100 tons of supplies and arms confiscated by the 1st Squadron.

Going home

But time was running out for the American forces in Cambodia. President Nixon had declared that all U.S. forces would leave the country by June 30, two months into

Snuol lies in ruins after air strikes, artillery, and the firepower of the 11th Armored Cavalry virtually obliterated the Cambodian city in May 1970.

the incursion. In addition, the arrival of the monsoon rains slowed the tracked vehicles. Thus operations wound down as the month progressed. On June 25 the land-clearing companies crossed the border to Katum, followed the next day by the 1st Squadron. On June 27 the 3d Squadron of the 11th ACR rolled out in column formation from Route 7 to Katum. Farther north, the 2d Squadron quit Cambodia at Loc Ninh.

After fifty-eight days of service in Cambodia the Blackhorse Regiment was back over the border. Many had appreciated the opportunity to strike the enemy in his sanctuary, but most were relieved to return to somewhat more familiar territory. "You know, it was funny," recalled platoon Sergeant George A. Hutchins, "nobody liked Vietnam, but we were all happy to get back."

The Cambodian incursion was the last serious flexing of American ground combat muscle in the war. During the

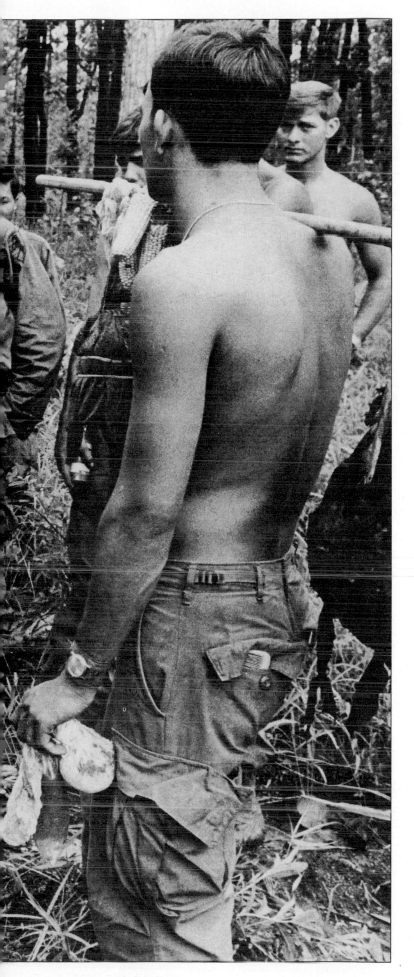

previous twelve months future American policy in Vietnam had become clear: the U.S. military was turning the war over to South Vietnamese forces and pulling out. In the months after the Fishhook operation, the 11th ACR increased the number of operations undertaken in support of Vietnamese forces. From their new base camp at Di An, close to Saigon, troops moved out with a comparably sized ARVN or Regional Forces unit, as the American commander tried to give his Vietnamese counterpart an equal role in the execution of each mission.

The new role of the 11th ACR was consistent with the Vietnamization policy of the Nixon administration. When it was first announced in 1969, General Creighton W. Abrams, Westmoreland's successor as MACV commander, formed a task force to study methods of troop withdrawal. One of its members was Col. Starry, who later recalled the directions of Abrams, himself a legendary World War II tank commander: "Save the armor units out until last, they can buy us more time." Starry was struck by the irony: "Thus armor units, specifically excluded from the buildup until late 1966, would anchor the withdrawal of American combat units from Vietnam."

On December 20, 1970, the 11th Armored Cavalry received orders to prepare the 1st and 3d squadrons, as well as a number of support units, to return to the United States by March 5, 1971. The 2d Squadron, reinforced by the regimental air cavalry troop, remained in Vietnam for another year, operating from Long Binh in support of American and ARVN units.

In early February the 1st and 3d squadrons withdrew from their areas of operation. Excluding the assets of the 2d Squadron, the 11th ACR turned over 44,000 pieces of equipment, including more than 900 wheeled and tracked vehicles, to the U.S. Army command. The various facilities at Di An—including the service club, swimming pool, and miniature golf course—were closed down in late February and early March and the base was turned over to the Vietnamese marines. Two-thirds of the 11th Armored Cavalry, numbering 3,196 officers and men, were reassigned to other units in Vietnam or in the United States.

Upon its return to the U.S., the 11th ACR was deactivated, only to be resurrected later on the Army rolls. Within a year the personnel and equipment of the 14th Armored Cavalry, based in Germany, were used to re-form the 11th Armored Cavalry. The Blackhorse Regiment, at least as those in Vietnam had known it, was gone, but now on the other side of the world its history of "mounted" combat continued—a tradition it had fought to maintain in Southeast Asia.

Outside Snuol, Blackhorse troopers gather around a VC who presented a chieu hoi card indicating his intention to rally to the GVN during the 1970 Cambodian incursion.

141

Patrolling the Delta

The 9th Infantry Division first served in World War I but built its reputation as the "Old Reliables" during World War II. Specially trained for amphibious assault, it formed the spearhead for Allied drives into North Africa, Sicily, France, and across the Remagen Bridge into the heart of Nazi Germany. One of the division's officers in the European campaign was a promising artillery colonel named William C. Westmoreland. Shortly after the war ended, he rose to command the 60th Infantry Regiment. General Westmoreland always held his old wartime formation in high esteem even though the 9th Infantry Division was deactivated in 1962, just before the Vietnam conflict intensified.

When planning was under way in the early 1960s for the contingency of U.S. intervention in Southeast Asia, the U.S. military examined the option of sending American combat troops into the Mekong Delta of lower South Vietnam to confront the Vietcong guerrillas. However, the same wet, marshy conditions that ensured the vital production of rice

The 9th Infantry Division headquarters at Dong Tam sits upon what was originally flooded rice fields. Barely visible on the horizon is the Mekong River.

General Westmoreland persisted in his conviction that the military situation would not improve until substantial American combat troops were committed in the delta. His staff developed an elaborate joint Army-Navy Mobile Riverine Force concept, drawing both upon recent French experience in the First Indochina War against the Vietminh and river campaign lessons learned by Union forces in the American Civil War. In support of this effort, military engineers conducted intensive delta surveys producing hydrographic charts and soil analysis data for locating possible military installations. In December 1965, MACV presented proposals for American intervention in the area that were costly but feasible. The Department of Defense and, later, the State Department approved.

The mobile riverine force was to be a contingent of Army troops housed in Navy barracks ships, propelled to the battlefield on modified landing craft, and supported by artillery lashed on towed barges. A base of operations could be created by dredging sand from the marshland near a main branch of the Mekong River. This new base could be sustained in the heart of VC-dominated delta territory without overtaxing established logistical facilities. The effort required one light Army brigade and a specially tailored naval task force.

The recommendation for a modern Army riverine force coincided with the reactivation on February 1, 1966, of the 9th Infantry Division at Fort Riley, Kansas. Major General George S. Eckhardt, the new commander, had traveled from Iran to the traditional cavalry post of Fort Riley the previous September to prepare to raise the division. Chief, the last cavalry horse on the rolls of the Army, watched over the division's formation from his stable, but the mobility of the 9th was destined to be provided not by horsepower but by a new matrix: U.S. helicopters dominating the air lanes and armored assault boats chasing the enemy through the waterways.

The new division was designated the 9th Infantry Division, largely in deference to General Westmoreland's past service in the unit. It was secretly scheduled for Vietnam. Although organized as a standard infantry division, one of its three brigades would function as a mobile floating force. The division was organized with one reconnaissance cavalry squadron (3d Squadron, 5th Cavalry), and nine infantry battalions (three each from the 39th, 47th, and 60th infantries). Four artillery battalions, an engineer and a signal battalion, an aviation battalion, and a support command augmented the ground forces.

Because of a shortage of both men and equipment, the division was formed in increments. The headquarters staff of the major commands formed first, then combat battalions were phased in until the early summer. Training time

throughout the region imposed considerable geographic obstacles to conventional forces dependent upon a sophisticated supply network. There were no proper anchorages or suitable landing fields, and the few roads could barely support heavy American trucks. Because of extensive seasonal flooding, local transport was usually limited to small sampans that could thread through the maze of shallow rivers and narrow canals.

After American combat troops landed in Vietnam in 1965, these logistical concerns paled when compared with the objections posed by the State Department and the U.S. Embassy in Saigon to the introduction of American forces in the delta. They feared that it would be impossible to avoid unpleasant incidents between American soldiers and the local people of the densely populated area. Further, the diplomats thought that the deployment of an American division to the area, the one region of the country for which the South Vietnamese retained sole responsibility for security, would lower ARVN's already drooping morale. So the U.S. Army suspended for the time being its plan to field a division specifically trained and equipped for delta operations. As a consequence, the Vietcong continued to attract the loyalty of many farmers who resented the aloof rule and unwelcome taxation imposed by the Saigon regime and rendered the South Vietnamese army divisions posted in the delta flood plain ineffective in combatting the guerrillas.

9th Infantry Division

Arrived Vietnam: December 16, 1966

Departed Vietnam: August 27, 1969

Unit Headquarters

Bear Cat   *Dec. 1966–July 1968*

Dong Tam   *Aug. 1968–Aug. 1969*

Commanding Officers

Maj. Gen. George S. Eckhardt   *Dec. 1966*
Maj. Gen. George G. O'Connor   *June 1967*

Maj. Gen. Julian J. Ewell   *Feb. 1968*

Maj. Gen. Harris W. Hollis   *April 1969*

Major Subordinate Units

6th Battalion, 31st Infantry	5th Battalion, 60th Infantry (Mechanized)	9th Medical Battalion
2d Battalion, 39th Infantry	3d Squadron, 5th Cavalry	9th Signal Battalion
3d Battalion, 39th Infantry	Company E, 50th Infantry	9th Supply & Transport Battalion
4th Battalion, 39th Infantry	Company E, 75th Infantry	15th Engineer Battalion
2d Battalion, 47th Infantry (Mechanized)	2d Battalion, 4th Artillery	709th Maintenance Battalion
3d Battalion, 47th Infantry (Riverine)	1st Battalion, 11th Artillery	9th Administration Company
4th Battalion, 47th Infantry (Riverine)	3d Battalion, 34th Artillery (Riverine)	9th Military Police Company
2d Battalion, 60th Infantry	1st Battalion, 84th Artillery	335th Army Security Company
3d Battalion, 60th Infantry (Riverine)	Battery H, 29th Artillery	9th Aviation Battalion

2,624 KIA
(Casualty figures are "Vietnam Era.")

18,831 WIA

10 Medals of Honor

was compressed so that with the completion of division field tests in December the unit would be able to enter the wetlands at the beginning of the delta's dry season.

The division shoulder patch displayed a bright red-and-blue double quatrefoil rimmed in olive drab, and it induced such derogatory labels as the "Flower Power" or the "Psychedelic Cookie" division.

The first element of the 9th to reach Vietnam was the 15th Engineer Battalion, which arrived on October 19, 1966, to help construct the main division campsite at Bear Cat, close to Saigon. The rest of the 9th Infantry Division went to Vietnam in stages. Advance troops arrived by air on December 8, and the rest of the division sailed in naval transport ships. The division's official entry into the Vietnam War was recorded as December 19, 1966, when Major General George S. Eckhardt led 5,000 soldiers down landing craft ramps across the beaches of Vung Tau to be welcomed by General Westmoreland himself. By the time the last troops landed little more than a month later, division strength had grown to more than 15,000 men.

The 9th joins the war

The site of the division's southern delta base lay within a vast area of rice fields sixty kilometers south of Saigon on the Mekong River. The first soldiers assigned to the flooded rice fields during the fall of 1966 pitched tents atop log rafts in the oozing mud that had been under six feet of water only a few weeks before. To build a military camp there seemed next to impossible. The *Jamaica Bay*, one of the world's largest dredges, anchored in the Mekong River and pumped sand into the rice fields to raise the level of the campsite. Within a few months more than ninety acres had been reclaimed with 2 million cubic feet of fill, and the ground level had been elevated ten feet. Just as the base neared completion, the Vietcong put a temporary stop to the work. In the early darkness of January 10, 1967, VC sappers sank the *Jamaica Bay* with explosives, but two more dredges were brought in to continue operations.

In mid-January the first infantrymen—from the 3d Brigade of the 9th Infantry Division—arrived to provide security. Three engineer battalions were now working around-the-clock to complete the base. The division's 15th Engineer Battalion built mess halls, latrines, and troop billets while the 69th and 93d engineer battalions labored on the road network and drainage system. At last, during March, the bulk of the riverine 2d Brigade was able to occupy its base.

Eventually the once-flooded expanse of rice land was transformed into 600 relatively dry acres as two-story barracks replaced tents. Cement was poured on the roads to preserve them against monsoon rains. A large turning basin was dredged adjacent to the base, while an outlet on the Mekong River provided for the vessels of the Mobile Riverine Force. General Westmoreland himself named the new installation Dong Tam, which the Americans translated as "United Hearts and Minds." From its discouraging beginnings, Dong Tam grew into the largest Army outpost in the delta.

The deployment of the troops of the 9th Infantry Division eventually stretched across the southwestern flank of the protective ring around the capital city of Saigon. One brigade was stationed at Bear Cat near Saigon, another was located inside the muddy delta at Dong Tam, and the final brigade was posted between them at Tan An. The division quickly became fully engaged in its formidable task of seeking out and destroying the Vietcong in the flat marshes and dense swamp forests.

The northernmost 1st Brigade served in the multidivisional Operation Junction City, until then the largest drive of the war. Thus the Old Reliables, who had been trained and equipped largely for delta missions, ironically fought their first important battle in the jungles of War Zone C along the Cambodian border. In the predawn hours of March 20, A Troop of the cavalry squadron was attacked in a furious six-hour firefight. The men claimed victory when the enemy finally fled the battlefield.

In early April the division saw its first action in the delta region, scoring a stunning victory near Rach Kien in Long An Province. A preplanned air strike exposed underground VC positions and forced the enemy to flee their damaged hideouts. Immediately, the 3d Battalion of the 39th Infantry and all three battalions of the 60th Infantry boxed in the disorganized Vietcong defenders and reported that they had inflicted heavy casualties.

On May 2, deeper in the Mekong Delta, elements of the 2d Brigade collided with the 514th VC Battalion at Ap Bac, site of a devastating ARVN setback in early 1963. Displaying exceptional resourcefulness, the 3d Battalions of the 9th Division's 47th and 60th infantry encircled the enemy as helicopter gunships and fighter-bombers rained rockets and bombs on the VC positions. The enemy battalion attempted to flee the battlefield but was badly mauled. Another violent firefight erupted in the Cam Son Secret Zone, thirty kilometers west of Dong Tam, during a combined reconnaissance by two battalions of the 47th Infantry, elements of the 7th ARVN Division, and several naval river assault teams.

The May fighting in the delta confirmed the need for a combat strike force capable of navigating the Mekong waterways. After months of preparation the Mobile Riverine Force (MRF) finally became operational in June 1967. The force was composed of two battalions from the 2d Brigade and Naval Task Force 117, which provided the necessary armored Monitors, assault patrol craft, and armored troop carriers. Working together, they initiated extensive combat operations in the Mekong Delta, but it

Soldiers of Company B, 3d Battalion, 39th Infantry, 9th Infantry Division, watch an air strike intended to flush out hiding VC during an operation near Rach Kien in April 1967.

was not until late June—six months after the division had arrived in Vietnam—that the MRF saw its first real combat.

Major General George S. O'Connor, who served as assistant division commander for four months, assumed command of the Old Reliables that month. Under his leadership, the division's area of operations expanded to 275 square kilometers dotted with more than 1,610 hamlets. Frequently joining forces with Vietnamese marine or army elements, the 9th Infantry Division engaged VC forces in a series of sharp actions.

Warfare in the marshes

During these summer months the 2d Brigade steadily improved its riverine tactics, hoping to strike the Vietcong in some of their most heavily fortified delta strongholds. By the time Colonel Bert A. David assumed command of the riverine 2d Brigade in September 1967, the MRF had learned some valuable lessons. For example, surprise was essential in riverine operations since the delta terrain limited maneuverability; preparatory air and artillery strikes in advance of earlier missions revealed that the Americans were about to attack. As Col. David planned Operation Coronado V, a strike into enemy base areas in the Cam Son and Ban Long Secret Zone forests near the My Tho River, he forbade aircraft flights over the target area and withheld artillery fire until his landing craft had moved upriver close to the shoreline where he intended to attack.

On the morning of September 15, an armada of armored troop carriers of River Assault Squadron 11 under Navy Lieutenant Commander Francis E. "Dusty" Rhodes, Jr., followed a vanguard of mine sweepers up the channel. The lead assault craft, each crowded with troops of Lieutenant Colonel Mercer M. Doty's 3d Battalion of the 60th Infantry, were approaching the landing beaches when Vietcong rockets and automatic weapons suddenly lashed the vessels from both sides of the river. Several assault boats were set on fire. Temporarily out of control, the boats began to run amuck. Some tried to maneuver through the smoke and returned fire with their own machine guns and cannon. In the confusion, one boat overtook the mine sweepers and landed a lone platoon on the hostile shore.

Col. David, overhead in his command helicopter, saw this single landing and ordered the rest of the force to follow. However, Lt. Comdr. Rhodes had already ordered an immediate withdrawal because of the heavy crew losses and damage to the boats. The Navy squadron reorganized downstream and reattacked, this time supported by helicopter gunships and heavy artillery. The landings were made in the face of sustained enemy fire. One thirty-man platoon of Company A suffered eighteen men wounded. Clouds of riot control gas smothered the enemy bunkers, producing an effective smoke screen that at last allowed Lt. Col. Doty's soldiers to form a defensive perimeter.

Col. David brought three other battalions into the battle from other directions. Although these combined forces surrounded the VC positions and the area was lit by continuous flare illumination, most of the enemy in the 514th VC Battalion escaped into the darkness. Col. David's forces swept the battlefield the following day—too late. They found few defenders. Operation Coronado V, which ended in the first week of October, was a nasty initiation into riverine warfare for Col. David. Most of the 9th Division's 427 casualties suffered during that month came in the Coronado fighting. The Navy sustained losses as well.

Because they were unique and so attention grabbing, mobile riverine operations became synonymous with the 9th Infantry Division. In fact, however, only one of its three brigades, the 2d, was engaged in this manner. The other two brigades operated more or less as conventional infantry units with only small modifications made for the delta terrain. Like other infantry formations, the hunt for the Vietcong by these brigades began with airmobile assaults followed by long marches through open fields in search of the enemy hiding in nearby woods, paddies, and huts. The 9th Infantry Division also initiated far-ranging sweep operations deep into Vietcong territory, marching through previously unsearched rubber plantations and dense jungle and using flimsy sampans or rope bridges to traverse the myriad streams and water channels. In the upper delta, grenadiers and riflemen sloshed through the head-high marsh grass and thigh-deep mud of the Plain of Reeds in pursuit of the elusive Vietcong. Within the populated districts, including the approaches to Saigon and the main delta, division ambush (nicknamed Aquabush) patrols prowled the dangerous canals at night, snaring suspect sampans and inhibiting VC resupply efforts.

The enemy was hard to detect, often found only by accident. Private First Class Billy G. Crisp of Irving, Texas, was point man for Company B, 3d Battalion, 39th Infantry, as it marched through a wooded area near Rach Kien. As he began to radio his platoon leader to tell him about the rugged terrain, he noticed a pair of legs sticking out from a pile of palm leaves. He stopped and the legs slowly disappeared into the foliage. "The figure started to move and I knew he was aware of being discovered," Crisp recalled. "Just before he disappeared I unloaded my weapon on him." The dead enemy soldier was identified as a North Vietnamese Army platoon leader who had been sent south to lead VC militia.

The 4th Battalion of the 39th Infantry disrupted Vietcong activity south of Saigon with airboats whose crewmen called themselves the Swamp Cavalry. The airboats were equipped with radios and M60 machine guns mounted on their bows. In swift formations they combed the flat lowlands and made small assault landings. The airboats were not strictly confined to the canals and waterways. When incoming tides swelled the sponge-dry rice fields, "this is when we really kicked in," an airboat platoon

Mobile Riverine Force

The Mobile Riverine Force (MRF) was a joint Army-Navy task force organized for combat operations against the Vietcong in the Mekong River delta. A region of marshlands, rice fields, and swamps, the delta was a logistical nightmare, but Vietcong strength in the densely populated region forced American troops to develop a means of challenging them there.

Using a concept from the American Civil War, when Union Army forces had operated with Navy gunboats, the MRF combined the

Men from the 2d Brigade, 9th Infantry Division, assigned to the Mobile Riverine Force, leave an armored troop carrier during an operation in November 1967.

9th Infantry Division's specially trained 2d Brigade with the Navy's Riverine Assault Force (Task Force 117). The soldiers of the 2d Brigade were stationed on floating barracks ships, around which docked an array of landing ships, landing craft repair ships, harbor tugs, and net-laying ships. For operations, they were ferried to shore by armored troop carriers, escorted by well-armed and nearly impenetrable Monitors. Artillery barges, helicopters, and fixed-wing aircraft stood ready to support the soldiers.

Together, the 2d Brigade's 5,000 infantrymen and the Navy's resources, which could move the force 240 kilometers within 24 hours, made the MRF a powerful mobile unit. After its activation in June 1967, the MRF launched a number of combat operations, most prominently the Coronado series, that took the MRF from Saigon to Ca Mau Point at the tip of South Vietnam. Its missions were varied. It kept shipping channels open and hit Vietcong sanctuaries; it also protected the cities of My Tho, Vinh Long, and Can Tho during the Tet offensive.

The MRF did not break the Vietcong's hold on the delta, but its operations hurt the enemy in a region where most other units had proved ineffective. In April 1971, the duties of the last elements of the MRF were transferred to South Vietnamese forces.

A Monitor and two armored troop carriers of the Mobile Riverine Force cruise down a delta canal, November 1967.

leader, First Lieutenant Richard Strasser, remembered. "The boats rev their engines to full speed, race into the paddy dikes, jump them, and cruise as fast as 70 knots per hour. Usually we can get the boats up to 50 knots in canals, but in the rice paddies, with their mirror-smooth surface, we really move!" The airboats of the Swamp Cav allowed the division to speed infantry into action faster than previously considered possible and extended its maneuverability and firepower over formerly inaccessible terrain.

The slow but steady progress of the 9th Infantry Division cleared sufficient ground south of the capital to allow General Westmoreland to field other "Free World" forces in the area. On September 21, 1967, the 2,000-man Royal Thai Army Queen's Cobra Volunteer Regiment was brought into Vietnam under 9th Infantry Division tutelage. Operating out of Bear Cat, the Queen's Cobras began combat and civic action operations in the Nhon Trach jungles, thirty

kilometers southeast of Saigon. Throughout its Vietnam service, the 9th Infantry Division maintained a close affinity with the Thais, which eventually expanded to division-size and earned an excellent fighting reputation.

A tidal wave

The 9th Infantry Division's heaviest fighting in Vietnam took place during the NVA/VC offensives in February and May 1968. Before the Vietcong tidal wave subsided, division soldiers found themselves engaged on many unaccustomed fronts and in unrehearsed actions. During the night of January 31 the division countered the first Vietcong Tet attacks throughout the countryside with all of its units. The 1st Brigade responded from its jungle base to fighting in the Mekong Delta. Tanks and armored personnel carriers from the 3d Squadron, 5th Cavalry, helped repel a

determined VC attack against Bien Hoa airport just west of the capital. Troops of the 2d and 3d brigades, who normally sloshed through the Mekong mire, fought for control of My Tho and Ben Tre, tracking down marauding bands of city fighters and charging concrete pillboxes in urban combat, reminiscent of World War II street fighting. Other delta-based units flushed Vietcong infiltrators from the rubble of downtown Saigon-Cholon.

In the midst of the hard fighting in February 1968, Major General Julian J. Ewell took command of the 9th Infantry Division, bringing with him a penchant for judging progress by statistics. For instance, the 15th Engineer Battalion kept Highway 14, the main artery into Saigon from the delta rice lands, open, often under fire and despite repeated VC attempts to interdict the critical road. The combat engineers filled more than 250 craters, some large enough to swallow an entire truck, and dismantled

258 VC nighttime roadblock and ambuscade positions in a single month. During the same period the engineers repaired nineteen destroyed bridges and built four new ones. The engineers' accomplishments were real and provided the material General Ewell liked to see in all the division reports submitted to him. Unfortunately, "chalkboard progress" was not always a true reflection of battlefield reality.

On March 3, 1968, troopers from Company B of the 47th Infantry's 2d Battalion discovered a large Vietcong tunnel complex only three kilometers from division headquarters at Bear Cat. Soldiers on a reconnaissance mission noticed holes at the base of a hill. Carefully disarming numerous

Soldiers of the 9th Infantry Division push forward on foot and in APCs toward Vietcong positions near the Long Binh post on the first day of the 1968 Tet offensive.

A Minor Language Barrier

Two riverine soldiers slosh through the delta's muddy water while on a search-and-destroy mission, September 1967.

While coordination between Army and Navy personnel in the 9th Infantry Division's Mobile Riverine Force was generally excellent, the services' different dialects created a minor language barrier in the Mekong Delta, causing both problems and humorous incidents.

Army Sergeant Mike Barnes arrived to join the riverine force from North Highlands, California. When he first heard the term "scuttlebutt," he thought it meant some kind of floor mop. Later he was politely informed that scuttlebutt was sailor talk for a drinking fountain or the latest rumor.

Riverine force Specialist Fourth Class Paul Cherkas of Woonsocket, Rhode Island, returned to his barracks ship and was informed by the sailors that a "field day" was in order. Cherkas smiled, assuming that it meant "some kind of Navy holiday." He quickly learned that it was the seagoing answer to the Army scrub brush party. When Cherkas was directed to the "void tank," he expressed his ignorance of Navy talk with disgust, believing that the tank meant "a cesspool connected to the latrine" (to the Navy, the "head"). He was relieved to find out it simply meant a large storage area for the ship's gear.

An Army helicopter pilot attempting to land on a mobile riverine vessel was thrown into temporary confusion while being guided in by Navy crewmen. "My flight deck is green," the sailors relayed. Not realizing the phrase meant the deck was safe and clear, the Army pilot continued to circle while he thumbed through his codebook for the new word. Finally he radioed back, "I only see white!" which indeed the decks were.

The 4th Battalion of the 47th Infantry became so mixed up by Navy jargon that the infantry unit resorted to a battlefield measure. The battalion required that a Vietnamese interpreter be present whenever captured Vietcong suspects were questioned. In an effort to alleviate misunderstandings with the Navy, the battalion directed that an Army translator be appointed. Specialist Fourth Class Thomas J. Hain of Chicago was selected and learned the Navy jargon in eight

months. He even wrote a dictionary of Navy terms for battalion use. "It's enough to blow anybody's mind," he recalled and tried to mimic naval orders: "Reveille, reveille, heave out and trice up! Knock off ship's work! Sweepers, sweepers, man your brooms!"

The Mobile Riverine Force's language problems were further complicated by the arrival of Private First Class Lieutenant Norals, an eighteen-year-old rifleman of the 3d Battalion, 60th Infantry, during 1968. The riverine force commanders grumbled that he must have been the only Army enlisted man with an officer's rank as his first name. (Actually he wasn't; Army ranks in Vietnam included at least one private with the first name of Major.) When the Chicago native was assigned to the barracks ship USS *Benewah* and introduced to his new platoon, the soldiers thought they misheard his actual title, snapped to attention, and saluted him. When the call, "Hey, lieutenant," was heard, Private Norals naturally answered, only to learn that it was an actual lieutenant that the company commander wanted. The problem was resolved after Norals was allowed to be addressed only by his last name.

The joint Army-Navy Mobile Riverine Force never quite mastered its language differences. Perhaps such difficulty was only to be expected in a formation where a fresh Army mobile riverine captain, on his first tour of battle duty, carried a title of rank equal to that of a grizzled battleship skipper, who in the army would be regarded as a full colonel.

booby traps along the way, they climbed a 500-meter-long trail leading through dense foliage to a circular bunker system guarding the tunnel entrances of an underground VC hospital. The subterranean system was seven levels deep and contained many rooms. Each passage had numerous trap doors. The walls were blackened from the soot of lanterns. One of the volunteers who searched out the newly found tunnels was platoon Staff Sergeant Winston W. Butler, who later remarked, "We searched the complex and never found the bottom. The tunnels were over six feet tall and we had no trouble standing upright in them. They looked as though they had been used very recently."

The proximity of such a large enemy complex, plus the expectation of a new wave of VC attacks in May, called for more manpower. Accordingly, the division received its tenth infantry battalion on April 7. Nicknamed the Bearcats, the 6th Battalion, 31st Infantry, was organized at Fort Lewis, Washington, in November 1967. It trained for Vietnam combat in the cold of winter. The battalion commander, Lieutenant Colonel Joseph Schmalhorst recalled, "Watching the men search a mock-up Vietnamese village in the snow was a strange sight." The battalion was rushed to Vietnam at the end of March and immediately entered a crash course in tropical warfare at the division's Reliable Academy. The new soldiers received advanced instruction in weapons firing, patrol tactics, medical evacuation "dust-off" procedures, the disarming of booby traps, and field hygiene.

The May offensive

The newly arrived Bearcats were soon in battle. The long-predicted second 1968 Vietcong assault on Saigon erupted on May 7. Although this offensive was minor compared to the January attacks, Main Force VC units seized strong positions at the southern edge of the capital. The enemy quickly entrenched themselves in the suburban ruins where the Y Bridge crossed the Kinh Doi Canal and prepared to push their attack into the Chinese community of Cholon. The Bearcats and four other battalions of division infantrymen, closely supported by armored personnel carriers, helicopter gunships, and Air Force fighter-bombers, smashed through heavy enemy resistance in five days of grueling combat.

Members of the 3d Battalion, 34th Artillery, aboard floating artillery barges, fire 105MM howitzers at a Vietcong supply point along the My Tho River, April 1967.

The Y Bridge was secured by mechanized troops, while other enemy forces were sealed off and destroyed in the rubble of a nearby factory complex. Sergeant Darwin Gault was among several members of the 5th Battalion, 60th Infantry, who faced a predawn VC counterattack on the bridge defenses. When a torrent of fire from the shielded APC weapons opened up, the VC fell back and tried to knock out the vehicles with antitank rockets. Sergeant Gault spotted two rockets being fired from the window of a building about 150 meters away.

The first projectile slammed into the bridge railing, and the second whizzed high and detonated harmlessly in the canal. As the Vietcong took aim for another shot, Gault picked up a spare M79 grenade launcher. "I had never fired one at the Cong before," he later admitted. Yet, his first shot was right on target, turning the window entrance into a blinding ball of fire. Multiple explosions from a stockpile of rockets followed. With the local VC rocket support destroyed, the APCs posted to the bridge were secure. A subsequent Vietcong ground attack was also defeated.

The division's 2d Brigade Mobile Riverine Force performed well throughout the Tet offensive. The brigade soldiers fought through crowded cities, an unfamiliar environment for infantrymen trained primarily in amphibious methods. After intense fighting around Saigon, the brigade moved to the relief of the critical delta port city of Can Tho. In three weeks of virtually continuous house-to-house combat, the brigade smashed the heaviest enemy attack of the Tet offensive in the delta.

During this battle, MRF Sergeant John Blanchfield of the 4th Battalion, 47th Infantry, covered the evacuation of a wounded comrade. "The firing was so heavy that we couldn't stand up and the man was too badly hurt to be dragged," Blanchfield, who came from Perry Hall, Maryland, explained. He held up the head and back of the wounded man while Specialist Fourth Class Robert Schultz from Glen Cove, New York, acted as a human packhorse by moving on his hands and knees with the man on his back. After carrying the man just a few meters, Blanchfield saw bullets striking the ground nearby. Holding the wounded man's head with one hand and firing with the other, Blanchfield killed the enemy sniper.

Another sniper opened fire from the rear, and Blanchfield whirled around to aim. "I just touched the trigger and the next thing I knew, I was flat on my back." An AK47 round had struck his rifle magazine first, exploding the weapon. Blanchfield saw another M16 on the ground and quickly grabbed it. He killed the second sniper while carrying the wounded man another fifty meters to safety. Blanchfield then noticed he had been wounded by several of his own bullets that had exploded from the magazine. The brigade received the Presidential Unit Citation in recognition of its battlefield valor in a ceremony on June 6, 1969—appropriately aboard the barracks ship USS *Benewah*, anchored in the My Tho River.

The efforts of the 9th Infantry Division in such close proximity to Saigon also received recognition from the grateful South Vietnamese regime. During the division's fiftieth anniversary celebration on July 18, 1968, Lieutenant General Le Nguyen Khang, the commander of III Corps and the Vietnamese Marine Corps, attached the coveted red-and-yellow streamer of the Vietnamese Valor Award, Army Level, to the division colors in appreciation of its clearing operations in Saigon during the enemy offensive. Khang next pinned the Cross of Gallantry on Gen. Ewell, signifying an award to all Old Reliables who served in Vietnam through June 1968.

The next month the division relocated its main base headquarters to Dong Tam. However, its subordinate units still engaged in heavy fighting in their old sectors as part of the U.S. and South Vietnamese Tet counteroffensive. The 1st Brigade adopted jungle tactics using sniper teams and ambush patrols to assault surviving VC units in Long An Province. This style of warfare placed a high premium on small-unit proficiency and individual tracking and jungle warfare skills. The unit's successful activities earned the 1st Brigade the salutory nickname of the Recondo (derived from reconnaissance commando) Brigade and the award of another Vietnamese Valorous Unit Citation with Cross of Gallantry, Army Level.

Behind the infantrymen

As was the case for every American division engaged in combat in Vietnam, the 9th Infantry Division's operations centered around the helicopter. The motto of the division's own flying unit—the 9th Aviation Battalion—reflected this presence: "Anywhere, Anytime." However, several other aviation units were so routinely attached from the 1st Aviation Brigade that they became almost accepted as part of the 9th. The 214th Aviation Battalion (Combat) and the 3d Squadron of the 17th Cavalry (Air) combined to give the division more than 480 pilots and 200 aircraft, ranging from AH-1G Cobra gunships and cargo-lifting CH-47 Chinooks to light observation helicopters and Huey transports. The 361st Aviation Detachment was assigned to supervise the three separate division airfields at Bear Cat, Dong Tam, and Tan An. This small but critical detachment controlled over 72,000 sorties and pumped an average of 40,000 gallons of fuel daily to keep the helicopters flying safely in the air.

While infantrymen trudging through the Mekong Delta measured their field time in operational days, aviators flying in their support measured their air time in hundreds of thousands of blade hours. Flying day and night, these aviators provided the division with the essential mobility and scouting services that brought all division components, even the riverine force, into contact with the enemy. The air crews also actively patrolled over hostile territory, preventing open Vietcong maneuvers through the search zones and severely restricting the movement of enemy materiel. Wherever the infantrymen went into battle, helicopters could be seen helping to destroy the enemy, bringing in supplies or reinforcements and taking out the wounded.

The 9th's artillery contained the most unusual arsenal of mixed cannon and howitzers to see action in Vietnam. The delta terrain and riverine capabilities of the division obliged the Old Reliable artillerymen to adopt unique tactics in order to continue their primary mission of placing steel on the target with first-round accuracy.

The endless winding waterways of Kien Hoa Province gave birth to the division artillery barges that allowed the artillery to tie up along the shore and to deliver fire support where needed. The barges became the artillerymen's home; the crews not only worked on the barges but also ate, slept, and relaxed on them. The 3d Battalion, 34th Artillery, was the only active Army riverine artillery in the world during the Vietnam era. All the light 105MM howitzers were either placed on barges or mobile firing platforms. Since the artillery barges were required to move along

narrow streams in support of riverine and airmobile infantrymen, the cannoneers were sometimes forced to leave their artillery pieces and fire machine guns and rifles for close protection.

The other three artillery battalions used more conventional fire support bases positioned on dry land next to the infantry. Chinook and Sky Crane helicopters enabled all of the division's towed howitzers to be lifted into airmobile action. However, the 1st Battalion, 11th Artillery, specialized in keeping their airlifted howitzers at the most advanced firing positions. Airmobile techniques were refined to the point where a battery could be slung underneath a helicopter with only a minimum of advance notice and during hours of darkness.

The medium artillery of the 1st Battalion, 84th Artillery, was bolstered by the large, tracked, eight-inch howitzers of Battery D. These heavy weapons were used almost exclu-

Two soldiers of the 3d Brigade, then under the control of the 25th Infantry Division, watch as their grenades explode enemy bunkers near the Cambodian border, January 1970.

sively around base camps. In contrast, the battalion's extremely mobile, light M109 self-propelled howitzers spent so much time on the roads that its Battery A was known simply as the Gypsy Battery. In sum, division artillery was specifically harmonized to render the widest array of weapons available to support the different division missions.

The mission of the 2,000-man division support command was to keep the infantry and artillery supplied and combat-ready at all times. This task varied from building bridges and base camps to moving men and equipment across contested territory. The crucial role provided by the support command included a host of services, many of which were complicated by the division's unusual delta requirements. These varied from assisting ship-to-shore communications to providing the 100 tons of variable munitions consumed by the division each day.

The 9th Supply and Transport Battalion contained only seventy-five trucks and other vehicles yet conducted eighty troop movements and moved 1,900 tons of supplies every week. The battalion was sometimes directed to deliver its cargo and ammunition despite the most hazardous circumstances. During the fierce Tet fighting, the battalion moved nineteen critical convoys carrying 11,154 tons of supplies through contested VC roadblocks and ambushes to the forward lines. The 9th Signal Battalion and 9th Medical Battalion excelled in rendering immediate responsive support throughout the scattered divisional command. Backing up all these division logistical efforts was the 709th Maintenance Battalion, which imported fifteen tons of parts a day into Dong Tam to repair anything from typewriters to trucks.

The 15th Engineer Battalion was primarily designed for light infantry combat support, but the peculiar delta conditions kept the unit working well beyond its intended levels. To supplement this lone battalion, the division was reinforced by the attachment of the 86th and 93d engineer battalions and the 67th Engineer Company. While in Vietnam, the engineers built or repaired more than 450 bridges and constructed 1,100 kilometers of road. The engineers also constructed and maintained all the facilities contained within the firebases and military posts under division control. The tremendous amount of engineering work performed was indicated by the 43,000 board feet of lumber used each week in various projects. Since much of the division work entailed operations around water, the engineers developed various boating skills in order to reach and complete their jobs.

The first to go home

Only two months after Major General Harris W. Hollis assumed command of the 9th Infantry Division in April 1969, President Richard M. Nixon announced that U.S. troop withdrawals from Vietnam would begin with the redeployment of approximately 25,000 men. Five days later MACV decided that a majority of the troops for the redeployment would come from the 9th Infantry Division. The division was chosen because MACV commander General Creighton W. Abrams believed that, in line with his Vietnamization directives, the security of the delta's population should again become the sole responsibility of the South Vietnamese.

The 3d Battalion, 60th Infantry, became the first unit to return from Vietnam to the United States. Within a month, on July 8, the battalion lined up at Tan Son Nhut Air Base where General Abrams gave them a farewell and South Vietnam's president, Nguyen Van Thieu, bestowed Vietnamese flowers and gifts. As the bulk of the division departed over the next few weeks, Maj. Gen. Hollis was reassigned to command the 25th Infantry Division.

The withdrawal of the 9th Infantry Division from Vietnam was not total. Its reconnaissance unit, the 3d Squadron, 5th Cavalry, had been dispatched to the northern DMZ area during early 1968, pending the arrival of the California National Guard 1st Squadron, 18th Cavalry, which was scheduled to arrive in Vietnam that November. When legal maneuvering kept the California unit from deploying, the squadron was forced to remain on duty in I Corps. Another unit of the 9th, the largest left behind in Vietnam, was the 3d Brigade, whose four infantry battalions continued to patrol Long An Province southwest of Saigon under the control of the 25th Infantry Division.

Unfortunately, the 3d Brigade suffered one of the worst tragedies to befall the division on September 17, 1969, at the outset of its independent service. During a brief skirmish in which one soldier was killed on the ground, the brigade command-and-control helicopter collided in midair with a Cobra gunship. Both aircraft were destroyed, and among the twelve men killed in the air were Colonel Dale J. Crittenberger, the brigade commander, and Lieutenant Colonel Leo P. Sikorski, commander of the 5th Battalion, 60th Infantry.

The separate 3d Brigade, the Go Devils, continued to battle nighttime movement of the Vietcong along the waterways between the Mekong Delta and Saigon. One ambush patrol of the 2d Battalion, 47th Infantry, was led by Staff Sergeant Ja Wa Thompson of Bronaugh, Missouri.

"About 8:30 we heard a sampan coming down the river. Some VC across the river began calling to them. We saw five of them in the boat and five on the bank, but there were more than that because we could hear them talking." The brigade soldiers waited until the Vietcong were within fifty meters of them and then opened fire with M16 rifles and M79 grenade launchers. Thompson said, "The VC were too surprised to do much. They hit back at us about five minutes later, but we had no casualties." The river was too swift to allow the men to cross and pursue the enemy immediately, but a later search found ten VC bodies in the ambush area.

The 3d Brigade became famous for this light reconnaissance and ranger-style pattern of fighting, which was referred to as bushmaster warfare. Contacts with the enemy were initiated by small, roving teams of men honed in sniper and ambush tactics. The brigade also contributed forces to the invasion of Cambodia in May and June. It finally returned to the United States from Vietnam in October 1970.

The 9th Infantry Division represented the most diversified American formation fielded in Vietnam, a unit specifically tailored for operations in the difficult and often inundated delta countryside south and west of Saigon. In many respects, the division served as a large laboratory for many concepts and studies not undertaken by normal line units. It was unique and made expensive use of men and equipment; thus, its effectiveness was hard to determine. Many prominent military strategists were quick to point out that Marines should have been used for MACV's riverine force and that the division was composed of too many dissimilar parts to work well as a single command. Since the 9th was never able to pacify the delta com-

pletely, and the division was selected by MACV as the first to leave Vietnam, other critics argued that the division's operations in Vietnam had amounted to a needless luxury made possible by the inflated war budget.

Many of these criticisms were probably valid, but the fact remains that the 9th Infantry Division served effectively to contest Vietcong presence in areas previously left to the enemy without challenge. During the fierce battles of Tet 1968, the division rendered invaluable emergency service in clearing the Saigon capital area and remote delta regions. Without the division's ability to respond in a multitude of ways, including the use of mechanized vehicles, airmobile assaults, and naval landing craft to deliver its troops, the enemy offensive might have been more successful, and the consequences for U.S. foreign policy and the resulting domestic crisis even greater.

In a memorial service at Tan An, officers pray for soldiers of the 3d Brigade, 9th Infantry Division, who were killed in the collision of two helicopters on September 17, 1969.

Mini-Tet

At 4:00 A.M. on Sunday, May 5, 1968, Vietcong rockets and mortars slammed into downtown Saigon, beginning the second major attack in three months on the capital city. On the same day, 119 other attacks throughout the country signaled a renewed nationwide Communist offensive. Though on a much smaller scale than the January Tet offensive, the so-called Mini-Tet, or second-wave, offensive once again shattered any illusions of security within the South Vietnamese capital and swept American troops into the fierce vortex of combat.

For nearly a month before Mini-Tet, the soldiers of the 9th Infantry Division had participated in a huge operation dubbed *Toan Thang* (Complete Victory). Involving more than seventy American and ARVN battalions, the operation formed a defensive ring around Saigon in an attempt to block further Communist infiltration and attacks. Within the city, responsibility for defense belonged to Lieutenant General Le Nguyen Khang, military governor of Saigon and commander of the III Corps area. To counter the Vietcong barrages on May 5, Lt. Gen. Khang at first relied on his elite Vietnamese marine, Ranger, and paratroop units. But during the next two days, as the bitter fighting spread southward into Cholon, Khang decided to request American assistance.

When two Vietcong Local Force battalions seized the crucial Y Bridge over the Kinh Doi Canal on May 7, the 9th Infantry Division's 2d Battalion, 47th Infantry, and 5th Battalion, 60th Infantry, were brought in to dislodge them. After the 9th Division troops retook the bridge and slowly began to move into Cholon, Vietcong snipers began firing at the Americans from rooftops and windows. In an effort to reduce the division's casualties, American firepower was brought to bear. As ARVN units patrolled through Cholon, 9th Infantry Division commanders decided to call for artillery and gunship strikes but forgot to warn their South Vietnamese allies. American bombs and rockets ripped through the city destroying Vietcong strongholds, and the ARVN troops barely escaped with their lives.

Many civilians did not. Some managed to flee to the safety of concrete animal pens in a Cholon slaughterhouse, but nearly 250 died in the counterattacks, while 2,000 homes were destroyed. Although most enemy positions were wiped out, local residents quickly became bitter toward what they perceived as an American overreaction. As one discouraged soldier of the 9th noted, "They're pretty angry with us in Cholon today."

During the next six days, troops of the 2/47 and 5/60 continued to weed out remaining Vietcong positions in bitter street fighting around Cholon. By May 13, most of the fighting in the city had subsided, and 9th Infantry Division troops began mop-up operations in villages south of the Kinh Doi Canal. The capital city was for the moment secure, the enemy routed. Soldiers of the 9th had successfully beaten back the Vietcong, but for many caught in the crossfire, victory came at a high price.

American troops take cover while fighting for the Y Bridge. ARVN units bore the brunt of the enemy attacks in Saigon during Mini-Tet, but elements of the 9th Infantry Division also saw fierce fighting.

After cordoning off a block near the Y Bridge, men of the 9th Division continue to receive sniper fire from behind their APCs. Their call for artillery support turned against them, however, when the friendly fire mistakenly killed two Americans and wounded three others.

As his company begins to withdraw after the errant friendly fire, a soldier of the 9th crawls through a ditch to safety.

A 9th Division soldier wounded in the head during the battle in Saigon receives emergency treatment.

A light observation helicopter searches for pockets of resistance among the charred and bombed-out remains of a section of Cholon at the end of the week's fighting. Heavy American firepower reduced much of Cholon to rubble.

The civilian toll. 9th Infantry Division soldiers mop up around Cholon while a child looks for family and the remains of her home. During Mini-Tet fighting, 2,000 homes were destroyed, leaving tens of thousands of new refugees.

The Tattered Banner

Most of the divisions that fought in Vietnam had long histories of service in several of America's previous wars. When units such as the 1st and 4th infantry divisions returned from Southeast Asia, they added to battle and campaign streamers that dated to World War I, cherished trophies of years of service.

One Army division, however, had virtually no history prior to the war in Indochina. Formed in Vietnam in 1967, the 23d Infantry Division (Americal) took its number and name from a unit formed in World War II, but that was all it had in common with its predecessor. None of its infantry regiments had served in the original division. The composite unit in Vietnam received an instant past in the hope that it would take a proud place alongside other units in American military history.

The reincarnation of the 23d Infantry Division did become famous but not so much for stirring victories as for embarrassing controversy. Though thousands of soldiers served their division and country well, others attracted greater public attention because of

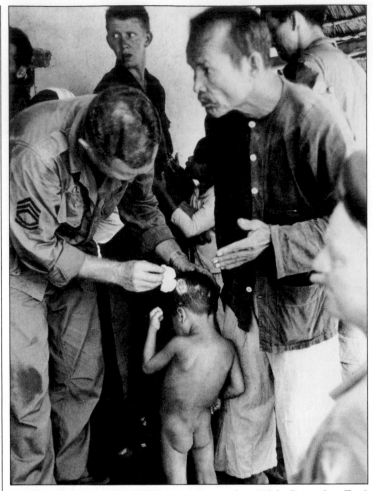

Pacification in action. A sergeant in the 196th Brigade, Task Force Oregon, provides medical treatment to a Vietnamese child in Le Thuy, near Chu Lai, May 1967.

their misconduct, lax discipline, or lack of ability. While the problems were not unique to the division, the Americal was saddled with the burden of becoming a symbol of military failure in Vietnam. Along with the streamers that were added to its flag came anger, shame, and uncertainty as to its ultimate place in the Vietnam experience.

Detour

The first unit of what would later become the 23d Infantry Division was intended not for service in Asia but the Caribbean. In April 1965, a month after the first U.S. Marine battalions landed in Vietnam, fighting broke out in the Dominican Republic after a coup against the ruling junta. As the two sides fought to establish a new government in the streets of Santo Domingo, President Johnson, suspecting Communist involvement, dispatched 23,000 American military personnel, including a brigade of the 82d Airborne Division.

Preceding page. A squad leader in the 4th Battalion, 21st Infantry, 11th Infantry Brigade, shouts instructions after coming under sniper fire southeast of Chu Lai, January 1971.

An international force made up of Caribbean nations restored order in the capital and the U.S. withdrew most of its troops by June, but the 82d Airborne remained there past the new year until Dominican elections could be held. The Pentagon wanted to bring the unit home and replace it with the 196th Infantry Brigade (Light), which had been raised specifically for Caribbean duty. As a light infantry unit it was organized with more men and less heavy equipment than a traditional infantry brigade, in keeping with its projected security role.

However, the brigade's state of preparedness was questionable. Immediately after its activation in the fall of 1965, 2,000 new recruits arrived at the 196th's headquarters at Fort Devens, Massachusetts, but the training personnel of the brigade were almost depleted by the demands for manpower of other Vietnam-bound units. Three high-priority levies claimed 120 sergeants and officers, and the brigade was left with a nucleus of only thirty-four officers and ninety NCOs and enlisted men. Due to the critical shortage of squad leaders, selected recruits were promoted immediately to private first class.

Just before the brigade's scheduled departure for the Caribbean on June 23, 1966, the Pentagon changed its plans. Elections held in the Dominican Republic on June 1 went smoothly, allowing the multinational force to withdraw. Because the 196th was considered ready for combat, however, the Pentagon rescheduled it for deployment to Vietnam within a month.

This change in plans required drastic alterations in a brigade that was originally trained for peace-keeping duty, not heavy combat. Although basic unit training at Camp Drum, New York, had featured counterinsurgency techniques, riot and mob control were emphasized. On the eve of embarkation for a year's tour of duty in Vietnam, soldiers hurriedly took advantage of leaves. All personnel judged unfit for combat were reassigned and replaced. The Army delivered more modern radios and the new M16 automatic rifle. Thus, with unfamiliar equipment and little training for their new assignment the men of the 196th Brigade sailed out of Boston Harbor on July 15, 1966, headed for war.

Departing from the East Coast meant a longer voyage: It took thirty days for the 196th to arrive at Vung Tau. The unit was initially slated for security duty in the Tuy Hoa area, but MACV decided instead to send it to Tay Ninh to secure lines of communication and to augment the efforts of the overworked 25th Infantry Division in the area. The 196th set up a base camp seven kilometers west of Tay Ninh City and prepared for further training and operations in War Zone C.

Its first taste of large-scale combat was hardly encouraging. On November 5, during Operation Attleboro, Vietcong sappers and infantrymen, bolstered by NVA regulars, pinned down most of two battalions from the 25th Division. The 2d Battalion, 1st Infantry, and 4th Battalion, 31st Infantry, of the 196th Brigade headed toward the battle

23d Infantry Division

Arrived Vietnam: September 25, 1967　　　　**Departed Vietnam:** November 29, 1971

Unit Headquarters

Chu Lai　Sept. 1967–Nov. 1971

Commanding Officers

Maj. Gen. Samuel W. Koster　Sept. 1967	Maj. Gen. Lloyd B. Ramsey　June 1969	Maj. Gen. James L. Baldwin　Nov. 1970
Maj. Gen. Charles M. Gettys　June 1968	Maj. Gen. Albert E. Milloy　March 1970	Maj. Gen. Frederick J. Kroesen, Jr.　July 1971

Major Subordinate Units

11th Infantry Brigade (Light) (3/1, 4/3, 1/20, 4/21)	American Scout Infantry Company	16th Aviation Group
196th Infantry Brigade (Light)	H Troop, 17th Cavalry	14th Aviation Battalion
(2/1, 1/6, 3/21, 4/31, 1/46)	6th Battalion, 11th Artillery	123d Aviation Battalion (Airmobile)
198th Infantry Brigade (Light)	1st Battalion, 14th Artillery	212th Aviation Battalion
(1/6, 1/46, 5/46, 1/52)	3d Battalion, 16th Artillery	23d Medical Battalion
F Troop, 8th Cavalry (Air)	3d Battalion, 18th Artillery	23d Supply & Transport Battalion
E Troop, 1st Cavalry (Armored)	1st Battalion, 82d Artillery	26th Engineer Battalion
F Troop, 17th Cavalry (Armored)	3d Battalion, 82d Artillery	523d Signal Battalion
Company E, 51st Infantry	Battery G, 55th Artillery	723d Maintenance Battalion
Company G, 75th Infantry		

808 KIA	8,237 WIA	11 Medals of Honor
(Casualty figures are "Vietnam Era.")		

area to reinforce the besieged men but were quickly engulfed in enemy fire as they haphazardly wandered through the jungle. The men made an urgent call for assistance and the 1st Division entered the area the next day, but the enemy melted into the woods, unwilling to face the larger force.

When questions arose regarding the performance of the 196th Brigade during Attleboro, MACV came to the conclusion that the brigade had cracked in the heat of battle. The 196th commander, Brigadier General Edward H. DeSaussure, was transferred to an artillery command; his brigade was judged too green for heavy combat. It was a jarring introduction to war.

A new division

Regardless of the doubts about the brigade's battle capabilities, the 196th was needed elsewhere in Vietnam. Increased enemy infiltration and attacks near the DMZ signified that the war in the north was escalating after a few months' respite. To counter the new threat General Westmoreland decided to concentrate his two Marine divisions, the 1st (based at Chu Lai) and the 3d (at Da Nang), closer to the DMZ. Although for two years only Marine units had seen action in I Corps, the American commander planned to send an Army force to Chu Lai.

With stateside forces already at a minimum and the military budget precluding the raising of another division within the 1967 fiscal year, Gen. Westmoreland could not request another division from the United States for immediate deployment in I Corps. So MACV decided to raise a provisional task force comprising units already in Viet-

nam. Westmoreland directed his chief of staff, Major General William B. Rosson, to form this group, designated Task Force Oregon after Rosson's home state.

Rosson quickly went about gathering units that could be spared with a minimum of risk. Three infantry brigades were selected for temporary duty: the veteran 3d Brigade, 25th Infantry Division, and 1st Brigade, 101st Airborne Division, as well as the "orphan" 196th Infantry Brigade. The brigades and their support units rushed to Chu Lai, where Task Force Oregon was activated on April 12, 1967, with General Rosson as commander. The 1st Marine Division moved to Da Nang, and the 3d Division established a new base camp farther north at Dong Ha.

The new task force was assigned the former 1st Marine Division area of operations, encompassing Quang Ngai, Quang Tin, and much of Quang Nam provinces. Its basic mission, Rosson recalled, was "to secure the Chu Lai base and to work with South Vietnamese forces in providing a security posture that would allow pacification to forge ahead." For the next several months Task Force Oregon shuttled over the coastal plain and mountains on search-and-destroy missions. For the two veteran brigades, it was business as usual, but the 196th was still learning.

Meanwhile, Westmoreland was planning to make the Army presence in the area permanent. The brigades from the other divisions were on loan, so only the 196th could stay there indefinitely. The Army promised to provide two new brigades from the United States, and on September 25, 1967, Task Force Oregon became the 23d Infantry Division (Americal), a reactivation of the old Americal Division formed in New Caledonia in the Pacific in 1942 (hence the name, an abbreviation of "Americans in New

Caledonia"). The new Army division, commanded by Major General Samuel W. Koster, was the seventh fielded in Vietnam and, like its namesake in World War II, the only one organized overseas.

Though the American Division was activated in September, only one of its planned three infantry brigades, the 196th, was then in Vietnam. To fill out the permanent force, MACV looked to two new units trained in the United States, the 198th Infantry Brigade (Light) and the 11th Infantry Brigade (Light).

It was a rather unconventional beginning to what many came to call the worst American division in Vietnam. But while later events and deeds of its soldiers might be seen as the chief reasons for the 23d's bad reputation, many of the causes of the division's poor performance in Vietnam had already been set in motion before the American ever went into action. These factors, some beyond the control of the division, inhibited performance and helped to make it a star-crossed unit.

From the outset, the training of each of the division's three infantry brigades lacked adequate planning and preparation. The 196th, the senior of the three infant brigades, had been given a crash course in Vietnam warfare after being diverted from Caribbean security duty. The 11th Brigade, activated in Hawaii in 1966, was not yet up to full strength or capability when the Pentagon curtailed its training schedule and ordered it to Vietnam by the end of 1967. As many as 1,300 of its men were found to be "undeployable," either physically unfit for combat or near the end of their enlistment. Hundreds of replacements arrived at Hawaii even as the final deployment date arrived. "Many of the men hardly knew one another, and there was a lack of cohesion in all the units," wrote Lieutenant General William R. Peers, who later directed an Army commission that studied the training of the brigade. The unit training schedule was cut in half, from eight weeks to four, depriving many of adequate orientation for possible combat. New M16 rifles arrived just two weeks before deployment, and the need for range practice cut further into other training.

Still, on December 5 the first units of the 11th Brigade set sail from Hawaii for Vietnam. For all the hasty effort to fill its ranks, the brigade was still more than 700 men short of its authorized strength of almost 4,000. One battalion that had been added late stayed behind for more training and did not make the trip until April 1968. Even after the brigade's arrival in Vietnam, new recruits continued to join it and then required in-country training, further inhibiting the 11th's ability to fight to its full capability. Manpower and training deficiencies, the Peers Commission reported, "resulted in considerable confusion and caused significant turmoil in the brigade's personnel status which was detrimental to deployment preparation."

The preparation of the new 198th Brigade was more suited to Vietnam than that of the 196th, though not particularly for combat. The Pentagon viewed it not as qualified for heavy fighting but rather for a modified security role, specifically to serve as the "Practice Nine Barrier Brigade" in Vietnam, manning observation posts and monitoring electronic sensors planned to be strung along the DMZ. Designed to prevent North Vietnamese infiltration, this application of technology became known as the McNamara Line, after Secretary of Defense Robert McNamara, its principal proponent. Because this line was projected as a static position, the soldiers assigned to it did not need to be a premier fighting outfit—simply an adequate guard detail.

U.S. Marines operated one section of the "fence" in 1967 but ceased work after several NVA attacks suggested that the plan was unfeasible, so there was no McNamara Line for the 198th to defend. Some other assignment was inevitable when it arrived in Vietnam in October 1967, made up of men who were hardly ready for heavy combat.

Even if Gen. Westmoreland was concerned about the training deficiencies and inexperience of his newest brigades, he was more concerned with getting troops to Vietnam as quickly as possible. In the case of the rushed deployment of the 11th Brigade, the general later claimed that his hand was forced from above. The brigade was sent to Vietnam prematurely at the order of the White House, he wrote in his memoirs, "in order to get the troops there in advance of an agreement the President was hoping—vainly, as it turned out—to achieve with the North Vietnamese for a cease-fire and a freeze in troop strength." Westmoreland explained that he committed the 11th Brigade to Duc Pho, in a "quiet sector," for further training under the 3d Brigade, 4th Infantry Division, but the latter brigade was needed for operations elsewhere. Before further training could be completed the Tet offensive forced the 11th into combat. Contrary to Westmoreland's claim, however, the 11th was actually committed to its first operation on January 22, a week *before* Tet.

The accelerated and inappropriate preparation of the American brigades was complicated by their assignment to a region that had bedeviled the Americans since their arrival in Vietnam. "Both Quang Ngai and Quang Tin Provinces had been Viet Cong strongholds for years," the Task Force Oregon commander, General Rosson, recalled. "Both contained remote mountain base areas of importance, and the population, particularly in Quang Ngai Province, traditionally had been a source of recruits and support for the enemy." Working among 1.5 million people in the densely populated coastal lowlands, the U.S. 1st Marine Division had been frustrated by the intransigence of both the peasant and the guerrilla—as well as the inability to distinguish the two—and had never effectively subdued either one. Now, with the shift of the Marines closer to the DMZ, the formidable task of securing one of the most challenging areas of Vietnam was pressed upon the newest division in the Army.

The third factor that restricted the American Division's success was the lack of effective coordination and unity within its ranks. Unlike other divisions in Vietnam, which were generally made up of unified, organic brigades, the 23d was an amalgam of three independent, disjointed brigades that had never worked together. Rather than fusing into one efficient fighting force, the brigades, whether because of each commander's intent, a weak divisional command, or simply bureaucratic inertia, largely operated with little overall administrative and tactical supervision. A colonel who later served as division chief of staff recalled that as a consequence of the Americal's hodgepodge make-up, "The three independent brigades got together and ran things pretty much as they wanted to—with little control and coordination at division headquarters." At more than 20,000 men, the 23d Infantry Division was the Army's largest, but its unwieldy composition and inherent organizational shortcomings threatened to make it one of the most inefficient and ineffective. Soldiers derisively referred to the hybrid outfit as the "Metrecal Division," after the low-calorie meal-substitute drink then being sold in the United States. Another play on

Artillerymen from the 196th Infantry Brigade fire on enemy positions even as a CH-47 Chinook helicopter ferries in another 105MM howitzer at the beginning of Operation Junction City, February 1967.

the unit's name labeled it "The Miracle Division," meaning it would be a wonder if it worked.

Though some expected the division to work out its problems once it had experience in Vietnam under its belt and better-trained troops in its ranks, other factors conspired to prolong these difficulties. The veteran troops of each U.S. division provided in-country orientation and extra training to new arrivals, but in the 23d this arrangement often exacerbated bad habits and ineffective tactics. In addition, the most promising leaders rarely reached the Americal. Officers slated for new combat assignments frequently lobbied to be sent to more established divisions, such as the 1st Cavalry Division (Airmobile) or the 101st Airborne Division, or to respected commanders, who were in turn able to choose the best prospects and leave the rest to less-established units farther down in the pecking order, like the 23d. Thus, with little tradition upon which to draw and lacking clout within the Army bureaucracy, the young American Division was sometimes a dumping ground for officers and NCOs who could not gain assignment to more prestigious divisions. Given this almost perpetual cycle of mediocrity, it was perhaps inevitable that the division was largely unable to better itself in Vietnam. Its subsequent poor performance only fueled the criticism of what was already an ill-fated unit.

Massacre and aftermath

Even as the 198th and 11th brigades arrived for service in late 1967, the 196th was in the field on the first official Americal operations. On November 11, 1967, the brigade took over Operation Wheeler/Wallowa, which was originally two separate operations undertaken by Task Force Oregon against Vietcong guerrillas in Quang Nam and Quang Tin provinces. The 196th concentrated on the Que Son Valley in Quang Tin, assisted by the 1st Squadron, 1st Cavalry, the divisional armored cavalry, and F Troop of the 17th Cavalry, the brigade's ground reconnaissance unit.

Wheeler/Wallowa and other Americal operations over the next several months were characterized mostly by light, scattered contact with guerrillas, punctuated by frequent mining, booby-trap, and sniping incidents. Such was the case on Operation Muscatine, a search-and-destroy operation in Quang Ngai Province initiated by the 198th Brigade and the 3d Brigade, 4th Division, and taken over by the 11th Brigade in January as its first combat operation. The area of operations included two sectors. The 4th Battalion, 3d Infantry, took the western portion while the eastern sector, along the South China Sea, was assigned to a task force commanded by Lieutenant Colonel Frank Barker. Making up the so-called Task Force Barker were what were considered the three best rifle companies in each of the brigade's three battalions: Alpha Company, 3d Battalion, 1st Infantry; Bravo Company, 4th Battalion, 3d Infantry; and Charlie Company, 1st Battalion, 20th Infantry.

On January 22 Task Force Barker began operations north of Quang Ngai City. Though there were few direct confrontations with the enemy, by mid-March more than 100 men had been killed or wounded, mostly from mines and booby traps. A large proportion of casualties occurred in the vicinity of the village of Son My, known as Pinkville for its strong Vietcong presence. The toll from action around Son My was all too apparent to the men of Company C, 1st Battalion, 20th Infantry, as they gathered on the night of March 15. In seven weeks of scattered fighting, only one of its four killed and two of its thirty-eight wounded were caused by direct enemy contact, the rest from hidden explosives and snipers. Many saw a chance for retribution in the next day's mission, a sweep through a hamlet in Son My called My Lai (4).

It took more than a year for the world to learn what happened at My Lai (4) on that fateful day, March 16, 1968. Charlie Company of the 1/20 and Bravo Company of the 4/3, operating in adjacent hamlets, reported 128 enemy killed and three weapons captured. Though it was unusual to recover such a low number of weapons from such a high number of bodies, few seemed to notice and no one questioned the figure. In Saigon, Gen. Westmoreland sent a telegram to General Koster congratulating the men of the two companies for their performance, declaring that the day's action had "dealt enemy heavy blow."

But the action at My Lai was not directed against an enemy force. The men of Charlie Company had run amok in a rampage of murder and rape that left over 300 women, children, and old men dead. Also, at nearby My Khe members of Bravo Company had killed many civilians. As an inquiry panel later reported, Lt. Col. Barker, Colonel Oran Henderson (the brigade commander), and General Koster were aware that noncombatants had been killed that day, but contrary to Army directives these casualties were not reported to the I Corps command or to MACV. In response to later South Vietnamese government inquiries about these casualties, Koster asked Henderson to investigate. When the report reached the division commander's desk it stated that "no civilians were gathered together and shot by US soldiers." Koster notified the Vietnamese officials that the matter had been investigated and he was satisfied there was no substance to the suspicions. "I just didn't feel an incident like this was apt to have happened," he later testified.

But the matter did not die. In March 1969 a soldier who was not at My Lai but had heard of the incident from other soldiers wrote a letter about it to several officials, including Gen. Westmoreland, by then Army chief of staff. A resulting Army inquiry and a larger investigation, headed by Lt. Gen. Peers, former commander of the 4th Infantry Division, led to charges of dereliction of duty against twelve officers, ranging from lieutenant to general. Maj. Gen. Koster, then superintendent of the U.S. Military Academy, was censured and reduced one rank to brigadier general. His assistant, Brigadier General George Young, was also censured. Only Col. Henderson was tried and acquitted; the others charged with dereliction of duty never came to trial. Others involved were never charged: Lt. Col. Barker died in a helicopter crash shortly after My Lai, and many soldiers in his task force had left the Army and were thus exempt from court-martial.

In addition, four junior officers and nine enlisted men were charged with war crimes; all were either acquitted or never prosecuted, except for one. First Lieutenant William L. Calley, Jr., was convicted of the murder of twenty-two civilians and given a life sentence. The term was soon reduced to ten years, and in 1974 Calley was paroled.

For many, the My Lai incident was no surprise, given the 11th Brigade's poor training and leadership. General

Peers later expressed shock at the "lackadaisical" training given the men in Hawaii. Numerous soldiers later testified that they could not remember receiving any lessons in the Law of War. Only half of the brigade had received copies of MACV's "Nine Rules" and other conduct guidelines upon arrival. (In a bizarre yet prophetic typographical error, corrected after a few days, a regulation in the brigade's combat operations manual read, "Combatants will exercise utmost care to insure maximum noncombatant casualties and property destruction.") For the men of Task Force Barker and the 11th Brigade, acts of random or excessive violence were apparently common; some units in the 11th, wrote one military historian, "were little better than organized bands of thugs, with the officers eager participants in the body count game." In the field the 11th picked up a new sobriquet: The Butcher Brigade.

Though it was supposedly one of the finest units in the 11th Brigade, Charlie Company hardly met high standards. One former member recalled that while on training maneuvers in both Hawaii and Vietnam, his platoon kept getting lost because its leader could not read a compass.

Members of Calley's platoon derided their lieutenant: "Everybody used to joke about Calley," said Allen Boyce, an eighteen-year-old rifleman. "He was one of those guys they just take off the street." Charles W. Hall said, "Calley reminded me of a kid, a kid trying to play war."

For all the shock concerning the revelations of My Lai, however, little actual knowledge of the incident spread to soldiers in the 23d Infantry Division. The division never officially reported it to its men, and whatever else they learned came largely from letters or newspapers from home. When the story broke in November 1969, a *New York Times* reporter questioned Americal soldiers in the field and was surprised to hear that the vast majority had not heard of the incident and most were doubtful that it had taken place. When told some of the details of My Lai, many of the men interviewed expressed the same emotions voiced by men of Charlie Company: hatred of the Vietnam-

Soldiers of Task Force Barker begin the destruction of My Lai (4) on March 16, 1968, in this official Army photograph, part of the Army investigation's classified file.

ese, frustration with the nature of the fighting, and anger at the loss of comrades. "I'd have done the same thing," said one soldier. "The company must have been hit hard before the action," one private first class sympathized. "You get your buddy next to you blown away, you ain't gonna love the dinks."

Action in the mountains

After he had closed the book on My Lai—albeit temporarily—in the spring of 1968, General Koster had other concerns. Especially significant in May was the North Vietnamese pressure on the remote Special Forces camp at Kham Duc, 130 kilometers west of Chu Lai. As an NVA division gathered in the hills on May 10, Company A of the 1st Battalion, 46th Infantry, 198th Brigade, airlifted into the camp. Joining it was the 2d Battalion, 1st Infantry, 196th Brigade, which for the past week had been fighting alongside U.S. Marines near the DMZ. By seven o'clock that evening the Americans were dug in around the base.

A continuous rain of mortar shells hit the camp, causing frightened CIDG troops to flee from their trenches along the perimeter to bunkers within the base. The Americal soldiers remained in their forward positions and returned the fire. The division would ultimately claim 300 enemy dead at Kham Duc. But time was running out for the camp.

In the early morning darkness of May 12 the NVA attacked the outlying trench positions, four of which fell by 9:30. More than twenty U.S. soldiers were lost in the fight. The battered Americal troops fell back into the camp with orders to evacuate Kham Duc.

Panic broke out as evacuation aircraft landed. Some men of the 1/46 pushed past Vietnamese civilians to fill the aircraft first, leaving many Vietnamese on the ground. Outraged Green Berets loaded 150 civilians onto another Air Force plane, but that aircraft was hit by enemy fire as it was taking off and it crashed, killing all on board.

At 4:33 P.M. the last plane took off. The only people remaining on the ground at Kham Duc were North Vietnamese. A key outpost in Quang Tin Province had fallen, and many Americal soldiers had failed to distinguish themselves in the fight's final moments.

General Koster left for his new post at West Point in May and was replaced by Major General Charles M. Gettys, who continued the larger divisional operations for most of the year. The search-and-destroy sweeps of Operation Wheeler/Wallowa in Quang Nam and Quang Tin provinces continued into November and registered a final tally of 9,908 enemy dead at a cost of 683 American soldiers killed. In another ambitious operation, Burlington Trail, the 196th joined with troops of the 198th, the 1st Squadron, 1st Cavalry, and the 26th and 39th engineer battalions to open the road from Tam Ky to Tien Phuoc, a route that had been under enemy control for four years.

Both operations were terminated on the same day,

November 11, 1968, but Americal and NVA units continued to clash in the mountains west of Chu Lai, especially the Hiep Duc/Que Son area. On the morning of November 17, Company D of the 5th Battalion, 46th Infantry, 198th Brigade, was following a trail up a heavily wooded ridge in the Nui Chom range, thirty-five kilometers from Chu Lai, when it came upon an NVA base camp. After machine-gunners fired into the bamboo hootches and the camp appeared deserted, two platoons marched in. The enemy was waiting. Automatic-weapons fire pinned down both platoons and wounded the company commander and first sergeant.

Gunships of C Troop, 8th Cavalry, and artillery pounded the camp, enabling the Americans to pull back and establish a defensive position for the night. A two-company sweep into the area the next day confirmed that the enemy had withdrawn farther into the mountains, so on November 19 all four companies of the battalion hooked up for a pursuit northward up Nui Chom Mountain. Companies A and D took the western flank, Company C took the middle, and Company B covered the east.

Delta Company had the first contact when NVA gunners opened up from sunken bunkers covered with dirt, bamboo, and foliage. The Americal soldiers poured automatic fire and grenades on the enemy positions, but for several hours the going was slow as the men moved from bunker to bunker in the misty monsoon rain. "We more or less leap-frogged up the trail knocking out the enemy bunkers as we went," recalled Staff Sergeant Phillip Madlin. "One of our biggest problems, and the one that really slowed us up, was that the enemy bunkers were always above us. They were about three-fourths below ground, and when you first looked at them they looked like an ordinary rise in the ground. Our point men usually couldn't spot them until they were fired upon."

Meanwhile, Alpha Company had also become engaged by fire from NVA fortifications. Nineteen-year-old Corporal Michael J. Crescenz grabbed an M60 machine gun and ran 100 meters uphill toward a bunker, firing into the small enemy gun port as he went. Two NVA soldiers fell dead. Crescenz entered the rear of another bunker and killed two more soldiers, then headed for the remaining fortification. A bullet ripped through his right thigh, but he knocked out the enemy gun with a burst from his M60.

The other Americans rushed up behind the corporal, but automatic fire suddenly opened up from another position. Again Crescenz ran forward to stifle the enemy gun, but this time he never reached it. Five meters from the bunker he was felled by enemy bullets. Alpha Company overran the position, but Michael Crescenz died from his wounds. He was later awarded a posthumous Medal of Honor for his bravery.

For the next four days the men of the 5/46 continued up the hill, its sheer sections wet and slippery from the tropical rain. Climbing hand over hand in some places

Led by ARVN soldiers, heavily laden troops of the 5th Battalion, 46th Infantry, 198th Infantry Brigade, tramp through the woods of the Batangan Peninsula in October 1969.

and still challenged by enemy bunkers, the men took up to an hour to move 100 meters. Helicopter gunships strafed the area and fighter-bombers dropped 500- and 750-pound bombs on the top and north side of the mountain to soften enemy positions and to prevent retreat. Finally on the morning of November 23, the Americans rushed the hilltop and found a large NVA base camp, including a well-stocked hospital and pharmacy. The command post contained a large generator and telephone switchboard with wires running to each of the 200 underground bunkers.

The seven-day battle netted sixty-six NVA dead and a substantial number of enemy weapons and supplies. The 4th Battalion, 31st Infantry, lost four dead and thirty-three wounded. The slugging, hard-fought battles at Nui Chom and Hiep Duc were reminiscent of those fought by the division twenty-five years earlier. The story of Nui Chom, declared the division magazine, "sounds like it was taken from the pages of a World War II American history book."

While some Americal soldiers fought these vicious battles in the mountains, the division's primary purpose was pacification of the population, especially along the coastal plain. The troops took part in village visits, offering their services in the populated areas near Chu Lai and Quang Ngai but always remained on guard for hidden mines and booby traps. There, some soldiers seemed to forge good

relationships with many civilians. "We knew a lot of people in the villages," recalled Doug Fairchild, who was a sergeant with the 11th Brigade. "They knew us by name, and we developed some friendships, especially among the older children." The situation changed farther inland, Fairchild remembered: "In the mountains the villages were pretty much VC-controlled, so therefore you met a lot of hostility and suspicion."

But counterguerrilla operations in the villages were not restricted to peaceful visits, as was the case in Operation Russell Beach. On January 13, 1969, troops of the Americal Division combined with U.S. Marines and Navy Swift boats and ARVN infantry in a complete cordon of the Batangan Peninsula, a long-time Vietcong stronghold only twelve kilometers up the coast from Quang Ngai City. Along the fifteen-kilometer-long neck of the cape, the 4th Battalion, 3d Infantry of the 11th Brigade and the 5th Battalion, 46th Infantry of the 198th stood in the middle of a human chain designed to sweep across Batangan. The intention of the mission, said Lieutenant Colonel Jack C. Davis, commander of the 4/3, was "to clear the area on foot,

step by step, to locate every tunnel and bunker, destroy the minefields and empty 'Charlie's breadbasket.' "

By noon the soldiers had started their deliberate walk and were knee-deep, and in some cases waist-deep, in mud. One rifleman described it as "trying to walk through a mountain of C-ration peanut butter." But the action was timed to coincide with the rainy season, explained Brigadier General Howard H. Cooksey, Americal assistant commander and operation leader, "so the enemy's tunnels would be flooded and no good to him." Though the men cursed the rain, they saw Cooksey's point. Lieutenant Colonel Ronald R. Richardson, commander of the 5/46, recalled seeing VC suspects literally flushed out of flooded tunnels. "They had been in water so long that their skin was shriveled up like a prune."

While the infantry tightened the cordon, division psychological operations teams went into action to evacuate civilians from the area. A helicopter rigged with a 1,000-watt amplifier cruised over the villages blaring instructions telling people to gather for the trip to the Combined Holding and Interrogation Center (CHIC) near Quang Ngai, where the population would be screened for possible

Firefight in the Hiep Duc Valley. A soldier of Company B, 4th Battalion, 31st Infantry, races forward under fire to bring ammunition to a machine-gun position, August 1969.

Vietcong. The first group ferried out was confused and frightened, for the Vietcong had warned that anyone who went with the Americans would be forced into labor camps at Cam Ranh Bay. When the helicopter arrived at the CHIC, the refugees were convinced that they were at Cam Ranh and refused to disembark until the province chief assured them they were actually only a few kilometers from their homes and were not going to be held captive.

After four days of pacification and relocation, the cordon line began to move east. Staying no more than 10 meters apart, the men moved only about 500 meters a day, a slow pace made necessary, General Cooksey said, because they "looked under every rock and behind every bush." To facilitate the search, aircraft dropped an average of 600 flares every night, bringing almost around-the-clock daylight to Batangan. Most American and ARVN casualties were caused by mines and booby traps. A platoon leader with the 4th Battalion, 3d Infantry, was shocked by the frequency of mines: "I've been over here in the field for about eight months now, and this is the most treacherous area I've ever seen."

On February 3 the line reached the sea, and the men then backtracked. In scattered action more than 210 Vietcong were killed and over thirty tons of foodstuffs captured. One of the largest "relocation" efforts undertaken displaced almost 12,000 inhabitants of Batangan to Quang Ngai. Included in this total were almost 600 who were adjudged enemy soldiers or agents. One high-ranking American officer declared the operation "a definite success," though he admitted that "the resettlement of the peninsula and indoctrination of the people may take a long time." Russell Beach officially ended on July 21.

Hiep Duc and Khe Sanh

Action in the region tapered off in the summer months. General Gettys was replaced by Major General Lloyd B. Ramsey, who took steps to integrate the commanders and men of the nearby 2d ARVN Division into the operations of his division. ARVN forces, whose primary task had been pacification, assumed a greater role in combat missions. With disengagement as the newly announced American policy, the 23d Infantry Division became a training and security unit and wound down its offensive operations.

But the Americans and North Vietnamese still sparred over strategic areas like the Hiep Duc Valley, the location of a refugee center of 4,000 civilians near Que Son. Local Communist propagandists had bragged that Hiep Duc would be theirs by September, so patrols of the 4th Battalion, 31st Infantry, were especially wary as they moved from their firebase into the hot and humid valley. When Bravo and Delta companies came under fire on August 18, they withdrew and called in reinforcements. Companies from three other battalions—the 3d Battalion, 21st Infantry, 2d Battalion, 1st Infantry, and 1st Battalion, 46th Infantry—were airlifted into the narrow valley to face what was said to be 4,000 NVA regulars.

Late in the afternoon of August 18, helicopters of F Troop, 8th Cavalry, fired on enemy positions as a platoon of Company C of the 4/31 moved forward to assist Company B, which had been pinned down. "Shell casings from the gunships streamed down on us," recalled the platoon's commander, First Lieutenant James Simms. As the battered NVA withdrew, Simms's men advanced to an abandoned enemy position on a moist slope. "The gunships made another pass, so we had to hit the dirt," the lieutenant said. "It was then that we found out the ground was soaked with blood—not dew!" The NVA who just left the hill had clearly taken heavy casualties.

The NVA fiercely fought for each of the hills as the Americans pressed forward. On the morning of the nineteenth, a helicopter carrying Lieutenant Colonel Eli P. Howard, Jr., the 3/21 commander, and seven others, includ-

Teeth clenched from the tension of battle, a soldier at the Bravo Company command post peers out into the bush during the fighting at Hiep Duc.

A soldier awaits helicopter evacuation after being wounded in the head at Hiep Duc. Bravo Company lost twenty-eight men in one day of fierce combat.

What's in a Name

The 23d Infantry Division took pride in referring to itself as "the only named division in Vietnam." But while MACV and divisional documents labelled it simply the "Americal Division," the Army insisted on referring to the unit's numerical designation, unwilling to exhibit any favoritism by using the name.

Virtually every one of the other American divisions had at least one nickname, although unlike the Americal, they were not authorized for use in official documents. Monikers such as the "Big Red One" (1st Infantry Division), the "First Team" (1st Cavalry Division), and the "Screaming Eagles" (101st Airborne Division) signified a pride and, it was hoped, instilled ferocity in each of the members of those units. These and other names—"Tropic Lightning" (25th Infantry Division) and the "Old Reliables" (9th Infantry Division)—harked back to the units' service in two world wars.

Appellations of smaller units dated back even further. Prior to World War I, when the Army consisted of regiments lacking divisional ties, most units had names born in noted battles or campaigns of the previous hundred years. The 7th Infantry Regiment, for example, became known as the "Cottonbalers" after its men fired from behind bales at advancing British troops during the battle of New Orleans in the War of 1812. The men of the 35th Infantry called themselves the "Cacti" for their service in the western desert against Indians in the nineteenth century.

Some nicknames had more obscure origins. Service in the China Relief Expedition during the Boxer Rebellion of 1900 gave names to the 9th Infantry ("Manchus") and the 14th Infantry ("Golden Dragons"). The "Wolfhounds" of the 27th Infantry and "Polar Bears" of the 31st Infantry traced their names back to their participation in an abortive American expedition into Siberia in 1918-19, after the Bolshevik revolution.

Many other regiments obtained their designations during Twentieth Century wars. The "Ready Rifles" of the 52d Infantry and the "Lions of Cantigny" of the 28th Infantry gained fame for gallantry in France during World War I. In World War II the 75th Infantry, an elite ranger unit led by General Frank D. Merrill, called itself "Merrill's Marauders." For its staunch defense under siege during the Battle of the Bulge, the 327th Infantry (Airborne) became known as the "Bastogne Bulldogs."

Though reorganization before Vietnam broke up the old regiments into independent and sometimes scattered battalions, each battalion in the parent regiment retained its old nickname. Some even added new ones. After operations in the mud of the Rung Sat Zone east of Saigon in the fall of 1966, the "Vanguards" of the 1st Battalion, 18th Infantry, took on a new name: the "Swamp Rats."

---

ing a news-photographer, was hit by enemy fire and crashed beyond the American lines. For the next five days Col. Howard's troops fought to reach the wreckage, but the NVA held them back with vicious fighting. "It was hell out there," recalled Private First Class Barry Daniels. "The NVA were all over the place with weapons and packs. We couldn't move 100 meters without being attacked." Reinforced by the 1st Battalion, 46th Infantry, and the 2d Battalion, 7th Marines, the Americans reached Howard and the others on August 24 but found them all dead.

The fighting in the Hiep Duc area raged for five more days. The exhausted American soldiers continued to push through a labyrinth of enemy bunkers and trenches as artillery from three surrounding firebases cut into the rocky slopes. The strain of the protracted battle soon took a psychological as well as physical toll.

During the five days, Alpha Company of the 3d Battalion, 21st Infantry, had taken heavy casualties while assaulting a North Vietnamese position on Nui Lon Mountain. At dawn on August 25 Lieutenant Colonel Robert Bacon, who had taken over the battalion command upon the death of Col. Howard, ordered the company to make another attempt. The reply of Alpha Company commander Lieutenant Eugene Schurtz, Jr., was shocking: "I'm sorry, sir," he radioed the battalion commander, "but my men refused to go. We cannot move out."

Incredulous, Bacon asked Schurtz to repeat his message. "Have you told them what it means to disobey orders under fire?" he asked.

"I think they understand," Schurtz replied, "but some of them simply had enough—they are broken. There are boys here who have only 90 days left in Vietnam. They want to go home in one piece."

Bacon told the lieutenant to assure the company that the bunkers were now empty and its mission was only to recover their dead. Still the men did not move. Bacon ordered Schurtz to move ahead and sent his executive officer and Sergeant Okey Blankenship, a combat veteran, to the men of Alpha Company to "give them a pep talk and a kick in the butt."

Arriving at the position, the two men found a group of exhausted, frightened young soldiers. One of them complained that they had suffered too much and should not have to go on. Sgt. Blankenship told him that another company had only fifteen men but was still in battle (an exaggeration), then challenged the men: "Maybe they have got something a little more than what you have got."

"Don't call us cowards! We are not cowards!" the soldier shouted, running toward Blankenship. The sergeant simply turned and walked down the trail toward the ridge where Lt. Schurtz waited. The men of Company A stirred, picked up their rifles, and followed him, ready to fight again. Because a company commander is ultimately responsible for the performance of his men, Schurtz was later relieved of his command. The men of Alpha Company were never reprimanded for their refusal to obey orders.

Alpha Company was not the only unit to disobey orders or to refuse to fight in Vietnam. A few months later, a platoon of the 25th Infantry Division defied orders to advance into combat. In 1970 the Army reported an increase in both individual and unit refusals to fight. But Alpha Company's action was suggestive of the difficulties that dogged the Americal Division. Once again the 23d's record had been blemished and commendable performance on the battlefield was tarnished by a breakdown in discipline and doubts about the quality of its soldiering.

After Hiep Duc, combat in the 23d Infantry Division's area of operations dropped off significantly as the rainy monsoon and typhoon season brought flooding and heavy rains to the coastal and mountain regions. Most Americal operations in 1970 were small-scale security operations in Quang Ngai Province, conducted from the several firebases that covered much of the area and served as the battalions' headquarters. As the American role in the war diminished all over Vietnam, U.S. troops conducted fewer and less-ambitious operations and seldom strayed too far from their camps, a condition later referred to as "firebase psychosis."

This new use of American troops meant that South Vietnamese forces would now undertake the more ambitious offensive operations, with U.S. troops acting only in an advisory or support capacity. This relationship applied especially to Lam Son 719, the ARVN thrust into Laos in February 1971. Under the provisions of the Cooper-Church amendment, U.S. ground forces were to fight only in South Vietnam and not cross the border. American helicopter pilots, exempt from the ban on ground troops in Laos, could fly missions over the border in support of the Vietnamese.

So while ARVN units were in Laos during the fateful operation, American combat, engineer, and logistical troops maintained a rear security post at the former Marine base at Khe Sanh. In addition to its five assault helicopter companies flying over the border, the 23d Infantry Division deployed its 1st Squadron, 1st Cavalry, as part of the base defense force. H Troop, 17th Cavalry, and F Troop of the 8th Cavalry escorted convoys along Route 9. Two battalions from the 11th Infantry Brigade—the 4th Battalion, 3d Infantry, and the 2d Battalion, 1st Infantry—patrolled the area south of the DMZ, supported by brigade artillery at Khe Sanh.

The operation, unlike the May 1970 push into Cambodia, was a virtual disaster on both sides of the border. The enemy was only too willing to defend its bases in Laos, and by March ARVN units were fleeing back toward Khe Sanh, leaving damaged armor and helicopters behind. Along Route 9 two platoons of B Troop of the usually reliable 1st Squadron, 1st Cavalry, suddenly refused orders to move ahead to secure a downed helicopter and some crippled APCs and had to be replaced by another troop that carried out the assignment. The troop com-

23d Infantry Division (Americal) Area of Operations

mander was relieved of his command, causing journalists to recall Alpha Company's refusal to fight at Hiep Duc nineteen months earlier.

The soldiers at the Khe Sanh base also came under daily mortar attacks and, like their Marine predecessors in 1968, dug in while their casualties mounted. An especially crippling blow came in the early morning hours of March 23, 1971, when NVA sappers slipped into the camp and blew up the main ammunition dump. Explosions and fire lit up the sky for three hours. Three Americans were killed and another thirteen wounded. Finally on April 7, after the last ARVN soldiers had quit Laos, Khe Sanh was once again abandoned, an unwanted outpost in a waning war.

U.S. forces were in a defensive posture and the South Vietnamese army was shell-shocked from the debacle in Laos, so the enemy became more audacious, continually attacking firebases throughout 1971. The most notorious and damaging attack came, as misfortune would have it, on a 23d Infantry Division base.

Located fifty kilometers west of Chu Lai, Fire Support Base Mary Ann was then the westernmost Americal outpost in Quang Tin Province. The 1st Battalion, 46th Infantry, now under control of the 196th Brigade, used it as its base for patrols in the area but had encountered no evidence of enemy regulars, and the camp was due to be turned over to the South Vietnamese. Many of its men and

much equipment had already been shipped out, and a feeling of lethargy seemed to have imbued most of the remaining 231 Americans, who were looking forward to redeployment to Chu Lai, then home to the United States. Staying at Mary Ann "was sort of like a stand down, a rest period," said one soldier.

The sense of security ended in the early morning hours of March 28, when at least fifty NVA sappers, clad only in shorts and smeared with black grease, breached the concertina wire, sensors, and trip flares around the camp, undetected by any of the guards. As Americans and South Vietnamese soldiers huddled in their bunkers from a simultaneous mortar attack, the marauders, armed with satchel charges, RPGs, and automatic weapons, roamed the camp virtually uncontested. They moved with brutal precision, knocking out the base's tactical operations center, helicopter refueling stations, howitzers, and other key locations within minutes. When an American captain tried to turn on the base alarm system and use the phone, he found that both lines had been cut and quickly realized the attackers "had an intimate knowledge of the firebase." Though the battalion had encountered no enemy troops, they had all the time been nearby, watching and waiting.

Traveling through the camp from south to north, small teams of sappers moved through the trench lines and tossed explosives and tear gas grenades at fifteen bunkers. Many of the Americans were unaware that the enemy had entered the camp until explosions rocked their own positions. Lieutenant Colonel William P. Doyle, the battalion commander, was unsure of what was happening until a satchel charge exploded nearby, wounding him in the legs. Some men stayed in the bunkers until the attack was over or until they were forced out by explosions. Others scrambled into position and immediately came face to face with gun-toting NVA. The surprise was total, the defense nonexistent.

Thirty minutes after the attack started, the intruders withdrew under covering fire. Newly arrived helicopter gunships caught some sappers on the wire, but most slipped away, leaving fifteen dead. FSB Mary Ann was in flames, its command centers and bunkers heavily damaged. All twelve officers lay dead or wounded. A total of thirty Americans were killed in the attack, and another eighty-two were wounded. Only one of the twenty ARVN soldiers present was wounded; ignoring their own inactivity, the Americans complained bitterly that the South Vietnamese had made little effort to assist them. But their help would have mattered little in the debacle. The action at Mary Ann was the Americal Division's largest single combat loss in over a year and one of the most damaging attacks on a firebase during the war.

An ammunition dump at the Khe Sanh base explodes, emitting a shower of rockets, during an enemy sapper attack in the early morning of March 23, 1971.

When the smoke had cleared in the morning, the shattered 1/46 started to pick up the pieces. The acting battalion commander, Major Donald Potter, flew into a rage and ordered the burning of the bodies of five sappers that had been taken earlier to the trash dump. For the next several days the corpses smoldered among the garbage while the Army tried to figure out what had happened at Mary Ann. "Somebody out there [at] Mary Ann screwed up," an Americal sergeant declared.

The MACV inspector general undertook an investigation and concluded that the camp's defenses had been sorely inadequate and many soldiers derelict in their duty. Because the enemy had never probed the base and the battalion was anticipating evacuation, its men had grown complacent and had ignored basic defensive procedures. Many were unfamiliar with the base's defensive plan or the location of claymore mines, trip flares, grenades, and M60 machine guns.

Much of the blame for the tragedy was placed on Lt. Col. Doyle, an eighteen-year veteran whose record up to then had been exemplary. The Army charged him with "substandard performance of duty" in failing to oversee proper defense of FSB Mary Ann. Doyle requested a court-martial hearing at which he could refute the charges, but his request was never granted. In April 1972 Lieutenant Colonel Doyle was formally reprimanded by Secretary of the Army Robert F. Froehlke.

Four other officers were disciplined, including Doyle's operations officer. The others were chastised not because of the attack but for the incineration of enemy bodies that took place the next day, a clear violation of the Geneva Convention. The inspector general reported that both Major General James L. Baldwin, the division commander, and Colonel William S. Hathaway, the brigade commander, had learned of the burnings on April 1 but had taken no disciplinary action. Baldwin admitted he had ordered the burnt remains buried and had not informed his superiors of the incident. The Army relieved him of his command in July and later placed a letter of admonition in his file. Col. Hathaway was denied promotion and, like Col. Doyle, was formally reprimanded.

While FSB Mary Ann was yet another stain on the record of the 23d Infantry Division, it also seemed to reflect more broadly the state of the American force disengaging from Vietnam. At the conclusion of his report, the inspector general urged that the incident be put into "the proper perspective," declaring that it

could very well have happened to other units of the 23d Infantry Division or to like combat units in Vietnam, today. The reduced level of combat activity and the increasing publicity by the news media focusing upon ending of the war tend to create complacency among both the troops and their commanders. Coupled with this is the effect of anti-Vietnam and anti-military attitudes within CONUS and the growth of permissiveness within the military establishment.

In the fall of 1971, as the repercussions of Mary Ann were still being felt in the 23d Infantry Division, the unit prepared to leave Vietnam. The huge compound at Chu Lai was scheduled to be turned over to the 2d ARVN Division, but before that was done the division suffered yet another blow, this time at the hands of the weather. On October 23 Typhoon Hester, the worst storm in twenty-seven years, swept in from the South China Sea and flattened half the base, including several of the division's supposedly typhoon-proof hangars. Most of the Americal's helicopters, desperately needed by the South Vietnamese, were lost.

Not all of the division was going home: The first unit in was to be the last out. The 196th Brigade became independent once again and was retained by XXIV Corps, the U.S. Army command at Da Nang, for security in the rocket belt around that city. The rest of Quang Nam Province was virtually conceded to the enemy. "Damn," said Private First Class Billy Roddie while on patrol in the mud and thorn bushes near Da Nang. "People at home just don't know that we're still out here fighting and the Vietcong are still shooting at us." But contact was rare, avoided by both sides. Finally on August 23, 1972, the 3d Battalion, 21st Infantry of the 196th took down its colors at Da Nang. It was the last American infantry battalion to serve in Vietnam.

The 23d Infantry Division, born in Vietnam, was also deactivated there. More than 17,500 men in its ranks had been killed or wounded in the war, more than four times the number of Americal casualties in World War II. Eleven soldiers were awarded the nation's highest military decoration, the Medal of Honor, and thousands more had won lesser awards. This notable total, and the sacrifice it represents, were a source of pride for a much-maligned division.

The men of the 23d bristled at criticism of their division in later years. For them, as well as those who had served in other American divisions, what was to be treasured and remembered were their ties and loyalties to smaller units—brigades, battalions, companies, platoons—and to their combat buddies. In the scattered, sometimes isolated conflict that was Vietnam, these links were the truer sources of identification and pride. Years after coming home, C. Tony May, who served with the 196th Brigade, recalled, "The Americal was the umbrella of the 196th, and we had unit pride, but when you're there for a year, it's hard to say, 'Hey, I'm part of this whole division here.' We were a company, you know, which was part of a battalion, which was part of a brigade, and I had a lot of pride in my unit. I still do."

An Americal sniper team moves through the high grass after being dropped off by a UH-1 helicopter, November 1970. A silencer is attached to the M16 of the soldier in center.

Bibliography

I. Books and Articles

"Ap Bau Bang." *Danger Forward*, September 1967.

"Ap Nha Mat." *Danger Forward*, September 1967.

"Ap Tau O." *Danger Forward*, December 1967.

Apple, R. W. "McNamara Hints He'll Hold Down Troop Increase." *New York Times*, July 12, 1967.

Armstrong, Kenneth. " 'Bobcats' Beating Jungle for VC Are Refueled by Helicopters." *Cleveland Plain Dealer*, November 18, 1966.

Arnett, Peter. "Radioman Leads Defense." *Washington Star*, November 7, 1966.

"The Battle of Ap Gu." *Danger Forward*, March 1968.

"The Battle of Minh Thanh Road." *Danger Forward*, December 1967.

Becker, Sgt. Bill. "Operation Nets Eleven Hundred Cong Dead." *Tropic Lightning News*, December 2, 1966.

"Belmont Hero in Line for Medal of Honor." *Boston Globe*, November 8, 1966.

The Big Red One (division yearbook). 1967-1970.

"Billings." *Danger Forward*, March 1968.

Black, 1st Lt. J. N. "FSB Diamond Thwarts Fierce Attack." *Tropic Lightning News*, March 10, 1969.

"The Blackhorse in the Fishhook." *The Blackhorse*, Winter 1971.

Blumenson, Martin. *The Many Faces of George S. Patton, Jr.* U.S. Air Force Academy, 1972.

———, ed. *The Patton Papers.* 2 vols. Houghton Mifflin, 1972, 1974.

Buckley, Tom. "G.I. Force Evades Trap and Kills Ninety." *New York Times*, July 22, 1967.

———. "Offensive Is Said to Pinpoint Enemy's Strength." *New York Times*, February 2, 1968.

Butterfield, Fox. "War Hasn't Changed for the Men Who Stay Behind." *New York Times*, November 12, 1971.

Casey, SFC Ben. "NVA Die in VC Valley." *The Ivy Leaf*, January 12, 1969.

Chang, Al. "Viet Cong Springs from Earth To Attack Camp." *St. Louis Post-Dispatch*, February 8, 1966.

"Change of Command." *Danger Forward*, September 1968.

Crawford, Sgt. Bill. "In Defense of Hiep Duc." *Americal*, January 1970.

Devine, Robert A., ed. *Exploring the Johnson Years.* Univ. of Texas Pr., 1981.

Dunstan, Simon. *Vietnam Tracks: Armor in Battle, 1945-1975.* Osprey, 1982.

"Enari History Ended on April 15, 1970." *The Ivy Leaf*, November 1970.

Endsley, Mark C. "Ninth Infantry Division Activated." *Army Information Digest*, March 1966.

Faas, Horst, and Peter Arnett. "Co. A Cries: No! We've Had Enough." *New York Daily News*, August 26, 1969.

Farago, Ladislas. *Patton: Ordeal and Triumph.* Ivan Obelensky, 1964.

Farley, Col. Roy W. "Blackhorse Report II." *Armor*, March-April 1968.

First in Vietnam. 173d Airborne Brigade, 1969.

Foner, Jack D. *Blacks and the Military in American History.* Praeger, 1974.

"Fourth Carson-Bound." *The Ivy Leaf*, November 22, 1970.

"Fresh U.S. Units Struck by Forces of North Vietnam." *New York Times*, October 30, 1966.

"FSPB Julie." *Danger Forward*, March 1969.

"FSPB Rita." *Danger Forward*, March 1969.

Goldstein, Joseph, et al. *The My Lai Massacre and Its Coverup: Beyond the Reach of Law?* Free Pr., 1976.

Gooding, 2d Lt. Mack. "Manchus Halt VC Regiment." *Tropic Lightning News*, January 13, 1969.

Green, 1st Lt. Cecil. "The Noose Around Batangan." *Americal*, May 1969.

Greene, Robert E. *Black Defenders of America: 1775-1973.* Johnson Publishing Co., 1974.

Gunderman, Capt. George L. "Ambush!" *Armor*, May-June 1967.

Hawkins, Sgt. George. "Nui Chom Mountain." *Americal*, May 1969.

"The Hell at Mary Ann." *Newsweek*, April 12, 1971.

Hersch, Seymour. *My Lai Four: A Report on the Massacre and Its Aftermath.* Random, 1970.

"History of the Blackhorse." *The Blackhorse*, December 1968.

Hybel, SP5 Alex, and SP4 Charles Zewe. "Fourth Called into Cambodia." *The Ivy Leaf*, May 24, 1970.

Hymoff, Edward. *The Fourth Infantry Division in Vietnam.* M. W. Lads, 1970.

Johnson, Lyndon B. *The Vantage Point: Perspectives of the Presidency, 1963-1969.* Popular Library, 1971.

Jones, Maj. Mel. "Cambodia Blitz." *Armor*, January-February 1971.

Just, Ward. "Soldiers." Part II. *Atlantic Monthly*, November 1970.

Kamm, Henry. "G.I.'s Near Song My Doubt Any Massacre." *New York Times*, December 1, 1969.

Karel, 1st Lt. Albert R. "CRIP: A Combined Effort." *Lightning 25*, November 1967.

Kearney, PFC Doug. "Sgt. Tells of VC 'Waves.' " *Tropic Lightning News*, November 11, 1966.

———. "Six-Hour Mad Minute." *Army Digest*, February 1967.

Leach, Col. James H., et al. "Montana Raider." *Armor*, September-October 1971.

"Loc Ninh IV." *Danger Forward*, December 1968.

"Loc Ninh Plantation." *Danger Forward*, December 1967.

"Loc Ninh III." *Danger Forward*, December 1968.

Low, W. Augustus, and Virgil Cliff, eds. *Encyclopedia of Black America.* McGraw-Hill, 1981.

McDuff, James M. *U.S. Army Shoulder Sleeve Insignia of the Vietnam War.* Privately pub., 1986.

"Manchus Battle by Night: Lost AP Sweats It Out." *Tropic Lightning News*, January 20, 1969.

"Manchus Praise Officers' Valor in Frontier City." *Tropic Lightning News*, June 2, 1969.

Mangold, Tom, and John Penycate. *The Tunnels of Cu Chi.* Random, 1985.

"Manhattan." *Danger Forward*, March 1968.

Martin, 1st Lt. Gary. "VC Valley—Scene of Enemy Defeat." *The Ivy Leaf*, January 12, 1969.

"The Massacre at Fire Base Ann." *Time*, April 12, 1971.

Middleton, Drew. "First Black U.S. Division Chief." *New York Times*, May 19, 1972.

Oberdorfer, Don. *Tet!* Doubleday, 1971.

"One Thousand Reds Raid Camp, GIs Kill One Hundred and Ninety-eight." *Philadelphia Inquirer*, April 16, 1969.

"Operation Toan Thang." *Danger Forward*, December 1968.

Patton, Col. George S. "Blackhorse Operations." *Armor*, July-August 1969.

———. "Pile On." Parts 1 & 2. *Armor*, January-February and March-April 1970.

Peers, Lt. Gen. William R. *The My Lai Inquiry*, Norton, 1979.

Pepke, Donn R. "Economy of Force in the Central Highlands." *Military Review*, November 1970.

Pizer, Lt. Col. Vernon (ret.). *The United States Army.* Praeger, 1967.

"Quyet Thang." *Danger Forward*, September 1968.

Randolph, John. "He Felt God's Presence After Tacoman Baited Trap." *Los Angeles Times*, n.d.

Robinson, Douglas. "Third Negro General Gets His Star." *New York Times*, September 16, 1968.

Russell, Lee E., and Volstad. "Tigerstripe Camouflage of the Vietnam War." *Military Illustrated*, April-May 1967.

Russell, 1st Lt. Roy C. "Lieutenant General William R. Peers: The Jungle Fighter." *Typhoon*, March 1969.

"Shenandoah II." *Danger Forward*, June 1968.

"Sixty Days to Remember." *The Blackhorse*, Winter 1971.

Smythe, Mabel M. *The Black American Reference Book.* Prentice-Hall, 1976.

"South Vietnam: A Terrible Price." *Time*, March 31, 1967.

"Srok Dong." *Danger Forward*, December 1967.

Stanton, Shelby L. *Green Berets at War.* Arms and Armour Pr., 1985.

———. *The Rise and Fall of an American Army.* Presidio Pr., 1985.

———. *U.S. Army Order of Battle: World War II.* Presidio Pr., 1984.

———. *Vietnam Order of Battle.* Exeter Bks., 1986.

"A Star for Davison: Combat Colonel Is Third Negro Promoted to General's Rank." *Ebony*, November 1968.

Summers, Col. Harry G. *Vietnam War Almanac.* Facts on File Publications, 1985.

"The Tet Offensive." *Danger Forward*, September 1968.

"Third Bde., Twenty-fifth Arrives Airlifted to Pleiku." *The Army Reporter*, January 14, 1966.

"Three Rebuked in G.I. Deaths." *New York Times*, April 22, 1972.

"U.S. Adding Seven Thousand to Vietnam Force." *New York Times*, January 19, 1966.

"U.S. General Relieved of Vietnam Command." *Washington Post*, July 13, 1971.

Vehnekamp, 1st Lt. Billy. "Ivy Thrust Successful." *The Ivy Leaf*, June 7, 1970.

"Vietnamization Is What's Happening." *The Blackhorse*, Winter 1971.

Votaw, Capt. John F. "The Blackhorse Kicks Back." *Armor*, July-August 1967.

Weinraub, Bernard. "Enemy Batters South Vietnamese Ranger Unit." *New York Times*, June 30, 1967.

———. "U.S. Attempt to Use Vietnamese in G.I. Units Is Partly Successful." *New York Times*, August 13, 1967.

Wellard, James. *George S. Patton, Jr.: Man Under Mars.* Dodd, Mead, 1946.

Westmoreland, Gen. William C. *A Soldier Reports.* Dell, 1976.

"Westy Calls Fourth Div Fight Major Victory." *Tropic Lightning News*, April 10, 1967.

Wolf, Col. Duquesne (ret.). *The Infantry Brigade in Combat.* Sunflower Univ. Pr., 1984.

"Xa Cam My." *Danger Forward*, September 1967.

"Xom Moi II." *Danger Forward*, December 1968.

"031820Z May 70 Mission." *Thunder*, Fall-Winter 1970.

II. Government and Government Sponsored Published Reports

Albright, John, et al. *Seven Firefights in Vietnam*. U.S. Army Center of Military History, 1970.

Fulton, Maj. Gen. William B. *Riverine Operations, 1966-1969*. Department of the Army, Vietnam Studies Series, 1973.

Hay, Lt. Gen. John H., Jr. *Tactical and Materiel Innovations*. Department of the Army, Vietnam Studies Series, 1974.

Mahon, John K., and Romana Danysh. *Infantry, Part 1: Regular Army*. Office of the Chief of Military History, U.S. Army, 1972.

Rogers, Lt. Gen. Bernard W. *Cedar Falls-Junction City: A Turning Point*. Department of the Army, Vietnam Studies Series, 1974.

Sharp, Adm. U.S.G., and Gen. William Westmoreland. *Report on the War in Vietnam (as of June 30, 1968)*. GPO, 1969.

Starry, Gen. Donn A. *Mounted Combat in Vietnam*. Department of the Army, Vietnam Studies Series, 1978.

Stuckey, Col. John D., and Col. Joseph H. Pistorius. *Mobilization of the Army National Guard and Army Reserve*. Strategic Studies Institute, U.S. Army War College, 1984.

III. Unpublished Government and Military Sources

The following documents are available through the Department of the Army, Office of the Adjutant General. Most can also be found at the U.S. Army Military History Institute, Carlisle Barracks, Pennsylvania.

Combat After Action Reports
1st Infantry Division
Operation El Paso II/III, 2 June 1966-3 September 1966.
17th Military History Detachment, 1st Infantry Division
The Battle of Prek Klok II, 10 March 1967.
4th Infantry Division
Battle for Dak To, 3 January 1968.
Keystone Robin-B, 1971.
Operation Francis Marion, 25 November 1967.
Operation Sam Houston, 16 May 1967.
25th Infantry Division
Battle for Tay Ninh City, 7 February 1969.
Fire Support Base Crook, 30 June 1969.
Operation Junction City (4th Infantry Division), 12 May 1967.
173d Airborne Brigade
Operation Atlantic City, 15 December 1966.
Operation Denver, 17 June 1966.
Operation Greene Lightning, 28 April 71.
Operation Greene Storm, 8 May 1971.
Operation Greene Sure, 20 May 1971.
Operation Toledo, 15 December 1966.
Operation Waco, 2 January 1967.
Operation Walker, 2 March 1969.
Operation Washington Green, 15 May 1971.
Operation Winchester, 4 January 1967.
Company B, 1st Battalion, 503d Infantry, 173d Airborne Brigade
CAAR, 20 November 1965.
Company D, 4th Battalion, 503d Infantry, 173d Airborne Brigade
CAAR, 1 February 1968.
Troop E, 17th Cavalry (Armored), 173d Airborne Brigade
Small Unit Action: E/17th Cavalry, 25 February 1967.
199th Light Infantry Brigade
Long Binh/Saigon Tet Campaign, 12 January-19 February 1968.
11th Armored Cavalry
Operation Atlas Wedge, 15 August 1969.
Operation Dong Tien II and Toan Tang 43, 9 December 1970.
Operation Junction City II, 1-15 April 1967.
Operation Montana Raider, 3 November 1969.

Operational Reports—Lessons Learned
4th Infantry Division
Quarterly periods ending 31 January 1967, 30 April 1969, and 31 January 1970.
23d Infantry Division (American)
Quarterly period ending January 31, 1969.
25th Infantry Division
Quarterly periods ending January 1969 and July 1969.
173d Airborne Brigade
Quarterly periods ending 15 October 1966, 15 August 1967, 15 November 1967, 15 March 1968, 15 May 1968, 15 August 1968, 15 November 1968, and 15 May 1971.
Task Force Oregon
Quarterly period ending 30 April 1967.

Senior Officer Debriefing Reports
Maj. Gen. Edward Bautz
Maj. Gen. Harris W. Hollis
Maj. Gen. Samuel W. Koster
Col. George S. Patton
Lt. Gen. William R. Peers
Maj. Gen. Ellis W. Williamson

Miscellaneous Documents
4th Infantry Division
Narrative Description of Events, 28 October-30 November 1967 (1st Brigade). n.d.
Recommendation for Presidential Unit Citation (3d Brigade). 1 April 1967.
23d Infantry Division (American)
Report of Investigation to Assess the Effectiveness of the Functioning of Command Within the 23d Infantry Division as It Pertains to the Attack Against FSB Mary Ann. Office of the Inspector General, U.S. Army, July 1971.
Exit interview with Col. Alphus R. Clark, 1 April 1971.
173d Airborne Brigade
Historical Summary, 1 January-31 December 1964.
Historical Summary, 1 January-31 December 1965.
Historical Summary, 1 January-31 December 1968.
11th Armored Cavalry
Cross Border Attack into Cambodia. n.d.
Redeployment After Action Report. 5 March 1971.
Casualty Information System, 1961-1981, Record Group 407. National Archives and Records Administration.
Letter from Col. John A. Bender to Maj. Gen. William R. Desobry. n.d.

U.S. Army Military History Institute, Carlisle Barracks, Pennsylvania
Oral History Collection
Conversations between General Bruce Palmer, Jr., and Lt. Col. James E. Shelton and Lt. Col. Edward P. Smith.
Conversations between Lieutenant General Jonathan O. Seaman, USA, Ret., and Col. Clyde H. Patterson, Jr
Interview with Lt. Gen. Arthur S. Collins, Jr.
Interview with Gen. William E. DePuy.
Interview with Lt. Gen. John H. Hay, Jr.
Interview with Lt. Gen. William R. Peers.
Interview with Gen. William B. Rosson.
Interview with Gen. Melvin Zais
Unit History Collection
1st Infantry Division
The 1st Infantry Division. n.d.
Fundamentals of Infantry Tactics. 1st Infantry Division Pamphlet 350-51, 1 February 1968.
1st Brigade, 1st Infantry Division in Vietnam: October 1965-April 1970. n.d.
History of the Iron Brigade in the Republic of Vietnam. n.d.
4th Infantry Division
The Famous Fighting Fourth in the Central Highlands. n.d.
The History of the Famous Fourth. 1969.
Three Wars: A Pictorial History of the 4th Infantry Division. 1968.
Annual Historical Supplement: Calendar Year 1966. (1st Brigade), 23 March 1967.
Annual Historical Supplement: Calendar Year 1967. (1st Brigade), 25 March 1968.
Annual Historical Supplement: Calendar Year 1966. (2d Brigade), 20 March 1967.
Annual Historical Supplement: Calendar Year 1967. (2d Brigade), 18 March 1968.
Annual Historical Supplement: Calendar Year 1967. (3d Brigade Task Force), 1 March 1968.
25th Infantry Division
Tropic Lightning in Vietnam: 1 October 1966 to 1 October 1967. n.d.
Annual Historical Summary: 1 January 1966 to 31 December 1966. (2d Brigade), nd.
Third Year in Combat—1968, The Fire Brigade, 1 January-31 December 1968. (2d Brigade), n.d.
23d Infantry Division (American)
23d Infantry Division (American) History. n.d.
23d Infantry Division (American) Participation in Operation Lam Son 719. n.d.
11th Light Infantry Brigade: 1 January 1967-31 December 1967. n.d.
History of the 196th Infantry Brigade. 1970.
Annual Historical Supplement: 1 January 1966-31 December 1966. (3d Battalion, 21st Infantry), 21 April 1967.
11th Armored Cavalry
Howell, Col. Martin D. "Selected Combat Actions." n.d.
Annual Historical Summary: 1 January 1966-31 December 1966. (1st Squadron), 23 March 1967.
Annual Historical Summary: 1 January 1968-31 December 1968. (3d Squadron), 12 April 1969.

IV. The authors have consulted the following newspapers and periodicals:

Army; Army Digest; The Army Reporter; Army Times; Danger Foward: The Magazine of the Big Red One, Vietnam; Lightning 25; Newsweek; New York Times; Redcatcher!; Redcatcher! (yearbook)*; Sky Soldier Magazine; Thunder; Time; Tropic Lightning News.*

V. Interviews

Maj. Gen. Edward Bautz, Jr., former CG, 25th Infantry Division; John Blanchfield, former Sgt., 2d Brigade, 9th Infantry Division; Lt. Col. Thomas P. Curtin, former Capt., 199th Infantry Brigade (Light); Douglas Fairchild, former Sgt., 4th Battalion, 21st Infantry, 23d Infantry Division (American); Gen. Robert C. Forbes, former CG, 199th Infantry Brigade (Light); Robert Heier, former rifleman, Company B, 5th Battalion, 12th Infantry, 199th Infantry Brigade (Light); Maj. Gen. Harris W. Hollis, former CG, 25th Infantry Division; C. Tony May, former SP4, 3d Battalion, 21st Infantry, 23d Infantry Division (American); Garrett Meador, former Sgt., 1st Battalion, 14th Infantry, 4th Infantry Division; Marc Miller, former executive officer, 16th Aviation Group, 23d Infantry Division, (American); Charles S. Newman, former 2d Lt., 1st Battalion, 8th Infantry, 4th Infantry Division; Ronald Orem, former Sgt., platoon leader, Company B, 5th Battalion, 12th Infantry, 199th Infantry Brigade (Light); John F. Peterson, former Sgt., 1st Battalion, 6th Infantry, 23d Infantry Division (American); Col. George D. Rehkopf (USA, ret.), former commander, 199th Infantry Brigade (Light); Lyle Shargont, former radio telephone operator, 1st Battalion, 35th Infantry, 4th Infantry Division; Richard Strasser, former 1st Lt., 6th Battalion, 39th Infantry; Col. Harry G. Summers, Jr., former battalion operations officer, 1st Infantry Division.

Picture Credits

Cover photo:
U.S. Army

The Big Unit War
p. 7, UPI/Bettmann Newsphotos. p. 8, U.S. Army. p. 10, UPI/Bettmann Newsphotos. p. 14, © Tim Page. p. 16, Philip Jones Griffiths—Magnum. p. 18, AP/Wide World. p. 20, National Archives. p. 21, Robert Capa—Magnum. pp. 23, 25, U.S. Army.

The Fire Brigade
p. 27, AP/Wide World. p. 29, U.S. Army. p. 30, AP/Wide World. p. 32, © Tim Page. pp. 34-35, Co Rentmeester—LIFE Magazine, © 1967, Time Inc. p. 36, AP/Wide World. p. 39, UPI/Bettmann Newsphotos. p. 41, AP/Wide World. p. 43, U.S. Army.

Five Days on Hill 875
pp. 45-46, UPI/Bettmann Newsphotos. p. 48, AP/Wide World. pp. 50-51, Bunyo Ishikawa.

Highland Regulars
p. 53, AP/Wide World. p. 54, U.S. Army. pp. 56, 58, UPI/Bettmann Newsphotos. p. 62, U.S. Army. p. 63, UPI/Bettmann Newsphotos. p. 65, U.S. Army. p. 67, Shelby L. Stanton Collection. p. 68, UPI/Bettmann Newsphotos.

The Road To Saigon
p. 71, AP/Wide World. p. 74, U.S. Army. pp. 76, 77, top, Al Chang. p. 77, bottom, Al Chang—AP/Wide World. p. 79, Bunyo Ishikawa. pp. 80-81, Shelby L. Stanton Collection. p. 82, U.S. Army. p. 84, Shelby L. Stanton Collection. p. 87, AP/Wide World.

In the Field With the 25th
pp. 89-95, Bunyo Ishikawa.

Army Combat Uniforms
pp. 96-103, Illustrations by Donna J. Neary.

Defending the Capital
p. 105, U.S. Army. p. 106, AP/Wide World. p. 108, Shelby L. Stanton Collection. pp. 110, 113, Peter Gyallay-Pap Collection. pp. 114, 116, U.S. Army. p. 117, Peter Gyallay-Pap Collection. p. 119, UPI/Bettmann Newsphotos.

Tracks in the Jungle
p.121, AP/Wide World. p. 124, Library of Congress. p. 125, National Archives. p. 126, UPI/Bettmann Newsphotos. p. 129, U.S. Army. pp. 131-133, Co Rentmeester—LIFE Magazine, © Time Inc. pp. 134-135, © Tim Page. pp. 136, 139, 140, Philip Jones Griffiths—Magnum.

Patrolling the Delta
pp. 143-144, U.S. Army. p. 145, © R.D. Moeser. p. 147, U.S. Army. p. 149, © R.D. Moeser. p. 150, © R.D. Moeser. p. 152, U.S. Army. p. 154, U.S. Navy. p. 155, U.S. Army. p. 157, UPI/Bettmann Newsphotos. p. 159, Shelby L. Stanton Collection.

Mini-Tet
pp. 161-164, Philip Jones Griffiths—Magnum. p. 165, Bunyo Ishikawa. p. 166, Angelo Cozzi, Milan. p. 167, Philip Jones Griffiths—Magnum.

The Tattered Banner
pp. 169-170, U.S. Army. p. 173, AP/Wide World. p. 175, Peers Commission/Shelby L. Stanton Collection. p. 177, Shelby L. Stanton Collection. pp. 178-179, Sp. 4 Bob Hodierne, U.S. Army—Pacific Stars and Stripes. p. 182, Mark Godfrey/Archive. p. 184, © 1983 David Burnett/Contact.

Map Credits

All maps prepared by Diane McCaffery. Sources are as follows:

p. 12—"Danger Forward," The Magazine of the Big Red One, Vietnam.

p. 37—Map by Shelby L. Stanton

p. 61—Department of the Army.

p. 111—"Redcatcher, Yearbook." Department of the Army.

p. 122—Department of the Army.

p. 138—U.S. Army Center of Military History.

p. 181—U.S. Department of Defense.

Acknowledgments

In addition to acknowledging the kind assistance of the following people, Boston Publishing Company gives special thanks to George Daniels, former executive editor at Time-Life Books, for his guidance and support.

Mr. Herbert Garcia, curator, Tropic Lightning (25th Infantry Division) Museum, Schofield Barracks, HI; Peter Joannides, executive director, Redcatcher (199th Infantry Brigade [Light]) Association; Morris S. Jordan, former sergeant and combat correspondent, 4th Infantry Division; David Keough, U.S. Military History Institute, Carlisle Barracks, PA; Colonel Rod Paschall, director, U.S. Army Military History Institute, Carlisle Barracks, PA; Robert L. Reynolds, former captain, 199th Infantry Brigade (Light); John Slonaker, chief, Historical Reference Branch, U.S. Army Military History Institute, Carlisle Barracks, PA; Dr. Richard Sommers, archivist, U.S. Army Military History Institute, Carlisle Barracks, PA; Colonel Harry G. Summers, Jr. (U.S. Army, Ret.), military correspondent, *U.S. News & World Reports*.

Index

Note on U.S. Military Unit Organization

The following chart summarizes the general organizational structure of the U.S. Army in Vietnam, with the approximate number of men in each unit. Note that after World War II the Army eliminated the regiment (except in the case of armored cavalry) and replaced it with the comparably sized brigade, composed of various battalions of former regiments. The battalions, however, retained their regimental designations for purposes of historical continuity (for example, 1st, 2d, and 3d battalions, 22d Infantry) but were usually scattered to different brigades.

Army Structure

Unit	Size	Commanding Officer
Division	12,000–18,000 troops or 3 brigades	Major General
Brigade/ Regiment	3,000 troops or 2–4 battalions	Colonel
Battalion/ Squadron	600–1,000 troops or 3–5 companies	Lieutenant Colonel
Company/ Troop	150–160 troops or 3–4 platoons	Captain
Platoon	40 troops or 3–4 squads	Lieutenant
Squad	5–10 troops	Sergeant

Names, Acronyms, Terms

ACAV—armored cavalry assault vehicle.

aero rifle platoon—heliborne infantry unit assigned to troops of the 1/9 Air Cavalry, also known as Blue team.

aero scout platoon—observation unit assigned to troops of the 1/9 Air Cavalry, also known as White team.

APC—armored personnel carrier.

Arc Light strike—code name for a B-52 combat mission in South Vietnam. First Arc Light mission took place in June 1965.

ARVN—Army of the Republic of (South) Vietnam.

AVLB—armored vehicle launched bridge. Mobile bridge capable of supporting sixty tons and spanning sixty feet of water.

Capital Military District—Saigon and the immediate surrounding area.

CIDG—Civilian Irregular Defense Group. Project devised by the CIA that combined self-defense with economic and social programs designed to raise the standard of living and win the loyalty of the mountain people. Chief work of the U.S. Special Forces.

civic action—term used by U.S. military forces for pacification programs in South Vietnam.

CONUS—Continental United States.

COSVN—Central Office for South Vietnam. Communist military and political headquarters for southern South Vietnam.

CP—command post.

CRIP—Combined Reconnaissance and Intelligence Platoon. The effort to train and equip local ARVN forces, composed of an ARVN Province Intelligence Platoon plus half of a U.S. Reconnaissance Platoon.

CTZ—organizational unit of two or more divisions designed mainly for control of combat operations. U.S. established four CTZs in South Vietnam: I Corps (northern provinces), II Corps (northern provinces and adjacent lowlands), III Corps (southern highlands and adjacent lowlands), and IV Corps (Mekong Delta).

DMZ—demilitarized zone. Established by the Geneva accords of 1954, provisionally dividing North Vietnam from South Vietnam along the seventeenth parallel.

dustoff—helicopter medical evacuation missions in Vietnam named for call sign of an early medevac pilot.

FAC—foward air controller. Low-flying pilot who directed high-altitude strike aircraft engaged in close air support of ground troops.

Field Force—command subordinate to MACV that exercised direct control over all U.S. Army units operating in a particular corps tactical zone. Field Force I commanded II Corps and Field Force II commanded III and IV Corps.

firebase psychosis—condition describing U.S. Army units that by 1970 had become so dependent on FSBs for security that they seldom strayed from the base, thereby limiting Army mobility.

FSB—fire support base. Semifixed artillery base established to increase indirect fire coverage of an area and to provide security for the firing unit. Also known as fire support patrol base (FSPB).

GVN—Government of (South) Vietnam.

H&I—harassment and interdiction. Artillery fire used to deny the enemy free and open movement.

HEAT—highly explosive antitank type of artillery round.

HUT—Hamlet Upgrading Team. U.S. Army program aimed at training and upgrading RF/PF forces.

Iron Triangle—nickname for VC stronghold less than thirty-two kilometers northwest of Saigon. Served as a supply station and base of operations against nearby targets.

Joint Chiefs of Staff—consists of chairman, Army chief of staff, chief of naval operations, Air Force chief of staff, and Marine commandant. Advises the president, the National Security Council, and the secretary of defense.

KIA—killed in action.

LAW—light antitank weapon.

LIFT—Local Improvement of Forces Team. See HUT.

LRRP—long-range reconnaissance patrol. Pronounced "Lurp." Unit first organized by the U.S. Special Forces whose missions included gathering intelligence on enemy troop movements, coordinating air and artillery strikes, and conducting special raids.

LZ—landing zone.

McNamara Line—plan conceived by Secretary of Defense Robert McNamara that involved stringing barbed wire, land mines, electronic sensors, and observation posts along the DMZ to block NVA infiltration.

MACV—Military Assistance Command, (South) Vietnam. Commanded U.S. Forces in Vietnam.

Main Force unit—regular forces of NVA/VC military.

medevac—see dustoff.

Mobile Riverine Force—joint U.S. Army-Navy unit formed in 1967 to conduct amphibious operations in the Mekong Delta.

montagnards—the mountain tribes of Vietnam, wooed by both sides because of their knowledge of the rugged highland terrain and fighting ability.

MSR—main supply route.

NCO—noncommissioned officer.

NVA—U.S. designation for North Vietnamese Army. Officially PAVN (People's Army of Vietnam).

operational control—authority granted to a unit over others not organic to it. Normally granted for a specific mission.

OSS—Office of Strategic Services. Created in 1942 under the U.S. Joint Chiefs of Staff to obtain information about enemy military operations. Disbanded in 1945, many of its functions were absorbed by the CIA.

psyops—psychological operations. Wide range of activities such as loudspeaker broadcasts and leaflet drops intended to lower the enemy's morale and to rally defectors.

rallier—enemy agent or soldier who defected to the side of the GVN.

RF/PF—GVN Regional and Popular Forces. Paramilitary units organized to provide provincial and rural defense. The U.S. nickname Ruff-Puffs is derived from the abbreviation.

Rome plow—large tractor with a bulldozer blade, especially developed for land-clearing operations. Also called a "jungle-eater."

RPG—rocket-propelled grenade.

SAM—Stamina, Accuracy, and Marksmanship. See HUT.

stand down—period of rest and resupply. Also refers to a unit's preparation for deployment back to the U.S.

TAOR—tactical area of responsibility.

tunnel rat—U.S. soldier, usually of small build, who searched VC tunnel complexes; originally armed with as little as a flashlight and a .45-caliber pistol.

Vietcong (VC)—originally derogatory slang for Vietnamese Communist; a contraction of Vietnam Cong San (Vietnamese Communist).

Vietcong infrastructure (VCI)—local Communist apparatus, responsible for overall direction of the insurgency including all political and military operations.

War Zone C—imprecise term used to describe an area of VC guerrilla activity northwest of Saigon and bordered by Cambodia.

War Zone D—imprecise term used to describe an area of VC guerrilla activity northeast of Saigon.